Psychotherapy and the Quest for Happiness

Emmy van Deurzen

Psychotherapy and the Quest for Happiness

Los Angeles • London • New Delhi • Singapore • Washington DC

First published 2009

SAGE Publications Ltd
1 Oliver's Yard
55 City Road
London EC1Y 1SP

SAGE Publications Inc.
2455 Teller Road
Thousand Oaks, California 91320

SAGE Publications India Pvt Ltd
B 1/I 1 Mohan Cooperative Industrial Area
Mathura Road
New Delhi 110 044

SAGE Publications Asia-Pacific Pte Ltd
33 Pekin Street #02-01
Far East Square
Singapore 048763

British Library Cataloguing in Publication data

A catalogue record for this book is available from
the British Library

ISBN 978-0-7619-4410-2
ISBN 978-0-7619-4411-9 (pbk)

Library of Congress Control Number: 2008925338

Typeset by C&M Digitals (P) Ltd, Chennai, India
Printed in India at Replika Press Pvt Ltd
Printed on paper from sustainable resources

For all those who yearn for happiness

and for Digby always

I dream of a green garden
where the sun feathers my face
like your once eager kiss.

Soon, soon I will climb
from this blackened earth
into the diffident light.

Sue Hubbard (*Ghost Station, Salt*)

Contents

Introduction: Happiness and Psychotherapy

It is not death that a man should fear,
but he should fear never beginning to live.

Marcus Aurelius

Where are we now?

We live in difficult times. Though we thought that civilization and culture would bring us ease, comfort and happiness it has turned out to be a little more complex than that. In the Northern hemisphere we are certainly more prosperous than ever before. We now have plenty of personal possessions and we consume many commodities. We can boast of a myriad of technological achievements. We know so much and we control even more. We have access to multiple and varied resources and exploit them to the hilt. Our economies are based on constant growth and expansion. Yet we have not achieved a state of permanent bliss and are not likely to do so in the near future. There is nothing new under the sun. Life is still not easy. It never was and never will be. Each acquisition comes with new drawbacks and introduces new responsibilities and problems into our lives. It is still hard to live a good life and get it right. Many of us feel rather lost in the world today, because of its increasing complexity and stress. We want happiness but do not really know how or where to find it. We spend much of our lives in worry, fear, depression, regret, doubt, confusion and anxiety. Even those of us who do well for ourselves feel stressed out and tired much of the time.

This is hardly a new phenomenon. People since times immemorial have found living a difficult challenge. Artists and authors have witnessed the miseries that are part and parcel of the human condition and they have taken their inspiration from the struggles and heartaches that ensue from it. For this is essentially what human culture is: the product of our attempts at overcoming our fundamental fragility, our fears and our frustrations. Today science and technology have come up with many ways of dealing with the dangers of the natural world and they are fairly effective in achieving their objective of taming and controlling the material challenges we all have to face. The overall aim is to constantly make our lives easier and safer. In strictly material terms this goal seems nearer and nearer, be it at the cost of having to run ever faster on the treadmill of economic growth. We are increasingly aware of the price the human race is paying for this progress however. At each step of the way we are confronted with the paradoxical and potentially threatening by-products and unwelcome consequences of our comforts. It is clear that a complete 360-degree review of our way of life is crucial for the future of the planet and mankind (see for instance Martin, 2006).

Science or art?

Such a review has got to include the way in which we live our mental, moral and emotional lives. It is profoundly alarming when scientists who are progressively more knowledgeable about personal and interpersonal interactions assume this automatically gives them the right to manipulate, control and manage our emotions and behaviour. An invisible revolution is underway in this field with unforeseeable consequences for the decades to come. As neuroscientists and social scientists become more capable of programming our minds and guide our actions, we need to make sure that we keep the reins in hand and that we are clear on what we do and do not want for our own future. Much more thinking is needed about how we can make sure that mechanical and factual knowledge serves rather than controls us. How are we going to protect human freedom, spontaneity and creativity? How will we decide where meaning is to come from and what we will believe and aspire to? What is our idea of transcendence and what shall we worship in future?

Classically, and for good reasons, these aspects of human living have been the domain of the arts, religion and philosophy rather than of the sciences. The arts are reserved for the creative expression of people's struggles with the human condition, whilst religion regulates and controls these struggles, giving them a purpose. Customarily philosophy used to oversee both artistic expressions and religious prescriptions, providing the space to reflect on them and make sense of the world. In this way philosophers were in a position to guide politicians and educators, safeguarding the moral debate in society. Who is guiding politicians in their ethical thinking today? That duty has been taken over by lawyers, industrialists and economists, who all have a stake in the continued growth of the economy. Philosophers used to claim a neutral place from which to reflect on human living and make sense of it. Their job was to rise above the interest of the moment and provide the bigger picture. We have more or less dispensed with such fundamental reference to human wisdom, even though the issues we are dealing with are increasingly vital to our survival. The scientific endeavour to pin human existence on concrete facts and figures has well and truly taken hold and has discredited the human capacity for discernment, reasoning and good judgement. Scientific values dominate philosophy today in the same way in which religious values dominated it in the past, obstructing its freedom and stopping its progress. Understanding and reflection on the human predicament are now secondary to rationality, if they are allowed at all. Will this make art, philosophy and religion redundant and eliminate human misery? It is highly unlikely.

Artists and philosophers have never been in competition with scientists. They cannot lose a battle they are not interested in fighting. Artists do not and never have proposed final solutions to the big questions of life. They do not seek to eradicate human suffering, finding plenty of interest in it. They rather describe and document it in their various ways, exposing the pain and joy of human existence and highlighting its contradictions, plumbing its depths, trying to fathom its endless mysteries. Art is the arena of human emotions and the artist's expression has often thrived on adversity, suffering and unhappiness because this is the fertile ground in which human ingenuity is rooted, grows and blossoms. It is in the depths and troughs of human experience that inspiration is to be found. Artists know that the richness of life is in its contrasts. For them the objective of living is not normality with its tedium of homogeneity, control and predictability; it is not the eradication of adversity they work towards, but the intensity and depth of passionate and radical human experience.

Similarly philosophers have never claimed that life could be smoothed out and made easy or brought under a simple rational common denominator. Philosophers seek to understand and make sense of the same human problems and difficulties that artists in their various ways explore and express, not in order to get rid of them, but in order to grasp their purpose. Philosophers do sometimes try to establish order in the chaos of the human condition, but not so as to eliminate conflicts and problems but so as to make sense of them and get better at resolving them. Philosophers, in the radical sense of the word (as lovers of wisdom), aim to deal with difficulties wisely, with a calm and full awareness of what is the case and what is desirable. Their pursuit is somewhat similar to that of world religions and indeed some world religions are known as Eastern philosophies. Unlike most religions however philosophies do not prescribe a particular way of life and they do not establish a dogma that needs to be obeyed to the letter. Their objective is rather to encourage people to learn to think for themselves.

Why is it that we get inspired by artists and philosophers? It is because they are in touch with what matters and they remind us to heed what is precious. Good artists and philosophers work from the inspiration and direct experience of personal confrontation with reality. This often means that they use their emotional suffering and despair as a starting point. They document their own battles with life and their work is an attempt at transforming their anguish and agony into something of value. They walk on the firm ground of life itself. Art is a great leveller and we recognize the agonies of the artist even if we try to deny these to ourselves much of the time. Kierkegaard's philosophy is a case in point, since his work is so directly based in his own life. He was a master at transcending his suffering and he expressed it rather well:

> *My spiritual work satisfies me so completely and makes me come gladly to terms with everything if only I am absorbed in it. That's how I can see my life too: bringing to others good tidings of comfort and joy, while I myself remain bound in pain for which I can anticipate no alleviation – except for this one thing: that I can work with my mind in this way. (Kierkegaard, 1999: VIII 1 A 645)*

It is uplifting to note that Kierkegaard got relief from his work and that he derived inspiration from his suffering. In facing his pain he found the key to coping with the anguish of life. Van Gogh was not so lucky or able to make sense of his suffering. He could only express it. His despair was surely his inspiration, but ultimately he found no redemption in it.

> *It is just in learning to suffer without complaint, in learning to look on pain without repugnance, that you risk vertigo, and yet it is possible, yet you may even catch a glimpse of a vague likelihood that on the other side of life we shall see some good reason for the existence of pain, which seen from here sometimes so fills the whole horizon that it takes on the propor- tions of a hopeless deluge. (van Gogh in Bernard, 1985: 203)*

While some people feel deluged by their pain and others find inspiration in it, human beings have always striven to thrive on hardship and misfortune rather than be struck down by it. We have learnt to distil something good out of what is troublesome. But it is not always easy to hold on to such hard earned pearls of wisdom and they frequently lose their strength and power as they are passed on from generation to generation as hearsay or proverbs or common sense. Few philosophers or other authors would permit themselves to base their writing on such diluted insights into the human condition. We need to get better at drawing on the life learning of our forebears. It is surely one of the best things human beings achieve in this world: to struggle with the trials and tribulations of the human condition, transcend them and pass on this learning to the next generation. And this is traditionally the territory of the arts and philosophy: to observe, comment on, highlight and illustrate the human condition so that others may benefit and live it more fully. But this is not about seeking happiness *per se*, it is about the whole complex business of life which can never be exclusively about happiness.

Philosophy as an alternative

It is only recently that scientists have begun to take over this field of study in a more objective and factual manner. Cognitive scientists now claim that human well being and happiness can be measured, cultivated and taught as a skill to those who are unhappy. Such claims are based on a materialistic world-view that considers human existence as something that can and should be controlled. It is not surprising that such a view can take hold, when academic philosophy has become increasingly enamoured of the scientific tradition and emphasizes its own analytic role. Over the past decades it has often narrowed its field of study to linguistic observations and scientific debate, detaching itself from its original mission of existential and human understanding. Of course there are still some philosophers who remain committed to the radical ethical and moral brief, but they are increasingly in the minority.

So, the task of understanding the vagaries of everyday reality has been up for grabs. And it is psychologists, therapists and counsellors who have become the applied philosophers of our age. It is they who have stepped into the breach of the vacuum of meaning. Since they deal with people's daily problems and preoccupations they have become cast in the role of spiritual and moral mentors, even without realizing it and even though they did not apply for the job. Invariably they do so without any training in philosophy and their moral guidance is not to everyone's taste and is often implicit in their work rather than explicitly stated. They work mainly with psychological theories and apply these to their clients' dilemmas without openly acknowledging that it is often moral, spiritual and philosophical problems that people are struggling with.

It is high time that therapists ask themselves how to take seriously their new role as existential guides. Where should they place themselves in this respect? Should they follow and even emulate the scientists and apply simple evidence-based cognitive and behavioural principles? Is therapy to become a scientific endeavour with the very clear objective of making human beings act and think in line with established facts and values? Is it right that it should aim for normality and adjustment and that it should eliminate sadness and pain and provide a shortcut to happiness?

Undoubtedly there is much to learn from the scientific input in this field. New understanding of brain and cognitive processes can help us get a clearer picture of what goes on in the mind. New social science and psychological research can guide our explorations and provide important insights into mental illness or social isolation that are directly relevant to therapy. We need to take all these new sources of knowledge into our stride. But none of these can prevent human misery or cure mental illness or eliminate the predictable difficulties of existence once and for all. The new cognitive science only touches the tip of an iceberg that philosophers, artists and therapists alike have respectfully circumnavigated since the beginning of time.

Of course a hard scientific approach can provide a useful new angle on the old debates about how to help people. But it will be only one angle and it will leave a lot of human experience out and in the shadows of its hard glare. It seems somewhat ironic that an evidence based scientific approach ignores the evidence of the reality of people's everyday lives. What price will people have to pay for focusing so much on living by the quantitative standards defining their well being? It seems peculiar that those who are scientifically minded have not noticed that in the great meta-analysis of life it has been shown over and over again that we can conjure up new ideas and new products, but that neither of these can guarantee a happier life or eliminate hardship, dissatis-faction or mortality.

All the evidence shows that every time we acquire a new commodity or a new advantage in life this comes at a price. Our appreciation of life goes up momentarily and briefly, but soon goes back to the same level as it was before. New possessions or gimmicks may enchant us but they do not guarantee happiness. In the longer term they may also have undesirable side-effects and noxious and harmful consequences. We have long known that money cannot buy love, life, happiness or meaning; it can merely provide greater comfort and ease. It is a resource, a means to an end, but not a final answer. The same applies to science. It can enable our explorations of the universe, but it cannot alter the elemental course of nature or prevent the fundamental pain of human living and human dying. Even if for instance we achieved the elimination of senescence so that humans could survive for several centuries, this would only magnify the problem of dealing with a massively expanding world population, which would require us to introduce some other form of population control and selection. We may be able to make our difficulties more tolerable or learn to work with them in new ways, but we cannot remove them all together. They are part and parcel of our existence and though we may alter them we will continue to falter and fail in getting rid of them completely.

There is a real irony in all this. In the mid-twentieth century we were predicted a technological future of long, happy and idle lives as it was believed that by the beginning of the twenty first century our work would be performed by machines and we would need to expand our capacity for leisure with earlier and earlier retirements and shorter working weeks. The reality as we know it now is rather different. The greater the feats of our technological society, the more we rush around to try and keep up the pace of our ever expanding lives in a faster and more demanding global village. The greater our productivity, and the more we have to work to keep quenching our thirst for new gadgets. We can-not stop running on the big treadmill, lest we lose our momentum and fall off the edge of the world. People's lives have become more and more busy and stressful. We seem increasingly taken over by work and worry. We are less securely based in our communities and families, for we are more mobile and more independent. In consequence our personal values are often determined by necessity or by default. They are also increasingly regulated by socio-cultural and media images of what it is to live a good life. But it doesn't satisfy us and it doesn't feel right. More and more of us are realizing that it is time to look again, weigh up the past and take stock of the present and find a new and better direction before it is too late. We know that we have to take charge of our future and build a better world, somehow. But we feel daunted by the prospect of what this involves and we cannot do it on our own. In the middle of our great successes we feel like a failure, for we have become isolated, alienated from ourselves, our ideals, each other and from life itself.

Making sense of life

We know we need to establish a new collaboration, for we are all bound together and ahead of us is the Gargantuan task of making sense of life again, creating a new code for human living that can satisfy us more than the superficial values we seem to have settled for in the interim. The question is whether we want to slump into the moral vacuum or make this effort. And if the latter, how should we go about it?

If we want to keep pace with human progress we cannot simply return to the make believe of the old religions, though some will continue to do so with fanaticism and wishful thinking. The old religions are outdated and out of synch with the world we have created. They need to be reviewed if they are to be credible. For starters we cannot afford religions that go against the facts science has brought us. We cannot be asked to believe things that are an insult to our intelligence. We cannot go backwards. Scientific rationalism alone may not be a satisfactory option, but irrationality is not a viable alternative. The world religions are limited by the fact that they are by definition sectarian and necessarily dogmatic (Dawkins, 2006). They take positions. Each holds on to a superior claim to divine truth, which makes them contradictory with each other and unfortunately often intolerant of alternative views. The last thing we need is to increase this competition for religious dominance, which is so conducive to warfare and a lack of tolerance. Yet we cannot just discard our religions as Dawkins would have us do. Christianity, Judaism, Islam, Buddhism, Hinduism, Sikhism, Confucianism, Taoism, Zoroastrianism and other religions all have good and interesting ideas, beliefs, principles and practices on offer and many people continue to value these traditions. Human beings have a deep need to belong, not just with each other but also to something beyond themselves. They will always reach for the stars and for metaphysical principles that hold them safely together. Science has not yet provided us with a connectivity that sounds true and inspires confidence.

Therefore those who abandon religion and call themselves atheists often fall back into the realm of spirituality by the back door of superstition, for they no longer have satisfactory explanations for the things that matter to them. We have not yet arrived at a scientific theory that provides a satisfactory alternative to religious practice and belief, though some scientists do espouse science as a kind of minimalist religion. Science is not a viable substitute for our transcendental cravings, even though it requires a similarly religious commitment and devotion to a particular worldview (McGrath and McGrath, 2007). One of the problems is that the scientific view is an intellectual and rational one and does not address the deeper layers of existence. Science also lacks a satisfactory meta-theory and gets easily caught up in specialist explanations that are then generalized in a rather cavalier way that defies the imagination. Individual scientific disciplines certainly have strong claims to elements of factual truth and provide the building blocks from which philosophers of science can speculate about the earth and the material universe. Philosophers of mind similarly generate theories out of the building blocks of cognitive science. But this kind of theorizing remains specialized and abstract and rarely attempts to relate to experiential and existential factors. It bears little relation to people's personal experience of their emotions or their interests in art and religion. Such theories curiously fail to address our need for meaning, myth and morality (Midgley, 2004). When thinking about the big questions we seem to exclude the big question of why human beings are capable of consciousness and why we crave purpose, understanding and transcendence. These issues, with a few notable exceptions, are rarely addressed head on by physicists, biologists and cosmologists (Davies, 2007; Dennett, 2003; Martin, 2006).

Science provides us with an intellectual discipline, but it does not really satisfy our spiritual and moral aspirations. For science to come up with a truly credible theory of everything it would have to take our feelings and longings for meaning into account as well as our struggles with the big issues of existence such as time and death and our experience of suffering. It would also have to consider our need for community, belonging, love and intimacy rather than speaking in terms of competition and the survival of the fittest. It will also have to account for our deeply engrained sense of a purpose in life.

But as this is not happening it is not really surprising that so many of us are dabbling in alternative forms of spirituality during these times of confusion and loss of faith. We thirst for mystery and we crave the sacred so much that we grasp at straws. We need something to believe in and we do not know where to find it. The ecological path seems to satisfy our urge for meaning to some extent and going green can easily become a quasi religious commitment, but it is at the end of the day a material preoccupation with the earth and does not satisfy our more personal aspirations for a wider meaning. Meanwhile the old esoteric pursuits of astrology, divination and mysticism of all sorts have never been so popular. It is tempting to go for these quick solutions that promise spectacular results and sure-footed guidance in our everyday quandaries. How desperate we are to find respite from the tawdriness of our desacralized existence. In the long run though, such superficial options do not satisfy our need for deeper understanding and may well leave us more lost and confused. We are only too aware of their ephemeral nature and the superstition they involve us in. We cannot simply turn our backs on our own progress and hide in the explanations of a generation that lived in other times, in other circumstances and on other continents. We may have lost the divine, but divination is no substitute.

If we want more reality and more understanding we cannot stick our heads in the sand and remain stranded in a world devoid of scientific knowledge. We cannot just pretend we don't know what we know. There can be no easy or magical solutions anymore, much as we would like to think there are. We have to think things through carefully. We have to stick to what makes sense; we have to be able to account for ourselves. Our values and beliefs cannot be random or passive or we will go right back to the Dark Ages where people were ruled by fear and make believe. In order to avoid this fate (which some people seem to flirt with recklessly), our thinking has to be sound and our ideas have to be tested and tried over and over again. We have to pursue our own quest for truth and right living and cannot start from the assumption that human happiness is the only goal and the Holy Grail. We cannot afford to pursue the objective of maximum pleasure with the naivety of children who want to dine, live and sleep in the sweetshop and be happy ever after. If we do try to take a short cut to salvation, we are certain to go down the wrong path. Addictions of all sorts are rife and illustrate this point emphatically. There are no short cuts that work. We have to take the long laborious way instead and be responsible for our actions, thoughts and ways of life.

Asking new questions

The questions we then need to start asking ourselves are: where do we want to get to? What is our goal and destination in life? What is our task in human existence if it is not simply to obey a god? Is it simply to procreate or to favour the evolutionary principles? Is it to be as happy as possible? Or is there more to it? When people come to therapy they often indicate that all they really want is the achievement of happiness in their lives. Should we consider happiness to be a desirable goal for life and therefore for therapy as well? Or is there a better path to follow? This book will ask all these questions and seek to answer them in many different ways. These are fundamental issues for psychotherapists and counsellors. Is happiness possible? Should we actively pursue it? And if so, what role, if any, do the professions of counselling and psychotherapy have to play in this respect? Are these professions designed to enhance people's well being? Is their mission mainly to overcome the symptoms of depression and anxiety? Should they try to eliminate unhappiness at all costs? Or should they make people think about their lives and how they live without focusing exclusively on the objective of happiness or even without trying to eliminate their ordinary human misery? Clearly counselling has come a long way from its beginnings in pastoral and educational guidance and advice. It has become medicalized and professionally organized and after a period of rampant growth it is now being cut back sharply by evidence-based practice standards. But are we satisfied with the kind of evidence this new regulation is based upon? Do we want counselling and therapy to be reframed as a method of improving mental health and emotional well being? Do we want it to be a brief intervention that targets happiness? Or has the world gone mad and are we losing touch with our understanding of the complexity of the human condition? Traditionally counsellors and therapists never saw themselves as the providers of bliss and they have usually vigorously denied that their function was to make people happy. Why should we forget that now?

We need to settle this matter once and for all. What is the role that therapy and counselling play in relation to human well being and happiness? To answer that question we will need to address a number of other questions first. What is happiness? Do we all have different notions of happiness? Is happiness ever a suitable goal for psychotherapy? Is therapy a cure for the lack of happiness or merely a temporary cover-up for it? Is unhappiness an illness? Are people meant to be happy and should therapy follow in the footsteps of the positive psychologists? We will seek answers to all these questions but we will also consider whether the opposite may be true and whether unhappiness may be an essential part of every human life and perhaps even a good part, in the same way in which labour and pain play a central part in living. Should we just get better at tolerating unhappiness or should we perhaps find ways of perfecting our capacity for misery and deal with unhappiness more effectively? Should therapists teach people how to be happy or how to be unhappy or maybe both? Or should they be neutral about these matters and merely allow people to come to their own conclusions? Therapists of different persuasions have different views about the objectives of their profession. Their clients however rarely know this. It seems important therefore to clarify this basic issue of what the therapist's role is in the human quest for happiness.

The function of the book

This book will propose a philosophical exploration of what therapy and counselling can offer clients who seek to understand their own life better. It will consider why it is that therapists so easily fall into the trap of aiming to make people more happy even when they believe that this should not be the case. It will investigate the possibility that therapeutic culture is not really anything new and that for many millennia human beings have sought to improve their situation not just by finding out how to control nature, or create beautiful things, but also by understanding themselves and each other better and most importantly by trying to understand what it means to live a good human life.

This is what is usually referred to as the search for wisdom and those who practised the art of wisdom were called philosophers not therapists.

So we shall consider whether philosophy has a part to play in redefining psychotherapy and whether doing so helps or hinders the quest for happiness. These are important and timely questions to address as governments jump on the bandwagon of brief evidence-based therapeutic interventions and positive psychology. Before we all forget what psychotherapy and counselling are about in the first place let us remember the well established human evidence that existential misery persists regardless of our attempts at getting rid of unhappiness. There is nothing sure and simple about trying to make someone happier. Do we really want mechanical and manualized forms of therapy to instruct people in how to live? This smacks of a prescriptive approach which takes us into a dogmatic direction. There are resonances of Huxley's *Brave New World* in there. The solution is not social engineering either by the widespread popping of happiness pills or powders, be they anti-depressants, tranquillizers, amphetamines, cocaine, heroin, marihuana or alcohol. Nor is the only solution to be taught how to keep one's mind under control by cognitive means.

As our scientific knowledge expands it is high time that a new wisdom is reintroduced into the equation of human living. And therapists now have a central role to play in this. At the moment they seem to fall into two camps. There are those who are opting to go along with the cognitive revolution, either because they believe in it or in the hope they can make it work and that perhaps, whilst no one is watching, they can smuggle some messy humanity back into the therapeutic process anyway. They rightly argue that doing something is better than doing nothing and that the evidence-based brief interventions at least have the merit of being democratic and funded. And there are others who are staunchly fighting to maintain the old status quo of longer term dynamic or humanistic therapies, based on insight or catharsis. This book will promote a third option, which is to move beyond both these ways of approaching the predicament and to rethink therapy in a more radical fashion. After a century of therapy most therapists accept that they can learn from all the different approaches and methods and that some amount of integration is a good thing. But most of us are also aware that we have to be disciplined in our understanding and evaluation of what we are trying to achieve when doing so. We just need to take that reflection to a higher level and link it with a reflection on life itself.

The purpose of the book

This book sets out to enable such reflection. It does not propose any particular therapeutic methods, skills or technique. It proposes philosophical clarity and logical thinking instead. It appeals to mental health professionals and therapists and counsellors of all orientations to dare to stop and think again, not just with clients, professionally, but also in our own lives and in a personal capacity. This book sets out a path for those who are interested in the evolution of therapy in a radical and more philosophical direction. It neither condones nor sets itself against the CBT revolution. It neither favours the old psychodynamic or humanistic approaches, nor rejects them. It simply proposes that we learn from all these therapies and integrate their understanding of the human condition by taking the widest possible perspective. It sets out to reunite therapy with its own horizon. That is the horizon of human existence and the purpose of being a person. A disciplined therapeutic integration requires philosophical clarity and that is precisely what we will set out to achieve.

So, if you have been wondering how to live your life more fully and more truly and help your clients to do the same, this book is for you. It will get you thinking about the old issues in a new way, though it will not provide any easy answers. It will lead you right back to your human roots and from there to your personal and professional aspirations and your desire to recalibrate your life and your work on a more solid and robust, more real foundation. It will start by looking in Chapter 1 at the role of beliefs and values in psychotherapy and how human beings arrive at their beliefs. Then in Chapter 2 it will consider what the quest for happiness is actually about and what it means to live a good life. This will take us to a survey of positive psychology and its insistence on happiness and subjective well being in Chapter 3. This will lead us to revisit the predictable human difficulties that get in the way of a blissful existence in Chapter 4 and in Chapter 5 the unpredictable crises that make things even harder. From there, in Chapter 6 we shall put happiness back in context with other emotions and states of mind, whilst considering the therapeutic communication that is needed to work with such, often unspoken, emotions. Chapter 7 will consider what life is about if happiness is not enough. Throughout the book we will challenge the role and current status of the psychotherapy profession. Throughout the book the idea of happiness is dealt with as a potential goal, whilst it is being contrasted and compared with other objectives, such as that of well being, meaning, understanding, purpose or transcendence. After all our explorations we may discover that we have returned full circle to the values we started out with but had forgotten. But this time we should have some solid ground under our feet, since we will have gone round the houses before settling down. We can already put forward the hypothesis that after all our thinking and debating we will be no further ahead in finding happiness. For, it would be surprising if a few pages of writing and some reflections afford us what so many lives have not been able to obtain: a secure base of bliss. But we may discover why happiness is and will remain elusive and why in spite of all our new knowledge, insight and technology, there is still no magic fix for life. The path we are on then is not one that will lead us to a happy life somewhere over a sunrise horizon, but rather one that will allow us to get a sense of the map of human living, enabling us to find our own direction towards a right way to live.

Chapter 1

Opening Pandora's Box: Values and Beliefs in Psychotherapy

*The soul unto itself
Is an imperial friend,
Or the most agonizing spy
An enemy could send.*

(Emily Dickinson, 1994: 46)

So, what is the role of therapy in our elusive quest for happiness? What is it that people hope to get from counselling and psychotherapy? Do they seek to meet a friend who has their best interests at heart and who will help them live a happier life? If so, are their expectations realistic and is therapy up to the challenge? Is therapy a refuge where people come to create the illusion that they may be able to overcome all their troubles and live happily ever after? What is happiness anyway?

The *Cambridge English Dictionary* defines happiness as a feeling that causes pleasure or satisfaction. The internet-based encyclopaedia, Wikipedia, defines happiness as 'a prolonged or lasting emotional or affective state that feels good or pleasing' (Wikipedia, 2006). Is therapy meant to achieve such a positive pleasurable and lasting emotional state for clients? In other words should therapy make things better and people feel good? If so, is therapy based on wishful thinking and does it conjure up a kind of utopia, which is ultimately unobtainable or unsustainable? We need to find out whether therapy deals with the real human questions or whether it deals with the ephemeral and short-term effects of suggestion only. Does therapy tackle the fundamental human issues of good and evil, life and death, anxiety and despair for instance? We shall start our journey of understanding therapy and its quest for happiness by looking at the ideology and belief systems on which our society and its new therapeutic aspirations are based, for they define our expectations of happiness.

Culture and ideology

Every culture entices or forces people into its dominant ideology, even when it tolerates varied beliefs and leaves some people to live in the margins of society. It teaches us to believe certain things and to disbelieve others. It prescribes certain fundamental rules of conduct and it demands a usually fairly strict obedience to these principles and their code of honour. It does so by giving us a set of prohibitions on the one hand and a set of injunctions and objectives in the form of ideals and aspirations on the other hand. These conventions and values are usually neatly wrapped in the culture's religion, which links people together. It does so by being centred around one or more holy texts, which cannot be questioned, since they are defined as divine or holy. Such adherence to a prescribed worldview magically transforms chaos into order and confusion into meaning.

This sacred link uniting the culture can be many different things, but if it is to acquire religious and sacred status it has to be rooted in a mythology which refers to the culture's origin and which cannot be questioned and has to be taken on faith. We can only truly belong to a culture to the extent that we accept its framework of reference. Its ideas, rules, beliefs and conventions are effectively distributed through the network of families and institutions that form the substratum of the culture. They are passed on in the form of values and these values may change somewhat from one generation to the next according to the times and mores and depending on what is most desirable and sought after at any particular moment. Cultures draw their power from these underlying beliefs and give direction to the individual's actions by aiming for certain defined ideals and standards, which are themselves derived from the ideology of the society. Values are the principles that dictate what something is worth in comparison to everything else. Values allow people to evaluate their experiences or possessions and put a price on them. Values are the measure of what people come to expect for and of themselves and they provide clarity about the objectives and characteristics of a well lived life. Values are determined by how much we are willing to give up in order to acquire or keep the thing we value. An ultimate value is something you would give everything up for, including your own life. The ultimate value is the ultimate good of our society and this is opposed by its ultimate evil: its arch enemy, that which we fear most. Evil is essentially that which actively undermines or threatens the good that we value. Usually it appears to do so gratuitously.

Each culture incorporates a view about good and evil. This is necessary if people are to have a definite sense of what is desirable and undesirable so that

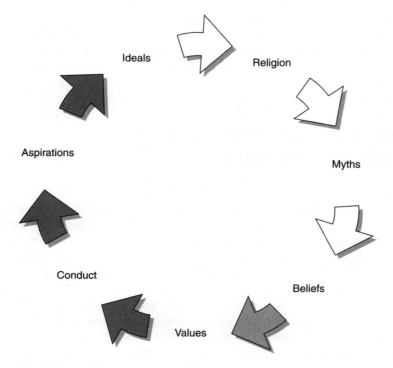

Figure 1.1   The cycle of ideology

they know how to act and what to aim for in life. The image of good and evil is graphically represented in the myth of creation that exists in a society, since this myth defines the fundamental conflicts out of which their world has grown. As such it lays the foundations of the sort of life an individual in this society can come to expect. So our lives are anchored from the outset in a clear and unambiguous explanation about the origin and purpose of human beings: we are told in no uncertain terms what the good and bad ways of acting are and how we should behave. We are offered a sequence of myths, values, beliefs and aspirations that keep us within a safe circle of good behaviour and which are summarized and organized by the edicts of our ideology or religion. We operate our lives within these parameters and find our evaluations within their boundaries.

Religions and their myths of creation are the magic circles within which cultures thrive. A myth of creation exists in every culture, but may not be present in an obvious way. In Western culture, in the twenty first century, we are divided in our mythology, for we are absorbing many varied myths and there are diverse groups amongst us, each living by their own legends and holy stories. Mostly our societies are still well embedded in the old established Judeo-Christian narratives about the origin of mankind in the Garden of Eden. Since Islam is also derived from the Old Testament, it too is compatible with that myth. Whilst Hindu and Buddhist notions are very different they have generally taken up a less prominent position in the Western world, quite likely because they do not include the same evangelical aspirations as the monotheistic religions do.

The core mythology and a new contender for the throne

Much of Western living is still set against the backdrop of our expulsion from an imagined paradise and the sense that things could be so much better if this had not happened. Deep down we attribute our fall to human frailty and failure. The purpose of existence remains that of the struggle with original sin and people hanker after a time when all will be forgiven and they will be admitted to a heavenly abode and rewarded for their hard work on earth. This myth is still written into most of our memories and drives us forward to great and small achievements and the best behaviour we can muster. We seek redemption and expect positive results if we do our best, aiming for better times to come later, either in this life or after our death.

What we often seem to forget is that in our cultural myth this endless striving is the result of Adam and Eve's inability to resist temptation; not the temptation of exquisite pleasure though, but rather the temptation to follow a natural curiosity and taste the fruit of the tree of knowledge. Their exodus from paradise is cleverly engineered by the seductive serpent who reminds them of their capacity to choose and eat the forbidden fruit. And they get precisely what they asked for: outside of the Garden of Eden they are exposed to the immediate knowledge of the gender differences between them, feelings of shame, regret and guilt and awareness of the contrast between life and death. They are confronted with human suffering, labour, conflict and responsibility. And so it is that human history and culture begin, in suffering; for outside of the Garden of Eden we have to survive by our own wits and the sweat of our brow. As soon as human beings come into the real world they have to learn to survive and record their learning to pass it on to the next generation. They also have to learn to suffer.

It is precisely because we have had to deal with all these existential problems over many millennia that we have evolved various ingenious ways of survival. And it is that same ingenuity that has ultimately led to a new global value system and a new set of beliefs, namely that of science and technology and its concomitants of industry and consumerism. All these are generated from the same desire to reduce suffering and achieve an easier way of life by applying our intelligence. The emphasis is now firmly on the human capacity for knowledge and understanding and the desirability of achievement and competition. Since the late nineteenth century Darwinian evolutionary theory has finally produced a suitable alternative myth of creation for this new religion, one that fits with the new spirit of optimism and belief in mankind's great capacity for scientific observation and technological prowess. Evolution is what we are about. The Big Bang theory of early twentieth century physics has at the same time provided the necessary cosmological backdrop to the new ideas and so the scene is set for a complete overhaul of our dominant ideology.

Science as religion

Few people are aware of the extent to which the contemporary scientific spirit has gradually taken on the guise of an ideology. It has been a gradual and surreptitious take-over bid. But it has been an extremely successful one, because the tenets of the new scientific belief system can be so easily distributed through the new churches, schools, media and universities and are so easily absorbed and so eminently sensible. Of course the new religion confuses us more than the old ones, for it is far less stable and commands a formidable authority based on the facts and products that it continuously generates. No church has ever been able to do such compelling magic. Science comes up with new ideas, data and theories on a regular basis and demands that we stay informed at all times: the objective is for us to evolve and to stay in touch with the latest inventions, theories and gadgets, lest we become outmoded, outdated and out of touch. The objective is to live ever smoother and more dynamic lives, striving to achieve as much of our potential as possible by basing our everyday activities on scientific data for maximum success. No wonder the culture of youth has got the upper hand. No wonder we are obsessed with longevity, fitness and happiness. The age of information has firmly replaced the age of knowledge, which had previously already replaced the age of wisdom. While wisdom can only emerge from maturity, fast changing information relies on immediacy and fits better with the vitality of youth. So now we no longer adjust our conduct to the old values and well established routines of our ancestors and forebears nor in terms of the word of our gods, but rather in line with the new evidence provided to us by the latest research. We live evidence-based lives and we take our cues from the media to keep us informed of the latest fashions and values to follow. One day we are told to eat or do one thing for a longer, healthier life, the next the evidence has changed and we are advised to pursue another new fad. Politicians have also learnt to use and manipulate scientific data to their advantage: they all dance to the same tune and propose new legislation in line with the new evidence available. No wonder they do not come up with widely differing views any longer. They steer a course between the scientific data and the popular opinions formed by the media.

And so we no longer worship the symbols of divinity and eternal life nor do we aim very much to emulate our elders. They are far too much out of date. We are not nearly as interested in universal values, but attracted by the glitter of the promise of immediate and direct results. So we worship the icons of glamorous and successful living proffered by society. We aspire to possess the latest gadgets and gimmicks and lifestyles, demonstrated to us by the stars and celebrities who seem to have the edge on this fast and high life. Though, unsurprisingly, many of us find this tyranny of celebrity and media culture with its heady mix of pseudo science, politics, soap, popular opinion and its daily parade of cars, clothes and beautiful people frustrating, unsatisfactory and irritatingly trivializing. It fails us by not addressing us as individuals with a real project or a personal part to play in the scheme of things. The secular values held out to us are so ephemeral that they do not bind us together in quite the same, profoundly spiritual and deeply emotional way that the old religions were capable of doing. In fact they divide us for we are now forever in competition with each other for those few rare places in the sun of an imagined Eldorado of fame and fortune.

In addition we have been left with a constant tension between the co-existing old and new religions. That tension has to be dealt with in some way. One of the ways of doing this is by coming up with a compromise solution. A possible compromise is to integrate the scientific theories with a satisfactory concept of purpose. One candidate for such a theory is that of Intelligent Design, which is the belief that God created the world (perhaps with a Big Bang) but then left this newly created world to evolve in accordance with Darwin's evolutionary principles. This is a solution favoured by those who want to save the old religions, but it dilutes these considerably and is not to everyone's taste.

There are other solutions to the puzzle. Nihilism is a popular solution, consisting of giving up on any spirituality whilst simply living in the secular sphere. Agnosticism is a weaker form of the same basic attitude. But many people find this negation of spirituality too extreme and harsh, so they simplify the problem by splitting their lives in two. They espouse the old religions with new intensity in private moments, whilst living their modern lives along secular lines. This makes it harder to know what personal or moral objectives to follow. It becomes ever more tempting to follow a simple and apparently attractive and straightforward objective like the quest for happiness. Indeed if we frankly opt for the values of the secular world, which are essentially based in the pursuit of maximum pleasure, comfort and ease in a material world, we become Hedonists. If we seek to remain true to some of the older values we may seek happiness by pursuing some form of Eudaemonia: the search for the good life by living in harmony with the demon, or the force of life. But we have a plethora of demons on offer to us and there is a multitude of new spiritual pursuits available to us as well.

Ideologies redefined

In the midst of all this confusion most of us now live with some form of hybrid belief, frequently without awareness of exactly what truths and objectives guide us. On the one hand we believe in human ingenuity and bolster our confidence by engrossing ourselves in technologically based and hedonistically orientated twenty first century pursuits. On the other hand we continue to worship the principles of some form of old fashioned religion or some new set of humanistic values. We may for instance foreground charity for others who are worse off than us or we may set stock by honesty or loyalty. The great televised charitable events like Live Aid or Children in Need appeal to many of us as they bind us together with a common purpose and make us briefly feel better about humanity and the world we live in. Most of us have some value that takes us to a higher plain, beyond that of purely monetary and sensory satisfaction. We tend to feel good about ourselves when we perform some action in relation to those principles, whereas we feel good in ourselves when we pursue the sensory pleasure principle. All the same the contradictions between these two modes of operating are glaringly obvious and it is no wonder that people often confess to being perplexed or confused about what the purpose of their life really is. They might believe in fame, success, wealth or pleasure as the ultimate principles to define their lives in a secular way, but underneath they will sense that this is not really enough and that by the standards of their hidden ideology a lot more is required of them. We end up living in a state of vaguely defined but constant existential guilt. The trouble is that most of us do not have the time or the opportunity to stand still long enough to think about the reasons for this. We do not really know what motivates our lives. More often than not people end up believing that all they want is to just be happy and if possible make some others happy in the process as well.

What people fail to see is that this search for happiness as a pure form of hedonism has enormous drawbacks since it makes it hard to accept any aspect of human living that involves deprivation, pain, sorrow, hardship, aging or failure: all things that religions normally seek to absorb, validate and integrate. Hedonism is often a form of Humanism, which is the belief that human beings are the highest form of life around and that the primary goal of life must be their happiness and fulfilment. It is one of the many forms of ideology people hold today. A variety of these are illustrated in Figure 1.2.

Ideologies provide us with a clear moral framework of values, beliefs and aspirations, for they tell us what the ultimate cause and objectives of life are, whether the ideology has been theistic or not. Humanity has had theistic ideologies for as long as history has been recorded or wherever on the globe we look. From Polytheism to Monotheism, there have long been religious explanations of our existence that place us safely within the lap of some God or gods. But there have also been other explanations of how the universe fits together. Buddhism and Taoism and many forms of Western philosophy have aimed to explain the universe without resorting to a god. Western thinking has of course been dominated by Christian thinking for millennia, though all this was changed at the end of the nineteenth century when religious ideology was replaced with scientific accounts of human evolution and motivation. Darwinism,

Figure 1.2 Ideological range

Marxism and Freudianism revolutionized human thinking; the notion of human purpose was drastically altered. We were cut off from our roots and from our skies all at the same time. Darwin questioned the very principle of creation and replaced it with his theory of evolution which could provide a more credible principle of explanation for our existence but left us believing that the main motivation and rather minimalist objective of our lives was that of the survival of the fittest. Marx threw all religious thinking out as mere addiction, calling it the opium of the people and preferring economic theory and a fervent belief in an egalitarian principle that would bring the oppressed masses into power: a profound belief in the human capacity for social evolution, foreshadowed by Hegel. Unfortunately the wisdom of the masses turned out to be less reliable than he had hoped. Freudian theories also eloquently rejected religious thinking as wishful and described it as the mere sublimation of the sexual instinct. This idea took root in the popular mind and together with other cultural developments, such as birth control technology, led to the sexual revolution which was predicated on the Reichian notion that sexual liberation and hedonism are better principles to live by than oppression and inhibition. When there is no longer a God to guarantee morality it becomes possible and desirable to experiment with new rules for living. As Nietzsche predicted we had to revalue all our values.

Rules and principles

On the whole we have sought, quite logically, to base our new rules on the principles provided by the facts. God has been replaced by human beings, by society and culture and it is these that now demand total obedience of us. The spiritual struggle of a growing person in the Western world is no longer defined by pleasing a god or a universal edict by tackling one's own inner turmoil. It is that of achieving maximum success and recognition in the eyes of our culture and society. It is not eternity but other people that are our horizon. From the moment we are born we begin to pick up the rules of the world around us, first through our families, but very soon through the input of television and other influences upon us, teaching us that the objective of life is to rise above the narrow confines of our own family and social group and reach for fortune, fame and triumph. No wonder it becomes so much harder to keep control over rebellious teenagers when the family is no longer a boundary they respect because their horizons reach so much farther. People who are redefined as instruments of survival rather than as instruments of God must assert themselves as much as possible instead of showing obedience as was demanded of them formerly. If only the fittest survive, we have to become as fit as is feasible. We have to make ourselves competitive, not only financially and professionally but also in the personal sphere: we have to be fit, attractive and happy. And yet we resent this.

But no matter how much we talk about it and find fault with the way of the world, blaming it on the media, broken families, the slackening of religion, drugs, sexual liberation and all the rest, it makes no difference where we seek the cause of all evil. The changes we have made cannot be undone and we have to learn to live with the new state of play. Most people continue to be rather confused about the world of today and find it hard to find meaning in it. We are confronted with the absurdity of existence and plunged into meaninglessness by being unhinged from our eternal northern star. So we seek to replace the old gods with new ones.

There are so many potential transcendental principles we can turn to. We can either put our faith in human beings, as in Humanism or Psychologism, or we can work for society, as in Marxism or Socialism. We may of course postpone a decision and refer to ourselves as agnostic, which is a way of saying that we simply do not know or do not want to think about it. Or we can reject the idea of ideology all together and call ourselves a nihilist. On the whole this means we have not yet made up our minds as to where to put our energy. Alternatively we may find the greatest advantage in using our energy to deconstruct or destruct, usually because we have not found a place for ourselves in the world. Nihilism is an increasingly popular stance for people in a post-modern world, with its corollaries of deconstructionism, scepticism and even anarchism or fanaticism. We are an increasingly cynical society and our children have less and less scope to dare to believe in transcendental principles, so that their vision often skips towards the pursuit of fame, fortune and happiness, which seem the most direct way of making room for oneself and rising above the clutter of the world. Once upon a time wisdom and maturity were symbols of virtues worth striving for, the prize of a life in tune with the higher purpose of human existence. Now youth, maximum enjoyment and fun are some of the most prized qualities of existence. Our undeclared value systems are riddled with short sightedness.

False prophets

As Western ideology is progressively more based in reductionistic objectives our prophets are often those who work with the new technology that provides us with new hope and dreams. Either they devise gadgets or technologies that simplify our lives or they hold out the promise of making our lives happier, healthier and longer. In spite of all our new knowledge and understanding of the physical world, we are arguably more alienated from the purpose of human existence than ever before. We rarely think about it. We may argue about the meaning of life or what makes a person happy, but we do not pose the question of what it is all for. We have not managed to come up with a coherent, credible and morally satisfactory story to replace the old myths. Instead we have the reductionism of a materialistic myth which tells us of the mechanics of human existence and at best shows us how to profit from it most. Seemingly people do not even try to challenge the norm of materialistic meaning, but speak instead of simple values like 'having a good time', as if the world is a great party and life should be experienced as a special treat. It is not always clear what is meant by 'a good time' though. People are often a bit vague or mixed up about their own happiness. They may overrate their unhappiness by comparing it to the expectation that life should be good and easy. We may confuse wealth, youth and success with happiness, so that our idols become those people who have acquired most of these attributes all at once. They appear to us to be happy because they are living the idealized life, though in reality they seldom are, as they struggle with the strange contradictions between their outward image of achievement and their internal sense of fraud and a failure to thrive. They may already have discovered that the happiness they have striven for was nothing but fool's gold. The real thing remains elusive.

Therapists need to understand these philosophical problems, so as not just to go along with people's spiritual bankruptcy and confusion. To begin with it helps for therapists to familiarize themselves with the personal convictions and theories that form the backbone of a person's life. They need to understand not just their clients' cognitive beliefs, but much more importantly their ideological and spiritual beliefs. They need to be able to work with the fundamental ideas that underpin their clients' moral judgments and self-evaluation.

Of course this means familiarizing yourself with ideas from the different world religions and their moral systems to get some perspective on different ways of looking at life. But even more important is to find a personal connection with moral thinking that is non-dogmatic in nature and that can help you understand where other people are coming from. In this respect it is illuminating to go back beyond the roots of dominant Judeo-Christian or Islamic morality and to investigate alternative worldviews in a playful manner. This is when we notice the similarities between so many religious stories of creation and human purpose. Remarkably many of the world religions, including Christianity, Judaism, Hinduism, Buddhism, Islam and Taoism, but also Paganism, Zoroastrianism, Heathenism and Hellenism, are based on comparable conceptions of the origins of mankind and the roots of good and evil. Many African and Maori stories bear a resemblance to these as well.

If we want to go to the bedrock of Western accounts of the creation of morality we can do a lot worse than to reinvestigate the Greek, Roman, Egyptian, Germanic, Celtic, Anglo-Saxon or Scandinavian myths that predate Judeo-Christian and Muslim belief systems. These early pagan beliefs are still with us to some extent, though very few people would say they take such religions seriously. This frees us to contemplate them, with enough familiarity and enough distance and without too much risk of offending or alienating anybody. When we examine the myth of creation of such religions we find that the old stories are more compatible with recent scientific accounts of the beginnings of mankind than we might expect, though they are a lot more imaginative. I shall illustrate this by briefly considering the relevance of the ancient Greek myth of creation.

Prometheus and the creation of man

Greek mythology provides us with a standard myth of creation, which tells us that in the beginning there was nothing but chaos. Everything was confused and shapeless; nothing was clearly defined or differentiated. The earth, sea, and air were all mixed together. The earth was not solid, the sea was not fluid, and the air was not transparent yet. When earth, sea and heavens were separated from each other the world as we know it came into existence. None of this is contradictory with current evolutionary thinking or with most other religious views.

In Greek mythology (Graves, 1992) each of the basic elements that the world consists of was represented as a God. It is quite clear that much of this is to be taken as symbolism rather than as literal truth. So at the start there was simply Chaos, the god of disorder, who gave birth to Gaia, goddess of the earth, who in turn gave birth to Eros, the god of love. So the principle of love is there from the beginning mediating between chaos and earth. Out of this love are created other gods, such as Ouranos, god of the heavens and Oceanos, god of the seas and Rhea, goddess of the rivers. With her son Ouranos (sky), Gaia (earth) then gave birth to the Titans, gods of the under-world, of which the youngest was Chronos, god of time. Again it is very telling that time is such an important parameter.

After this the Titans, and others, gave birth to more specific gods and demi-gods, like Thanatos, god of death and Hypnos, god of sleep and Nemesis, god of anger and revenge. It is fascinating that there were therefore gods repre-senting all the fundamental and significant human experiences, even those we might think of as negative. The same is true in Hinduism. Also, all of these negatives are related, which is interesting. Chronos, time, then fought his father Ouranos, the sky, and eventually this led to the separation of his mother, earth, and father, sky, who split up to never be one again. Here is an early example of the importance of the vagaries and conflicts of family life. It is because of this separation that Chronos, the god of time, became all pow-erful and got to dominate earth and sky. As is the case in daily life, it is time that does all the separating and dividing. This interesting metaphor of human living reminds us that it is time that human beings are made of and that dom-inates our lives, more than either earth or sky alone. Chronos then married his sister Rhea, the goddess of rivers (and flow), but ate all their children, for fear of being dethroned by them. Eventually the sixth child, Zeus (the living one), was rescued by his mother, who gave Chronos a stone to eat instead which made him regurgitate his other children (Hestia, Hera, Demeter, Hades and Poseidon), who promptly fled to mount Olympus with their brother Zeus. And so the conflict between family members is the essence of all human rela-tions and sets the scene for the future. Rather reassuring. A mother saving her children from the father's wrath by stealth: heroic but tragic, since there will be a price to pay. Tragedy is constantly present in this story about human origins. And it gets even better.

For when the gods and Titans had settled down they created new creatures in the shape of animals of all sorts and shapes. But they wanted to create a nobler animal and so man was made. It was Prometheus, one of the Titans who had taken the side of the gods on Olympus, who shaped man out of earth mixed with water. Prometheus is the representative of labour and industry. Man was thus shaped out of clay and immediately linked to the notion of having to work for his existence and create things out of earth. He was also from the start endowed with more abilities than the other animals. Prometheus made man in the image of the gods and gave him an upright stature. Unlike the animals that face downwards towards the earth, human beings face upwards towards the heavens. Such a lofty position and such high aspirations are certain to lead to trouble and the story of Pandora's Box is the story of the predictable and necessary downfall of human beings after they have become a little too proud. Let us note in passing that this downfall is not a punishment as is the expulsion from paradise in the bible, but rather an indispensable consequence of our desire to reach for the sky.

When Prometheus was given the task to create all the creatures, the animals as well as the human beings, he enlisted his brother Epimetheus to do all the hard work. Epimetheus did a good job, distributing all possible good qualities to the animals so that when he had finished there were none left. So when it came to making the human being he had run out of gifts and Prometheus had to help him out. Realizing that humans would be lacking so much by comparison to the other animals he decided to give them a special gift to defend themselves. This gift was that of fire, something which up to then had been strictly reserved for the gods.

Prometheus stole the fire from the sun, lighting his torch by it and bringing it down to mankind. Now people could make weapons and tools, cultivate the earth, defend themselves against animals and each other and warm their houses for comfort. This allowed human culture to develop and for human beings to learn crafts and sciences and arts that made them equal, or nearly equal, to the gods. Interestingly this is an exact illustration of the history of mankind, evolving its industry, science and technology. However, when Zeus realized what Prometheus had done, he was extremely angry. He had Hephaestus, the smith, shackle Prometheus to the side of a hill, high in the Caucasus Mountains. Prometheus hung there for centuries, having his liver pecked out every day by an eagle sent by Zeus. The torture was endless since the frosts at night would heal his wounds so that it could start all over again the next morning. In other words Prometheus was crucified so that human beings could benefit from the godly gift of fire. Yet they too were still to pay a price for their acquisition.

The story of Pandora

Zeus dealt with the advantages that Prometheus had bestowed on man by giving these mortal beings a gift that would counteract and destroy their happiness and their success. He decided to give them woman. He figured that woman could easily undo all that Prometheus had done. A beautiful young girl was created, named Pandora. This name meant 'all is given'. Indeed she had all the advantages the gods were able to bestow on her. She had a beautiful body and voice, given by Hephaestus. Athena gave her dexterity and inventiveness. Aphrodite put a spell of enchantment over her. Mercury gave her persuasiveness and so on and so forth until she was the most amazing creature on earth. Then Zeus gave Pandora to Epimetheus, Prometheus's brother. He could not resist temptation and took her in, even though he knew it would mean trouble.

Pandora brought a box with her, which contained a secret. She was told not to open this box. But one day she simply could not contain herself and in spite of Epimetheus's warning, she took the lid off. Immediately a multitude of problems, diseases and troubles escaped into the world. All the illnesses mankind knows suddenly spread all around. All the evil, hatred and spite that can affect human beings were distributed far and wide. Pandora was very upset about what she had set free and she put back the lid as quickly as she could. Then she realized that there was just one more thing in the box that she had not let out and that she could always keep in there safely. In this way it would always be preserved for human beings to rely on. Any person faced with the ills of mankind would still have this last quality to draw on. That last little but ever so important entity always at our disposal was: hope. It was the gift that makes human life liveable, even when everything seems hard and impossible. Hope is that which allows us to endure our fate, no matter how difficult it is.

Relevance of the story to psychotherapy

It seems as if this story of creation provides us with a credible myth to live by or explain our human predicament with. No one would actually believe that the story is an accurate representation of something that happened historically (unlike the myths of creation of currently practised religions which are still taken literally by many) but it serves us well as an illustration of the human struggle and of everyday human reality. It also provides a blueprint for the adventure of human living, for the story clearly tells us that it is up to us to make the most of our gifts, whilst overcoming our troubles. Also these are usually bestowed on us because of our hubris: in this case our over confidence in our ingenuity. The story reminds us that there is always hope to guide us even in the worst of circumstances. This account of human living allows for lots of interpretations and is not to be taken as fact. It is therefore even compatible with an evolutionary notion of the origin of human life. It emphasizes human wit and human struggle as interacting with each other all the time and leading to progress when people find a way to outsmart their fate. Greek myths always emphasize how temporary such victories are since human tragedy and fate always catch up with us providing us with large obstacles and troubles on the way. This never ceases and human living is essentially about finding ways of coping with these. This is true to some extent of biblical stories and of the Mahabharata as well of course and this is where religion and literature catch up with each other: such myths teach us about life and life is always an adventure full of conflict, adversity and strife that we somehow have to learn to master.

We may have evolved into a sophisticated culture but there are certainly no fewer difficulties and troubles to deal with now than ever before. The Pandora story, like the story of Adam and Eve, portrays the human challenge as that of labour in the face of multiple troubles that we have brought upon ourselves. It recognizes that the relations between men and women are often at the centre of the difficulties that arise. It also demonstrates that it is mankind's destiny to evolve further as our natural curiosity will continue to lead us into trouble. These are the kinds of emotional and ideological components that are badly missing from a purely 'scientific' account of what people are about. Therapeutic endeavours need to be based on some sort of narrative conception of the tasks that confront human beings on a daily basis. The notion that we are confronted with a multitude of problems that are not of our own making is quite useful. The idea that there is, at bottom, always this additional quality of persistence in human beings, based on hope, allowing us to overcome our trials and tribulations, is highly relevant to therapeutic culture.

The function of hope

Hope most certainly is necessary for any form of psychotherapy to work. Perhaps it is mainly hope that inspires people in the early days of a therapeutic relationship. Giving hope to individuals who have none is a minimal objective of successful therapy. Psychotherapists who work with disenfranchised people will know that without hope there is no strength and no possibility that real work can be accomplished. Without hope there is no confidence. Confronted with the evils of the world people need a quiet place to recover and have the time to discover, in the reassurance of deep and supportive human contact, that new hope and confidence can be found. They need to gain new courage and inspiration to go forward.

This is not to say that hope giving and encouragement are the sole objectives of therapy. Hope is a necessary component of therapeutic work, but it is only a first step. We still need to deal squarely with the difficulties that people are struggling with. Nothing can be a substitute for the work of confrontation with reality. The evils of this world have to be faced directly in therapy in the same way in which the problems of one's own character have to be dealt with. With some clients therapists may need to be a bit like Pandora: opening the box to let the evils fly around freely, where they had been hidden and suppressed. With other clients therapists may need to enable the person to make sense of all these difficulties and to organize and tame them. With others still all therapy can offer initially is hope and patience and the strength of endurance. Hope is reserved for the rock bottom of existence: it is only useful once we are faced with and are facing up to the human condition in its most raw state. Hope should never therefore be seen as a potential hiding place. Allowing clients to hope for a utopia where all their troubles will be over is not useful. That ideal place, where all is right with the world, is not going to come and does not exist. There is no paradise on earth and as far as we can tell there is none after this life either. If we create the illusion that there is an ultimate place of rapture that therapy can capture, we are not dealing with therapy but with wishful thinking.

Therapists have to be willing to address all the woes of the world even if they are unrelenting. For most of us it is hard to live resourcefully and well and much of the time we will feel weak or discouraged. Pascal said that human beings are so necessarily mad that not to be mad would be another form of madness. It is not really surprising that some of us cannot manage life at all. Even the best of us will encounter crises that get us down.

Kierkegaard had a pretty good idea about the extent of the problem and he accurately described the fundamental fears and anxieties, dreads and despairs that are part and parcel of being a human being. He also linked it with the notion of god forsakenness, something many of us live with everyday since we no longer believe in God.

> Deep within every human being there still lives the anxiety over the possibility of being alone in the world, forgotten by God, overlooked among the millions and millions in the enormous household. (Kierkegaard, 1999: A 363)

When we can no longer believe in a god or gods and we dread the lonely human struggle, the need to find another source of inspiration is on.

Despair and its destructive effect on human beings

So, if life is an inevitable sea of troubles and we can no longer turn to a god to save us, how are we to address problems in therapy? Are we to maximize the good things in life and let our clients aim to eliminate their problems and replace them with an enjoyment of what is pleasant? Is utopia to be found in such avoidant searches for good times? The answer is a resounding no. Though happiness seeking may work occasionally, it is not an enduring solution. For most of us it is not really an option at all. Truth and the good life are to be found not by avoiding life or by living in hiding, but rather by facing the daily struggle of human existence with courage and determination. Human truth is ambiguous and hard earned. As Merleau Ponty (1945/1962) said, we need to find out how to give our lives meaning through the incarnate experience of being alive. It is only by committing ourselves to life and engaging with the actions required in combating the problems we encounter that we can hope to achieve a modicum of happiness. Kierkegaard knew a thing or two about this as well. He recommended the so called negatives of anxiety and despair as good starting points for learning to live, even though this leads to a paradoxical position.

> *Consequently it is an infinite merit to be able to despair. And yet not only is it the greatest misfortune and misery actually to be in despair; no, it is ruin. (Kierkegaard, 1855/1941: 45)*

Kierkegaard ends up by distinguishing between two forms of despair: the despair of weakness and the despair of defiance. In the despair of weakness the person can see that they are capable of asserting selfhood, but they do not yet dare do so. In the despair of defiance the person is empty but trying to assert a self in spite of this and building castles in the air in order to do so. People go through both these experiences and can never assume themselves to be beyond despair, for as their circumstances change their capability for despair changes too. We would be fools to think ourselves above despair, as we would be fools to believe ourselves capable of always acting morally.

Frankl, through his experiences in concentration camps, discovered that people react in different ways to stress and despair and that they are capable of things they would not have thought themselves capable of in more favourable circumstances. We can surprise ourselves in both good and bad ways and should never assume we know how we will respond in new and harsher circumstances.

> *In the living laboratories of the concentration camp, we watched comrades behaving like swine while others behaved like saints; man has both potentialities within himself. Which one he actualises depends on decision, not on conditions. (Frankl, 1967: 35)*

In the therapeutic arena we soon discover that all is not as it seems and that perfectly good people are capable of having awful experiences or doing horrible things, whereas people who seem bad on the outside can find perfectly good moral principles and abilities in themselves as well or suddenly come to great advantage in their lives. We are all capable of both extremes and we may fall to unexpected lows at times. Yet it is also within human capability to improve by learning from experience and by aiming for values and projects that are worthwhile. This is so in spite of a current, post-modern tendency to nihilistic evaluations of the world. Human beings are capable of progress.

They are also capable of change and perfectibility (though not perfection) and they can certainly improve their conditions. What is more: it is when they are tested and tried by circumstances that they show their mettle and that their resilience comes into its own. But they have to find a way to reflect on their experiences and conduct so that they can come to a deliberate decision about how they should live.

Success is not important to freedom

Perhaps what people tend to lose track of these days is exactly that: the fact that they have to create their own meanings. They have to provide a *raison d'être* for themselves. They have to reclaim their freedom and find the best way of being they are capable of, whilst facing up to the worst. Freedom and success are not bound together. Those of us who are not afraid to fail and who are not afraid to suffer may be more free than those who think they are self-determining and in control because they constantly aim for success and live with the constant fear of failure. Sartre understood more about freedom than most and he said:

> to be free does not mean to obtain what one has wished (in the broad sense of choosing). In other words, success is not important to freedom. (Sartre, 1943/1956: 483)

To remember this is in itself liberation. It means that people even in the worst conditions can aim for freedom, or at least for a small measure of freedom in their attitude. To make sense of their world and to organize it for themselves in accordance with their beliefs is a greater freedom than to achieve the artificial and overrated goods of twenty first century culture. Whilst many people find themselves in conditions of penury and need, few find themselves in a position to turn their difficulties to the good that Frankl was suggesting was within their reach. Frankl thought there were basically three ways of finding meaning in life (Frankl, 1967). He suggested that people find meaning in the experiential values of the good things we can take from the world, in the creative values of the good things we can contribute to the world and ultimately in the attitudinal values of the way in which we choose to deal with the inevitable suffering that will be our lot in life at certain times when neither positive experiences nor creativity are on the menu.

It is not therefore misfortune but only human despair about misfortunes, or rather the lack of willingness to stand up and be counted, that makes evil go unchallenged and makes misery permanent. When Pandora's Box is opened and the evil escapes, something or someone needs to draw our attention to the possibility of improvement and overcoming. It isn't a bad bottom line for counsellors and therapists to build on. If as therapists we can understand, protect and enhance human freedom we may be able to play a significant part in helping people to find meaning where meaninglessness reigned before.

So perhaps we can now answer the question of whether it is right for therapists to be the guardians of human happiness or human contentment. The answer has got to be: only to the extent that therapists do so by addressing rather than by avoiding the realities of human living. But this may mean that the training and practice of therapists have to change considerably.

Historical perspective

Why is the role of the therapist shifting so much? Szasz, in his 1961 book *The Myth of Mental Illness*, concluded that in our society we will increasingly need to seek help with our problems in living. He says:

> *We are all students in the metaphorical school of life. Here none of us can afford to become discouraged or despairing. And yet, in this school, religious cosmologies, nationalistic myths, and lately psychiatric theories have more often functioned as obscurantist teachers misleading the student than as genuine clarifiers helping him to help himself. (Szasz, 1961: 273)*

Why is it then that people are turning to therapists to help them to live? If we want to set human endeavours in the context of their historical development, we find that Foucault's poignant analysis of the history of mental illness explains a lot.

Foucault's analysis of the archaeology of madness, which he sketched out in his history of insanity in the Age of Reason called *Madness and Civilization* (Foucault, 1965), gives us a handle on all this. He argued that madness is the limit of human reason in the same way in which death is the limit of human life. Both are sanctified and so both evoke horror and awe.

> *As death is the limit of human life in the realm of time, madness is the limit in the realm of animality, and just as that has been sanctified by the death of Christ, madness, in its most bestial nature, has also been sanctified. (Foucault, 1965: 81)*

There is always a need for opposites to be taken into account if we are going to be serious about our approach of the human realities that tax us the most. Yet, madness itself, Foucault proposed, is a way for us to escape from the stark realities of everyday life. It is something akin to sleeping or if we prefer something like simply being mistaken. More poetically put by Foucault himself as:

Madness is precisely at the point of contact between the oneiric and the erroneous (ibid.: 106). ... It is not reason diseased but reason dazzled. (ibid.: 108)

This sums it up quite nicely. For this is what happens to most of us: we are not ill but dazed and dazzled by the complexity and confusion of living. But we do not have to respond to this by thinking of ourselves as emotionally or mentally deficient. Foucault gave us a good way of conceiving differently of mental illness in relation to different human ideologies, which deal with the issue of wellness and illness in different ways. Many are familiar with Foucault's archaeology of madness. He was one of the first people to pinpoint the ways in which society has approached the phenomenon of otherness and difference at different times. He recognized that each phase of history had different moral principles and beliefs, or as he put it: different eras had different epistemes, or ways in which knowledge and problems were approached.

Below is an overview of his views. I have added an extra dimension to his list to bring it up to date (van Deurzen and Arnold-Baker, 2005).

Epistemes	
Middle Ages	Exclusion
Renaissance	Resemblance
Classical Age	Representation
Modernity	Self-reference
Post-modernity	Death of self
Virtuality	Inclusion

Figure 1.3 Foucault's Epistemes

In the Middle Ages people were preoccupied with the exclusion of a middle way: things were either good or bad and if you did not fit into the picture of the church about what was good, you were expelled as an outsider. This age was represented graphically by Brueghel's painting of the ship of fools, where mad people were sent off to sea to die. In the Renaissance (seventeenth century) there was a revival of the ideals of godliness: people aimed to be as similar to the virtues of religion as they could. Being god-like was a good value to follow. In the Classical Age (eighteenth and early nineteenth century) representation took over: people now wanted to find the representations of good and bad in nature, in the outside world: body and mind got split and scientific thinking took over. It led to a denial of what human beings are. Then, in the Modern Age, of the late nineteenth and early twentieth centuries, man became self-absorbed and enamoured with human achievements. People started believing they could do anything and that they could overcome any problem. This was the age of self-reference which was overtaken by the era of post-modernity and the death of the self in the atomic age, when individuals no longer mattered in the same way and mankind for the first time became capable of destroying itself. Now knowledge and values both suddenly became relative. Truth was no longer definitive and the new awareness that mankind could self-destruct or destroy the planet settled in. Everything had become temporary.

An age of virtuality

This is no longer true for our culture however. I have argued that we are now moving on from post-modernity into the Age of Virtuality and I have written about this elsewhere (van Deurzen, 2000; Van Deurzen and Arnold-Baker, 2005). The Age of Virtuality is the age when mass communication takes over from individual person to person communication and where values are constantly replaced with new values and have to be re-valued as Nietzsche predicted more than 100 years ago. It is also an age when there is a renewed interest in happiness and well being and where we may be on the verge of rediscovering the importance of community on a wider scale than before. For our virtuality also reconnects us and brings us closer to more people than ever before.

Perhaps this will be the age where we finally get the hang of the difficult art of living. As mentioned above, in the Middle Ages mad people were excluded from their community, while in the Classical Age they were locked away as criminals and in the Modern Age treated medically. In the Post-Modern Age they were sent back into the community, which sometimes meant negligence of the real needs of the individual. It was the age of survival of the fittest. In the Age of Virtuality and the global village, where communication and electronic connections are beginning to take over and insert us into a new and wider network of virtual relationships, there are new challenges and new possibilities. We know more and are more aware of multiple possible interpretations of any person's experience. On the World Wide Web we can always find another person who has had a similar experience to ourselves and we can feel ourselves included in a larger more diverse community across the whole world. Of course this also means that we need to work harder at making sense of things if we are to keep it all together. For here we come back to Pandora and her box full of demons. Because what she has set free is more than we bargained for but it may also be the beginning of something promising.

Dealing with the demons

As Pandora lets the demons loose from her box, we need to ensure that we shall not hide away from the consequences. We need to find sure ways of dealing with our demons, for we cannot avoid them. Carl Jung pointed out the need to face our own shadow. But before him Nietzsche spoke of accepting our capacity for the daemonic. To span between beast and god is what he thought we should aim for. Rollo May (1969a) also spoke of the importance of the daemonic element of human nature and the need to befriend one's own daemonic or powerful elements.

Freud only recognized one demon until 1929: libido, the sexual instinct. This is not really surprising against a Victorian background and perhaps more importantly against a Judaeo-Christian background. The bible's story of the expulsion from Eden sets the tone. Sexuality is the demon that haunts us. Freud did like to refer to various other Greek myths, and tragedies, the stories of Oedipus and his father Laius and mother Jocaste for instance, and he was clearly taken with the notion of inevitable human tragedy as crucial learning points in our development. But it was only at the end of his career that he introduced that other crucial human demon: death.

Indeed we need to recognize that we cannot reduce human suffering to one single kind of experience. We have many devils in our lives. There are many and various concerns that preoccupy and bedevil human beings. Human living is complex and often unpredictable and as Jaspers (1951) has shown much of it is defined by limit situations, where we come to the edge of our existence and have to take a stance.

Steady progress into the future

Heidegger was the philosopher who really put the ultimates and negatives at the centre of his thinking. He is the one who truly put death and human mortality on the philosophical map. He emphasized the significance of death as the point towards which human beings always progress through time (Heidegger, 1927/1962). Our mortality is that which defines us most definitely since from the moment we are born we are ready to die. We are creatures who essentially live in time and are always no longer what we were and not yet what we will be. Our ability to take our death into account defines the level of our aliveness, the intensity of our engagement with life. Heidegger coined the notion of constancy, which is the extent to which we keep our eyes on the objective and the reality of our loyalty to our own human existence. He also spoke of anticipatory resoluteness, which is the way in which we face up to the reality of dying. It is only when we are prepared to accept the way in which we die everyday that we can find the determination to claim our own life away from the influence of other people.

Tillich similarly emphasized how important it is to push ourselves to our limits and even beyond them. Tillich's idea of taking non-being into one's being is a most enlightening one. He argued that the more non-being or death or guilt or fate or failing we can face up to, the more we truly come to life.

Living is not about having an easy time. Far from it. It is about letting yourself be challenged to the maximum and rising to this challenge. It is to not
fear the negative but instead take it to heart.

> *Truth is found in the midst of struggle and destiny, not as Plato taught,*
> *in an unchanging beyond. (Tillich, 1966: 15)*

Human values have to be laboured for and this labour is worthwhile. It is
what makes human life meaningful. The phase of Post-modernism is coming
to the end of its useful life and is ready to be put behind us. Our children and
grandchildren will be able to go beyond the nihilism and scepticism that they
have inherited from the eighties, nineties and noughties. We need to open our
eyes to the challenges and opportunities of the Age of Virtuality and move
forward. We are now in a position to face up to human reality as never before
and we need to let ourselves do this vigorously. We need to think about the
new morality we are capable of.

Implications for therapy

But we have still not clearly formulated what that new morality would be and
that is precisely because it has to be discovered and created at each step of
the way (de Beauvoir, 2000; Sartre, 1983/1992, 1992). It is neither founded
on religious dogma nor simply on scientific data, though it takes these into
account. It brings all sources of information and reflection together through
philosophical insight and emotional and psychological understanding. It is
about the capacity to reflect about moral issues rather than refer to a set moral
code. It is what I have called mor-ability: the ability to create morality rather
than follow morality. And where does this thinking about living take place? I
would argue that it is often in the setting of counselling and therapy and certainly in the setting of counselling supervision and training. It is about taking
human living seriously, not taking it for granted, but thinking about it carefully
and deeply. It leads to an approach that is neither directive nor non-directive,
but directional, purposeful and searching instead. It will be an interactional,
reciprocal approach, in which human problems are debated. They are not
treated medically nor treated prescriptively, not punished by the penal system
nor condemned morally, but resolved and understood. This can only happen
in the context of an open and challenging relationship, in dialogue with
another human being, who is entirely and utterly available to this process.

For that is what is most needed when we are anxious or depressed: to find
someone who understands our troubles and puts them in a human context.
Psychotherapists then need to be prepared to encounter any or all of the demons

that Pandora or life has let out of the box rather than aim for a global state of happiness. They need to be capable of lucid and free thinking and helping others to think through their problems in living without imposing a doctrinaire view. This requires an openness and readiness to explore human existence without thinking in terms of the normal and the pathological and without aiming for happiness or cure. It means that therapists will have to get better acquainted with a philosophical exploration of what it means to live a good life. So this is what we shall turn our attention to in the next chapter.

Chapter 2

The Good Life: Philosophy as a Guide to Therapy

He'd agonised for a year and more, searched
for the truth about himself and his future.
A decision had gradually formed
and broken through his indecision.

(Henning Mankell, The Man who Smiled: 25)

Having argued that psychotherapy may have an important role to play in enabling people to live better lives, we need to consider what a better life would consist of and how it could be achieved. What are the parameters of good living that are appropriate and workable for people in a post-modern or virtual society? What are the realistic values that therapy can deliver with confidence in a new age of constant change where our point of reference is no longer the family but the global village? What is the role of the therapist in enabling people to find a new and satisfactory direction in their lives?

A post-modern world

Although we are on our way towards the virtuality I described in the previous chapter, our daily concerns are still very much those of a post-modern world, where the values of modern living have been questioned and changed. The rules of yesterday are no longer in vogue. Post-modern living requires a new attitude of unconcern. If we can muster a certain detachment and a slightly ironic attitude we can manage, or at least pretend to manage, rather well. If we care about old values, such as truth, loyalty and faith, we may well run into trouble as we get out of synch with the world around us. Much of the time the world is too fast for us to catch up, let alone to take enough time to think and re-orientate ourselves. We are busy all the time. We chase our own tails, getting dizzy in the process. With no time to think things through, people have lost their bearings and follow the morals of the media, which are often ephemeral and based on the fashions of the moment. The phenomenon of flavour of the month has pervaded much of human relations. It seems alright nowadays to switch allegiance, point of view or position, as long as one stays in line with the most fashionable perspective of the moment: the tyranny of popular opinion has replaced the dogma of organized religion.

The role of philosophy

Philosophers, who once upon a time would think through the moral questions of the time, have learnt to limit their investigations to questions of logic, contradiction or definition and they stick to narrow interpretations of the latest scientific facts. Philosophy used to be the discipline that took the broadest view of the world; it used to paint on the canvas of life and integrate all knowledge into theories that aimed for universal understanding and truth. Philosophers have long since given up doing so, for truth has become an antiquated and taboo concept, which is to be avoided like the plague. Few philosophers are willing to take a stance on the crucial matter of how people should live. This subject is left to the calculations of health economists or the imagination of journalists. Pop stars and soap operas interpret daily events with confidence and alacrity. Moral philosophers, with few exceptions, rarely commit themselves to a particular worldview these days and they seem to have little advice to give us (Blackburn, 2001).

The search for wisdom has been replaced with the search for knowledge. Departments of philosophy are being disbanded in universities at a rate of knots, for there is no money in philosophy and no career structure. Though there is a new movement of philosophical consultancy (Achenbach, 1984; Curnow, 2001; Herrestad et al., 2002; Hoogendijk, 1991; Lahav and da Venza Tillmanns, 1995; Le Bon, 2000) this is not generally valued in philosophical circles. Philosophical counselling remains a countermovement in the field of philosophy and stands out as an exception to the trend of dis-affectation and the isolation of philosophy as a handmaiden of scientific discourse. Philosophical counselling is itself at risk of being taken over by life coaching, which is often based on cognitive and pragmatic principles.

But it is not just the philosophers who have abandoned the search for wisdom. Most ordinary people have learnt to rely on ephemeral facts and fictions to orientate their lives. We are quite complacent about the standards we set for ourselves and even for those who still follow religions; rigorous spiritual discipline is mostly a thing of the past. No longer do we rely on the mythologies of our ancestors but neither have we replaced these with clearly formulated alternative mythologies. The closest we come to mythologies are the ones shaped out of best selling popular science books. We follow the apparent authority of the expert and buy into the notion that all humans are selfish or that life is essentially based around the survival of the fittest, for the Darwinian worldview with its new evolutionary narratives about selfish genes is the one that seems to have really taken root.

But that will change, for new ideas will replace the old ones and show the incorrectness of our perceptions. For that is one of the positive outcomes of our science-driven world. Worldviews are shaped and reshaped much more rapidly in our information processing, virtual world. This does however leave us without the sifting and integrating process that thinkers used to do for us. We are rushed off our feet trying to keep up with intellectual fashions. So, out of our depth we turn to the dummy guides that simplify this complex world for us and try to catch up with the new knowledge we require in order to survive. For life improvement has now become a commercial enterprise and we can do little else than follow the latest theories and best selling gurus. It is the popular scientists and authors of self-help guides as well as the media commentators who form our opinions and dictate our way forward into the future.

But how can people like that encompass the wisdom of ages and how can they interpret the new scientific data satisfactorily? Quite simply they can't and they don't. Science has become so fragmented and specialized, that even scientists themselves find it difficult to keep up with the explosion of information within their own speciality, let alone within their wider discipline, making it totally impossible to stay in touch with developments across the board. Interdisciplinary work is still rare and very difficult to get funding for. Nobody gets funding to do the thinking to bring all the disparate facts together and make sense of them.

Philosophy is not a lucrative business and it does not produce anything for the economy. Yet, science desperately needs to be interpreted and guided by a broader and overarching philosophy. It needs to be summarized and reasoned through in order to proceed from the facts and data to a new wisdom and arrive at a true understanding of what human beings can claim to know about themselves and the world. But nobody is doing this, least of all the politicians who use science in a piecemeal way to inform new societal developments and who cherry pick the bits that appeal to them for short-term success. The same is true of journalists, who are now often the interpreters of new information and who offer us the brave new world on a platter. So we are fed random morsels of scientific data on a daily, need to know basis. What is organizing this media frenzy is mainly marketability. We get served up titbits of information when they appear to be instantly marketable commodities. Science sells papers and programmes when it is presented as either sexy or threatening. We only find out about new drugs when they have hurt a sufficient number of people or when they promise greatly enhanced vitality. This makes the media scientists the sophists of our time. They are called on to

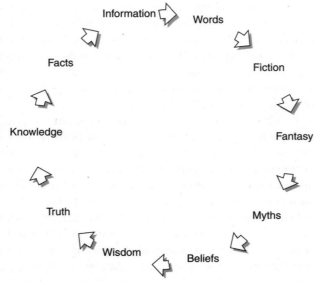

Figure 2.1   The Cycle of Facts and Fantasy

dispense guidance in a way similar to that of astrologers or other soothsayers: they base their predictions on soft facts that are manipulated for greater effect and made to say a great deal more than is warranted.

The cycle of facts and fiction

In reality scientific research provides us with lots of disparate and often contra-dictory facts. These have to be observed and tested for a long time and they have to be brought together with other facts and findings in different areas before they can be thought through carefully in a disciplined and morally responsible way. It is the latter two phases that are usually dispensed with these days. Civilization started with the use of an instrumental language, then moved to a capacity for story telling, then to the creation of whole mythologies, which turned into care-fully honed religious beliefs, which then were tested in order to arrive at greater knowledge about the universe, which in turn led to a search for truth and wisdom, which gave rise to the development of science, which has now led us back, full circle, to a new age of story telling, where the many data of scientific knowledge are used randomly to enchant and amaze us, rather than in order to piece together a coherent worldview which can help us make sense of the human condition.

Our lives are thus directed by a constant flow of changing information. When the Classical search for wisdom was replaced with the Enlightenment's search for truth, this may have seemed like progress. When the search for truth led to the investigations of science and the search for factual knowledge, this may still have seemed like a desirable step forward, in that people became aware of the relativity of the universe and the need to investigate it carefully. When the search for knowledge turned into a more specialized and detached search for exploitable data, things shifted out of our grasp.

This is probably to do with the commercialization of knowledge and the fact that only those things that make money get taken seriously. It eschews the picture and takes bits of information out of their context. Thus we lose track of the network of connections that keep the facts making sense. This leads to the loss of meaning we so acutely experience today. This loss of meaning in turn stimulates a process of questioning and relativizing: some of this is good, since it frees our curiosity to discover new things. But most of it has just led to the scepticism that is so evident in the cynicism of the new generation, fed on media hype, speaking in the tongue in cheek tones of mocking and self-mocking. With information overload it is sensible for us to guard ourselves from being seen to be taking anything too seriously, lest it should already be out of tune with our fast-moving times.

Post-modern crisis

Post-modern society is positioned in a stance of disbelief, where passion is suspended and the suspicion of potential error is rife. Many young adults now speak in phrases that end in question marks rather than in full stops or exclamation marks, even when they are asserting something. It is as if they are constantly on the look out for potential disagreement and will sarcastically reject any hint of commitment before others can dismiss their views. They remain reserved and at a safe distance from their own assertions. Everything has already been seen, said, done and heard, nothing has the capacity to bring us to wonder or reverence any longer. We now say something is awesome when it is merely interesting or new or striking. We are hardly aware of the profound seriousness or value of our own existence, for we have been indoctrinated to make light of our lives and think ourselves no more than a vehicle for a few genes competing with some other genes. We are no longer in awe. Our lives feel like an insignificant blip in the universe, an afterthought, a redundancy, a random variation on a predictable theme. Derrida spoke of the crisis of reason, and I quote here from his *Writing and Difference*:

> *But this crisis in which reason is madder than madness is more rational than reason, for it is closer to the wellspring of sense, however silent or murmuring – this crisis has always begun and is interminable. (Derrida, 1967/1978: 62)*

It is quite clear that in a post-modern world even facts are no longer taken seriously. Reason has gone crazy on us and perhaps this is a good thing, since it had begun to dominate almost everything. Facts these days are known as data, mere bits of information that can be manipulated and computed. Data can be generated so rapidly that we often end up with information overload. We experience ourselves as suffocated by reason and data and this leads us to becoming increasingly immune to new ideas. It would seem as if Post-modernism and its deconstructing of values have led us into a state of information fatigue and an era of sceptical disillusionment. But let us not blame this on the scientists and theoreticians, for they have merely formulated and implemented what societal movement became possible. How curious though that at the beginning of the third millennium of the history of Western civilization we are at risk of destroying the meaningful universe we have so carefully and arduously created over the previous 2,000 years. Post-modernism may have grown out of mankind's realization that we are now capable of destroying the planet, but it has itself spawned a frame of mind which is potentially ruining our moral and emotional landscape.

When the Hellenistic philosophers popularized the activity of seeking for eudaemonia, the good and well lived life, this was seen to be about a search for wisdom rather than a search for material ease or mastery over the physical universe. Aristotle's striving for the good life was based on virtue and the right way of conducting oneself and this was a very practical, concrete and down to earth activity accessible to all (Macaro, 2006; Richardson Lear, 2004). Eudaemonia was not just some theoretical state of mind, it was a concrete everyday experience based on how one conducted oneself and lived one's life. It was in many ways a practical application of the more philosophical wisdom of Socrates and Plato and a realistic option for all those who were interested in improving themselves. It was intended to provide a better alternative to demagogy and the following of empty opinions and superstitious beliefs. The movement from wisdom to truth, to science, to knowledge, to facts, to information, to data, has led us full circle back to an era in which people base their actions once again on popular opinion and superstition. For in a society where information guides every day decision making, little credence is given to universal, religious or ethical principles. It may be a great liberation to be freed of the shackles of moralising and dogma, but we have replaced them with emptiness and random choice and are yet to implement our new moral ability.

When the Internet provides us with an overview of what is available in human culture, this access to pluralism and diversity, which is active and on line, i.e. on tap, we get tempted to pick and choose values in the same way as we pick consumer goods. The virtual universe is becoming our new reality: it takes us beyond nihilism. The deconstructed universe has made room for the virtual space of unreality, where anything goes. We have become experts at relativity and unknowing and when nothing is certain and everything is in question we can generate virtually anything. Virtuality is an apt word that captures both the unreality and relativity of human life in this age and the pressing need to find a way to replace the old ideas about virtue with a new virtue-ality. All one has to ask in this age is whether the opinion one expresses is in line with the most recent data. The touch-stone of our orientation is thus: is this the latest, the most up to date view?

Virtuality in question

There is probably a lot to be said for this kind of dynamic, driven, open ended, consumerist, and versatile, inclusive, non-judgmental, well-informed way of life. Many thrive on it. Some of the advantages are that many more people can participate in the forming of opinion, in the creation of standards, in the upholding or breaking of rules. The problem is that this accessibility also means permeability: when everyone has access, the boundaries become fluid. This changes the nature of human relations considerably. There are fewer certainties, fewer commitments, and fewer universally accepted truths to lean on. The virtual community provides its own credo, loosely defined as 'anything goes as long as it goes'.

Take away the Internet, television, radio, newspapers, magazines, CDs, DVDs, Ipods and other mobile devices that connect this virtual society of the global village and you have an instant crater of boredom and confusion. As long as we run along with the constant stimulation, we lead hard working, hard playing lives, which seem to be the contemporary standard of good living: the fast life, where much is achieved and much fun is being had. The morality is one of high energy, high performance, high visibility and accountability, a morality that leaves no room for sentiment or even seriousness, unless in jest. There can no longer be any reliance on things established in the past. People have become as replaceable and easy to discard as the wrappers of their take away hamburgers, and yet they queue up to make their two minute contribution to public opinion or claim their little share of fame or recognition eagerly when given half a chance. Contemporary society is temporary. It is also often a con. The temporary nature of the everyday is so obvious that there hardly seems any point in making long-term plans. Those who are fast on their feet will be the first to pick up the new opportunities, jump on the right bandwagon, and drift in the most popular direction ahead of the crowd.

Those who can manage this do well and get pleasure in feeling part of the flow. But many cannot keep up with this kind of warrior lifestyle and they seek out other ways of coping. Hiding in hedonism is a popular twenty-first century activity. Those of us who do clinical work are well aware of the casualties of alcohol and substance abuse. But there are other signs on the wall as well. The flourishing of fundamentalist religions is another product of the lack of clarity and the craving for instant gratification and clear paths to follow. On the other hand, but very much along the same line, is the soaring interest in various cults and the popularity of old superstitious beliefs and practices, such as the reading of runes, tarot cards or tea-leaves. This is a fascinating phenomenon that continues to spread. Self-help and lifestyle books are bulging on the shelves of our bookshops. Psychotherapists and counsellors, the new moral guides of our era, write a good number of these as well.

But there are other sources of comfort available to young people today. Pop and rock music and their multiple ever expanding subcategories, with their videos and associated products, are hugely influential in determining fashion and lifestyle. Soap operas and advertising slogans similarly bend the ears of many and influence their way of talking and thinking by providing the stories and tunes of our lost mythologies and hymns that used to be the province of religion. I do not think we should be scathing or dismissive about this phenomenon. There is no point in panicking and mounting the moral brigade. Culture is an organic phenomenon and it fills its own gaps and finds its own solutions to problems. There is as much to be learnt about the craving for values from the lyrics of teen culture and soap opera scripts as there is in the learned books of the scholars of the day. What is startling is not that these new aspects of our culture are so dominant and quasi religious, what is staggering is that we do not take them more seriously and think that a superior and dismissive stance towards them is sufficient. It is, in my opinion, crucial for us to investigate what is happening to the need for purpose and value at the grassroots level. It is equally important to contrast and compare these popular values with the values of yore and with the age-old principles and beliefs that have guided the generations before us. We need to ask ourselves how they compare and how we might understand the wisdom of the future in light of our learning from the past and the present. So let's take a brief look at both aspects.

The values of youth culture

Teenagers today do not believe in the same things as their elders. There is nothing new in that. What is new is that the changes and differences between the generations are forever speeding up and are now so great that it is hard to keep up, day by day. The parents of this new generation themselves grew up in a post-war era and take consumerism for granted. But they have not understood how the delight they once took in consumables has been replaced by boredom and disinterest on the part of their own children, who do not value their possessions in the way we still expect them to. The new, virtual age generation are not interested in accumulation and possession and their discourse on the subject of values is largely nonchalant. They do not find it easy to accept any ultimate source of value and are opportunistic and relativistic. My daughter, when she was 13 years old, announced to me one day out of the blue that she was sure that the world did not really exist and that therefore nothing really mattered. Life, she thought, was no more or less than a dream or a nightmare. She had decided that its reality was fleeting and imagined, rather like that of a film or a videogame: something that could be altered and changed at whim. In this virtual world values were clearly relative and she had somehow found a way to cope with that relativity.

But how can we live when our values are ephemeral and change according to circumstances and the mood we are in? When people are depressed they do not think anything has a purpose. If they are in a normal state of mind they might consider that the meaning of life, if there had to be one, would be to have as good a time as possible, to be happy or have fun and get the most out of life. Alternatively you might get a rush from proving to people as you get older that what you said when you were younger is actually true, or has potential. No matter how old you are you can still be right and proving this might be an important motivation when you are considered too young to have anything of value to contribute. Rebellion no longer seems an attractive option, since it does not seem as if it would make any difference to the world anyway. People have lost the sense of being able to have a direct impact. So striving for fame and fortune seems a sensible objective, if one wants to achieve some influence. Also children are aware that most of what they do is what other people expect them to do. I was told by a reliable source that the only thing children feel they can do that they have not been asked to do and they might actually do against the parental wishes is watching television. It is quite extraordinary how the younger generation seems to have carved out its territory in the virtual world open to them, which is hardly surprising since the physical world with its many dangers and constrictions is now more closed to them than ever before. They live in a world of advertisements and material goods. Materialism is a pragmatic way of life to them: to have or not to have has become the question: for the have nots crime becomes the only serious option. The materialism is accompanied by a tremendous cynicism. Oscar Wilde's definition of the cynic as he who knows the price of everything and the value of nothing seems to apply to perfection.

New guidelines

And yet, somehow even these cynical young people need some principles, some values to live by, and it is not by chance that guidelines for living circulate on the Internet with alacrity. People crave tradition more than ever, even though our own is taboo. But these guidelines are interchangeable and non dogmatic. They are just something you pay attention to for a laugh, probably well aware it is a sales gimmick on the part of an Internet provider. It becomes a kind of experiment, just a bit of fun with the wisdom of the world. Young people glean a lot of their life's wisdom in this kind of half-serious experimental way and perhaps this is not a bad thing. They seem to acquire a knack for dismissing it if it seems trite or trivial. It seems to be the new way of gathering information, exploring and experimenting, without retaining much in a committed, permanent fashion. What seems good about it is the aspect of exploration, for it affords them a personal adventure in going around the houses, checking what is on offer in our fickle world. Yet there seems little to help them decide whether what they come across is worth taking seriously or should be dismissed as just another joke. No one teaches how to test and compare all this information that is available. It is not clear how to judge the level of authority that any of it has or should have. So what happens is that knowledge is acquired by aiming for that which rises in the popularity stakes and at the same time, realizing nothing is forever and nothing is holy, young people increasingly take everything with a grain of salt. But their pursuit of truth is not so different to that of people across the ages. Their wisdom may be rather pragmatic but a lot of it makes sense and rings bells. Here is the list of instructions for life that was circulating on the net at the turn of the millennium.

Instructions for life

1 Give people more than they expect and do it cheerfully.
2 Memorize your favourite poem.
3 Don't believe all you hear, spend all you have, or loaf all you want.
4 When you say, 'I love you,' mean it.
5 When you say, 'I'm sorry,' look the person in the eye.
6 Be engaged at least six months before you get married.
7 Believe in love at first sight.
8 Never laugh at anyone's dreams. People who don't have dreams don't have much.
9 Love deeply and passionately. You may get hurt, but it's the only way to live life completely.
10 In disagreements, fight fairly. No name calling.
11 Don't judge people by their relatives, or by the life they were born into.
12 Teach yourself to speak slowly but think quickly.
13 When someone asks you a question you don't want to answer, smile and ask, 'Why do you want to know?'
14 Take into account that great love and great achievements involve great risk.
15 Call your mother.
16 Say 'bless you' when you hear someone sneeze.
17 When you lose, don't lose the lesson.
18 Follow the three Rs: Respect for self, Respect for others, Responsibility for all your actions.
19 Don't let a little dispute injure a great friendship.
20 When you realize you've made a mistake, take immediate steps to correct it.

21 Smile when picking up the phone. The caller will hear it in your voice.
22 Marry a person you love to talk to. As you get older, his/her conversational skills will be even more important.
23 Spend some time alone.
24 Open your arms to change, but don't let go of your values.
25 Remember that silence is sometimes the best answer.
26 Read more books. Television is no substitute.
27 Live a good, honourable life. Then when you get older and think back, you'll be able to enjoy it a second time.
28 Trust in God but lock your car.
29 A loving atmosphere in your home is the foundation for your life. Do all you can to create a tranquil, harmonious home.
30 In disagreements with loved ones, deal only with the current situation. Don't bring up the past.
31 Don't just listen to what someone is saying. Listen to why they are saying it.
32 Share your knowledge. It's a way to achieve immortality.
33 Be gentle with the earth.
34 Pray or meditate. There's immeasurable power in it.
35 Never interrupt when you are being flattered.
36 Mind your own business.
37 Don't trust anyone who doesn't close his/her eyes when you kiss.
38 Once a year, go someplace you've never been before.
39 If you make a lot of money, put it to use helping others while you are living. It is wealth's greatest satisfaction.
40 Remember that not getting what you want is sometimes a wonderful stroke of luck.
41 Learn the rules so you know how to break them properly.
42 Remember that the best relationship is one in which your love for each other exceeds your need for each other.
43 Judge your success by what you had to give up in order to get it.
44 Live with the knowledge that your character is your destiny.
45 Approach love and cooking with reckless abandon.

This list now exists in many different forms and shapes and it bears some resemblance to Mary Schmich's famous 'Wear sunscreen' which was also circulated on the net around that time and eventually set to music by Baz Luhrmann. What can we say about such a list in relation to moral ability?

First, it deals with practical advice. It provides guidelines for living without dealing with any of the big moral prohibitions found in most cultures, such as those of lying, cheating, stealing, adultery, blasphemy, violence and murder. We must assume that these are nevertheless taken as read. These are areas religions used to take care of. The fact that people do not seem to attend to these basics explicitly is presumably related to the fact that we no longer feel the need to attend to things that are dealt with by the law. If it is illegal then I do not have to think about it anymore. You just do not do it. Except that there are those people who flout the law and who thus raise moral questions for us again. When is murder not murder but self-defence? When is cheating not cheating but creative business competition? When is lying acceptable, if ever? Surely these questions cannot be left to the lawyers but need to be addressed in a serious fashion, by those who think for a living? In addition law makers need philosophers to help them perfect the rules and make them fairer. They need them particularly in their thinking about new areas for legislation that raise new moral issues, such as genetic engineering, abortion or body transplants.

Secondly the above list does not deal much with the complexity of human emotions, the human condition, or human predicaments or special dilemmas. It gives the sort of topical advice that grandparents might have given on specific occasions. It does nothing to help a person monitor their emotions as part of a clarification of how to live in the right way. It is interesting that young people seek out such advice and crave it. Similarly clients ask for the therapist's opinion on such matters regularly. Even though most therapists hate responding to these demands they often find they have to take on these areas of expertise, for sometimes people are just too confused to work it out for themselves.

When therapists instead make interpretations based on their theories of personality or development they further confuse people by implying that their confusion comes from pathology or childhood trauma rather than from dis-orientation. It is unproductive to withhold discussion and it is misleading to interpret. When my client is wondering whether she should or should not stay with a boyfriend and become his wife the question is not whether she is mature enough to form a stable relationship. The salient question is whether she considers a stable relationship to be desirable in the abstract and feasible and worthwhile for her now in this particular situation. Perhaps even more pertinently what we need to explore is whether the formation and maintenance of a stable relationship with this man is a project that she would like to devote her foreseeable future to and whether she knows what it involves. Considering this question is a complex business and cannot be solved by a list of how tos or a list of character traits. Nor can it be reduced to the question of whether the relationship would make her happy. It will take substantial effort and time to achieve it. It will require the clarification of the fundamental principles by which a good life is conducted. This means defining and debating the values of a well-lived life. That means thinking about values rather than applying particular rules and regulations. It was more than a century ago that Nietzsche taught us how to do this and question all our holy cows.

What values and virtue are not

In his *Zarathustra* Nietzsche (1883/1933) confronts us with the re-evaluation of values that he sees as the foundation of the new morality that can revitalize us. He challenges the old values, which are worn out and dusty, and enumerates some of the ways in which people fool themselves into the belief that they are virtuous. He says that some people may do what they are told and think this is being good. Others are too lazy to do anything wrong.

> *Others are like household clocks, wound up and they stick to the tick-tock of a predictable boring and unthought out existence and call this virtue. These people can easily be wound up though ... (Nietzsche, 1883/1933: 118/119)*

Other people are righteous or self-righteous and they call this virtue. Others deprive or lower themselves and call this virtue. Virtue can also be a pose, pretence or mannerism. Most of the time virtue is something we impose on others and expect of ourselves only in principle. In practice it is too hard to be virtuous and we excuse ourselves. We find out from books what virtue is, but do not apply the rules. The reality is that virtue is hard to come by. It is life itself that makes *virtuous* when it is lived to the full. Then virtue coincides with health, a health of body and soul, even though the body may be injured or broken or old and even though the soul may have been much hurt and be tired and full of doubt.

Being able to tackle such questions takes consistent self-questioning. You cannot achieve virtue unless you are willing to see where you go wrong and what harm you do to others and yourself. Therapists cannot work on values with a client unless they have been confronted with the breakdown of values for themselves at some point. Unfortunately the only way to discover about value is to discover about loss and degradation. Every catastrophic event that happens exposes the gaping holes underneath the surface of our world. Some events make craters in the world that was taken for granted. Only then, when we count the cost of life, do we see the foundations of the world revealed for what they are at rock bottom. As old worlds explode and shatter, new understanding may be fostered. But it does not happen so quickly or so easily. The fall-out of one's misfortunes spreads over many subsequent years, altering familiar landscapes and shattering your inner confidence. In an individual life it often takes years before a person can find the energy and courage to start clearing the rubble of old ruins, let alone plan new constructions in their place.

At a macro-level we see the same thing happening to humanity. In the first decades of a new millennium human beings are often defeated by prevailing scepticism. It seems hard to find safe places for our aspirations and beliefs. Our faith in benevolent gods or superior powers has been largely undone.

There is no homeland in which we can hide from the reminders of our mortality, our guilt, our failure, our forsakenness. We can no longer just believe in goodness, since evil greets us at every step of the way. It is high time that we ask the question of what it is that can redeem us and help us carry on when all seems doomed and dark.

Penelope's shroud

It is a question I often asked myself when the fabric of my own life unravelled like Penelope's fabled shroud. The whys and hows of this upheaval are not pertinent to this discussion – suffice it to say that I went through a wretched phase of loss and mourning when the life I had painstakingly created came apart at the seams. Eighteen years of marriage and family life and 18 years of building up an academic institution with colleagues came undone all at the same time. It was a time when the blinkers that had guarded me from seeing certain aspects of reality fell from my eyes in the wake of a number of simultaneous bereavements. It was no longer possible to carry on with hypocrisies and self-deception. The contradictions of your life come to their climax eventually. I had to stand up and be counted. Crisis and catharsis are never far apart from each other and it taught me much about myself, others and life to be tried and tested by fortune. I have subsequently found it easier to resonate with clients who struggle with situations of distress or terminal loss. My unhappiness was an important experience and brought me back into the river of life in a way happiness had not been able to do.

The words we put to the events that happen to us are never the whole story though. They do not reveal the complex structures of events and emotions of all the protagonists in the narrative. We are silenced by grief. And this allows others to misrepresent and manipulate what has happened, minimizing the pain which to strangers always seems unbearable and which they try to avoid at all costs by avoiding you when you suffer. You learn that suffering has to be borne by yourself and alone or with those that are prepared to truly love you and stand by you. The narratives about the disasters are only the surface names on things, which enable us to accord them a particular place and status. It helps to speak the words, but they never exhaust the layers of pain underneath. Words can never cover that pain, never absorb it. For it is so far greater and cannot be seen or heard or redeemed. The actual events underneath it fan out over many proceeding years as well as the years to follow. The aftermath of the struggle reveals fault lines in the world and in self and other that had never been guessed at before and that may seem irreparable.

I now recognize so well in my clients' descriptions of their predicaments that sense of slowly breaking down; the chronic incapacity in relation to certain places, certain people, certain situations. Out of it grows a fear of one's own desire for retaliation, the deep instinctual wish to be avenged for the injustices inflicted and for having been deprived of one's basic human dignity. To have no livelihood, to be a single parent on the dole, to be shunned by others, any remaining self-esteem in tatters by the actions and words of some, who unthinking and unknowing, tread on you. Trying to keep up appearances, playing at being a hero or heroine sometimes, drawing nearer to those who have experienced this too, avoiding those who have not, for they do not understand and with their incomprehension endanger your inner balance. Soon you find that most people are repelled by the smell of failure, not wanting any part in defective operating. The many fade away from you in the same numbers in which they hung around you when you did well.

Discovering the flipside of life is instructive. Seeing the dark side of human nature in action is not a pleasant spectacle but nevertheless strangely edifying. How daunting it is to be confronted with the fickleness of human relations and the insipidity of self-important conversations or the writings of those who would rather be raiders or traitors than friends. Were you like this yourself once? Did you commit those sins as well? Is that why this has happened? Were you so self-deceived? Were you not the paragon of virtue you once thought you were? Everything is now in question, including your self.

Meaning seeps away through the cracks of your ram-raided life. It will be years before you can begin to ponder, wondering about the second chance you have actually been given. Then gradually a new day dawns revealing the realization that you have perhaps stumbled upon one of the secrets of life. Your life is no longer exempt from the terrors and horrors you were trying to avoid and you can now taste the exquisite flavours of existence at the edge of the world. Released of the burden of perfection and ambition, at least temporarily, you rid yourself of the hypocrisies and deceptions and of the lies of defective affections. What a relief to be free.

Then with renewed urgency the fundamental question presents itself: what to do with this hard-earned freedom? How to use it? Now the mind is nicely focused. The old ways of drifting along with the crowd or with one's best sense of what seems vaguely interesting or desirable are no longer enough. It becomes suddenly very obvious that some things matter more than others. Value is created in action. It is the measure of what one is willing to give up for what really matters. In dragging oneself through the desert of one's temporarily suspended life a new source of meaning is discovered at the back of one's mind. When so much reality has been sunk into our existence we discover many new pieces to the puzzle of good living. But they still have to be fitted into place. This requires nothing short of heroism and heroism is in short supply when one feels more like a victim, like a wounded heap of human misery, a target for the scorn of many. But perhaps that is the better starting point, to find oneself at the nadir of one's life.

As Merleau Ponty once stated:

Today's hero is not sceptical, dilettantish, or decadent; he has simply experienced chance, disorder and failure. (Merleau Ponty, 1964: 186)

This would seem to suggest that we can only be heroic if we have first experienced this total collapse of individuality and societal esteem. Deconstruction precedes existence and existence precedes essence. Only in the bedrock of our low water mark can we begin to build anything essential and solid. Dreyfus's view on Merleau Ponty's hero was that:

> this hero is condemned to follow out fragile meanings without either the triumph of an absolute or the relief of despair. (Dreyfus, 1964: XXVI, intro.)

How true this is. The hero today is not the person fighting a just war or crusade, not the valiant leader of yore, who would be considered deserving whilst being cheered by the crowds. Such comforts are reserved for those who play at being heroes and heroines in the limelight of the television cameras. Not even iconic leaders have the illusion of success these days. Real heroism takes place behind the drawn curtains of living rooms in which small human tragedies are played out in the dark of the night. The anonymity of heroism is almost its precondition. As soon as we have an audience there is a salve for our wounds. We can then afford the luxury of despair or grief once more. We can even begin to think in terms of retaliation or reparation. Once more the lines of public thinking can be pursued and one's destiny becomes meaningful. But as long as we suffer the isolation of the licking of wounds that no-one wants to know about, we have to invent our own compensations, make up our own values and carve our own steps in the hard rock of life. To get out of the pit we have to grit our teeth. The values of our reclaimed lives will not be handed down to us from a mountain. We have to dig them out of the mud and devastation of our broken lives. So, assuming we do this, what will we find? What will it mean to us now to live a good life?

Values for an age of virtuality

First of all in the age of virtuality, virtue is relative and virtual, not certain or absolute. Virtue is defined as that which makes a difficult life good. It is never about avoiding difficulty, pain or trouble and cannot be achieved without these. We have to discover virtue out of the mistakes and disappointments of our lives. Like Ivan Illyich, in Tolstoy's novel *The Death of Ivan Illyich,* we gradually discover the fickleness of human living and learn to look for value and virtue in places where we did not look at first.

> And in his imagination he called to mind the best moments of his pleasant life. Yet, strangely enough all the best moments of his pleasant life now seemed entirely different than they had in the past – all except the earliest memories of childhood. Way back in childhood there had been something really pleasant, something he could live with were it ever to recur. (Tolstoy, 1886: 119)

It took Ivan Illyich a lot of suffering to find out that he had wasted much of his life. Even then it wasn't obvious to him what good living would have consisted of. In virtuality good living needs to be worked out by every single person on every single day anew and there are many different ways to achieve it, but even more ways of getting it wrong. Baumeister's work on the meaning of life (Baumeister, 1991), after reviewing many separate studies, shows that people have given up on believing that they can achieve fulfilment or happiness once and for all. We have learnt the hard way that nothing will bring constant contentment. There is no single recipe for living the good life.

Good living is more like good cooking: there are many different good foods and many different ways to cook, but not all are desirable and not all ingredients are good. There are certainly issues of taste and preference involved in what cuisine or what life to choose. And we may not want the same menu all our lives. But there are certainly culinary secrets. There is an art of cooking and it can be learnt and perfected. We cannot all be chefs or cordon bleu cooks, but we can all learn to prepare palatable food and make a meal more tasty and satisfying. Life, similarly, can be served up with more zest and flavour when we know more about it.

There is not just one way to lead a good life. There are many possible virtual lives that are worthwhile. What is good is relative to what you want to achieve. Every definition of good needs to be put into its proper context. Something is only good in relation to the objective you have in mind: paprika is good for goulash, but not for rice pudding; yeast is good for bread or beer, but not for making chocolate. We can know quite a lot about desirable ingredients and activities when we know what our objective is. We can know quite a lot about the effect of mixing different ingredients together. It takes both experience and creativity to discover the relative virtues of things and to make them work to best effect in specific situations. Helping people to learn to live a good life in their own way is what existential psychotherapy aims to achieve. This is about learning to recognize what one's objectives and purposes are whilst understanding the ways of the world that provide the means to achieve them or the obstacles to block them. Making a necessity out of virtue and virtue out of necessity makes all the difference between failure and a well lived re-orientated life.

That is another interpretation of the idea of virtue-ality: that it is about creating meaning out of meaninglessness and turning bad to good. It is this ability to transform reality that is one of the most precious gifts of being human. It is a gift more available to us in the age of virtuality, this capacity to shift life and not just find resilience against adversity but liquid energy in the swamps of misfortune. It cannot be taught as a technique and it cannot be predicted or prescribed. Fortunately creativity cannot be bottled. But it is within everyone's means and different people have different means at their disposal to create pockets of meaning in sadness or craft rafts to cross the rapids of their torpedoed lives. All can do it, but few come to discover that they can.

Now the good life has to not just be discovered, or won, it has to be created and re-created all the time. It has to be affirmed for it to come into existence. The quest for good living and the search for meaning and fulfilment are one and the same thing. We can no longer expect to be given prescriptions on how to achieve these things. The onus on every individual is greater than before. The returns increase accordingly. The more I put in, the more I will take out when I succeed in creating a positive reality. Of course if I do not win the good life the failure may also be devastating.

What is it that we would want to win? Some time ago I might have said: being. But being alone is not enough. What matters is how this being is enacted. It is as Levinas said:

> *The question par excellence of philosophy is not: why being rather than nothing? But how being justifies itself. (Levinas, 1989: 86)*

Similarly when we ask the question about what a good life is the salient issue is not whether a good life is possible or what it consists of but how we might achieve it. The good life has to be created in action. Finding goodness in life is not a random activity. It requires careful planning and creativity. Meaning is not intrinsic, it is extrinsic: it has to be added, not found in what we experience or bring about in the world. It is like Merleau Ponty's definition of philosophy in *Phenomenology of Perception*:

> *Philosophy is not the reflection of a pre-existing truth, but, like art, the act of bringing truth into being (Merleau Ponty, 1945/1962: XX).*

So how do we bring truth into being? Nietzsche's answer was to learn to live one's life in such a way that its eternal recurrence would be a good thing. To live in such a way that you would love to repeat it over and over again if that is what you were doomed to do, seems a good motto for living with care. It is not so dissimilar to Heidegger's recommendation of living with anticipatory resoluteness. For Heidegger though this anticipation is largely the anticipation of death, which is rather the opposite of Nietzsche's anticipation of eternal recurrence of life. To live so that you are ready to die has been a recipe for the good life since time immemorial. To live for the sake of life may be a little harder to do.

To live the life of re-evaluated values means to live a life which is calibrated on the purposes that seem most right in light of what we know. Wisdom will not be based on opinion; it will be based on knowledge, knowledge on facts, facts on information, information on data. But the data will be interpreted in light of the purpose and values that we opt for in life and they will be evaluated in light of the new ethical principles distilled from the thinkers who are not afraid to think about life. Those principles will always consider the individual interpretation and they will address the subjective evaluation of a person's life as it is lived rather than dictate a general rule. This makes it difficult to lay down a moral law and sets the requirement of enabling people to evaluate their own morality. People need to acquire or perfect their own moral ability. I like to think of this as learning to perfect one's morability. Morability is the capacity to work out what is right and wrong in the context of the world you live in and in relation to the purpose you want to achieve. It has to take the physical laws into account and the laws of the society one lives in. It also has to obey the personal laws of the individual and finally the laws of ontonomy: the laws of human existence.

I am well aware of the tentativeness of the principles I am describing. I would like to suggest that in the art of living there is room for many good cookery books. My formulae will not be yours. Not everyone will want to follow recipes anyway. But here, for what they are worth, are some of my own ingredients and basic rules of thumb. In this I follow a model of four world dimensions, physical, social, personal and spiritual. We live life on all these dimensions at once and are continuously dealing with opposing forces on each. Our existence on the physical dimension confronts us with the pull between life and death, on the social dimension with the conflicts of love and hate, on the personal with the challenges of strength and weakness and on the spiritual dimension with the tension between good and evil. There are of course many variations on these themes and many complexities of the interactions between the levels and their paradoxes. I have written about this elsewhere and shall spare you the details (van Deurzen and Arnold-Baker, 2005).

Moral ability on four dimensions

In order to find one's way in the post post-modern world of virtuality we need to be capable of responding to a multiplicity of possibilities and demands. The old system of values that was based on certainty about what was desirable is long defunct. It was temporarily replaced with the nihilism of deconstruction and we could remain stuck in a post-modern attitude of deconstructing truths and realities, but there is not a lot of mileage in continuing to do so. When we have experienced the levelling process described above we soon discover the need to make meaning out of nothing and create new values. These values will necessarily be relative to the situations and circumstances that we are in. Values in an age of virtuality are context specific. This is what I refer to as morability: the ability to think in moral terms without being moralistic and rigid about our values. It is the ability to think in terms of givens, purposes and consequences before we decide what is worth giving up for the values we choose. There are only a few basic principles guiding our moral ability and I shall mention some of these.

	DESIRES	FEARS	VALUES
PHYSICAL	life	death	vitality
SOCIAL	love	hate	reciprocity
PERSONAL	identity	confusion	integrity
SPIRITUAL	good	evil	transparency

Figure 2.2   Human values rediscovered

A good life needs a good physical foundation. The principle at work here is that of vitality. Vitality is the capacity to live life creatively. A vital attitude leads to a creative use of our energies. This includes an ability to give into suffering and death when it comes. Vitality is about being as dynamic as is feasible or desirable in a situation. It requires us to look after our own physical well being, without damaging that of another. We have to learn what makes our physical life good. This is about creating cosiness and excitement in fair proportions. It is about protecting one's own safety and to have enough, not too much or too little. It is about staying nimble and alert and resting and replenishing oneself enough to maintain one's physical balance. It is about nurturing oneself in a manner that is pleasurable without being greedy.

In the social dimension we need good relationships with our fellow human beings. This requires several principles including responsiveness and equity. Generosity is good, but it works only as long as the other is going to be generous too, otherwise you get depleted. If you have been wronged you need to make sure there is compensation and restitution. A good standard for relationships is that of reciprocity or mutuality. Reciprocity leads to the creation of community. What works best here is to recognize the principle of kinship: what I do to you I do to myself. As Martin Luther King once said:

> In a real sense, all life is interrelated. All men are caught up in an inescapable network of mutuality, tied in a single garment of destiny. Whatever affects one directly affects all indirectly. (Luther King, 1963: 70)

You no longer need to follow Kant's moral imperative to do to others what you would have them do to you. Nor is it necessary to follow the Bible's instruction to love your neighbour as yourself. It is enough to recognize how we all are affiliated and how what I do to you I do to myself by the same token and by definition. It is one and the same thing. I am you and you are me.

The individuality of the person is much overrated. In the personal world we need integrity and resoluteness, but that integrity can only be respected as long as my self is inserted harmoniously into the world around it. I need the courage to recognize my connections and elaborate these in such a way that I create a self as I relate to the world. The ability to know who one wants to be becomes crucial. We need to develop a sense of authority in deciding when to let ourselves believe things about the world that are of use and when to challenge them instead. To be an individual requires an ability to be both anxious and capable of the quietude and comfort that come from illusion formation and self-deception. In the end it is an overcoming of self and its illusions that brings true freedom (Murdoch, 1970). As Iris Murdoch put it:

> *Humility is not a peculiar habit of self-effacement, rather like having an inaudible voice, it is a selfless respect for reality and one of the most difficult and central of all virtues. (Murdoch, 1970: 95)*

Thus ultimately the good life cannot be brought into being without a spiritual foundation and purpose. We need to release ourselves into a wider sphere than that of our narrow self and worldly interests. On the spiritual dimension of our existence we find the release of our tensions and worries as we begin to see ourselves in the context of the history of mankind and of what lies beyond us.

We discover the dialectical movement of our lives as we become aware of the greater good that surpasses us and that puts our temporary concerns in context and perspective. Giving in to this dimension beyond us allows us to be regenerated by it. This can only be done to the extent that we let ourselves become transparent, allowing the forces of life to shine through us. We can now move forward and discover something closely resembling good faith, as we learn to constantly re-evaluate the consequences of our own actions. This ability to see reality and place ourselves in it is what defines our new moral ability in an age of virtuality. In order to achieve this we have to become disenchanted with the ties that bind us to the past and our narrow self-interest. Our pride has to wear thin so that a true humility comes through, which is an openness to reality in all its complexity. The most important asset for our age of virtuality is our hard-earned ability to re-evaluate and see ourselves in the relativity of our circumstances and then move onward in a new direction.

It is perhaps not what we would have wanted, but the path of virtue ability is hard and not easy to pass over. We have to learn to bring our own limited freedom into existence and let ourselves be touched by the challenges of reality. And so, in fear and trembling and with doubt, but also with hope in our hearts, we shall discover the never ending truth of human existence that will not be changed by the passing of a millennium: that human living is to love and struggle, laugh and cry, live and die. Life is always shorter than we think it will be and we should not postpone living it well until it is too late. If life is to be lived well, it is up to us to create its goodness. This goodness is to be found in the individual interpretation of the ordinary everyday realities and challenges. Perhaps Henry James got closest to it when he pointed out that it wasn't so much living a *good* life as living itself that mattered, when he wisely reflected:

> *Live all you can; it's a mistake not to. It doesn't so much matter what you do in particular, so long as you have your life. If you haven't had that what have you had? (James, 1986: bk.V, ch. 2)*

Chapter 3

Positive Psychology: A Science of Well Being

*There is but one truly serious philosophical problem
and that is ... whether life is or is not worth living.*

(Camus, The Myth of Sisyphus)

All of this is easier said than done. Living to the best of our abilities in the midst of the noise and rush of the twenty first century is not a straightforward matter. Many of us get lost on the way and temporarily or permanently give up on life all together. More people than ever commit slow suicide by letting themselves be drawn into pockets of sham safety. They get mesmerized and taken over by the illusions of substance abuse or other undermining activities that erode their abilities gradually and by stealth. Addictions are rife and provide the illusion of shelter and protection from a world that not only seems harsh but also futile. We are not at all sure which values to live by. It does not seem unreasonable to try to take some short cuts.

Few of us have real clarity about the purpose of life. When asked what their goals are people come up with fairly general statements about wanting to travel the world, find true love or live a happy life. The reality is a little different: most people feel hassled by the stresses and strains of their everyday lives and wonder what went wrong. They get on with their jobs and their families for better or for worse and fantasize that one day it might all come right. It is not surprising that in this vacuum of meaning and purpose a new movement in psychology has quickly gained ground, since it claims to be able to increase subjective well being in record time. Positive psychologists propose nothing less than a scientific revolution: instead of focusing their efforts on curing emotional problems and mental illness, they aim to improve our well being. This seems entirely in line with the objectives of the constitution of the World Health Organization which state that:

> *Health is a state of complete physical, mental and social well being and not merely the absence of disease or infirmity. (WHO, 1946)*

Positive psychologists have taken this objective seriously and have tried to define the positive experiences, attitudes and emotions that can give us greater well being. Though some positive psychologists like Seligman (2002) speak of 'authentic happiness' as the objective, mostly the talk is of subjective well being or life satisfaction (Diener, 2000): concepts that are much broader and less controversial. They are connected though. Well being is defined in the dictionary as:

> *A good or satisfactory condition of existence; a state characterized by health, happiness and prosperity. (Oxford English Dictionary, 2005)*

And according to positive psychology (Carr, 2004) such goals can be achieved without relying on hard earned self-improvement or careful and slow reflection over a life time. Positive psychologists promise immediate results by applying simple scientific facts to emotional problems. They set the spark of cognitive behavioural therapy alight and fan the flames of the human desire for everlasting happiness. Their philosophical assumption is in line with that of dominant ideology where the main objective of human existence is to achieve the highest possible level of happiness and well being in this life. It also promises to deliver these goods quickly and efficiently.

Philosophical objections

Of course the premise that happiness is the highest human good and can be relatively easily achieved is highly questionable in light of the complexity of existence. Though the idea is initially attractive and while it is only a fool who would dismiss these claims out of hand, we know instinctively that the notion of a science of happiness sounds a little too good to be true. In fact it raises immediate suspicion, as do fairy tale endings in movies or books. Few of us have not yet discovered that real happiness tends to be rare, brief and short-lived. Even if it is attainable it is invariably interspersed with periods of unhappiness. No one can achieve it without a struggle and this struggle often turns out to be more interesting than the objective of happiness itself.

But there are other problems that come to mind in the face of the positive psychology claims. Is it really possible to teach people the skills of emotional well being? And even if it were possible would it be a good thing to do so? Does the pursuit of well being relieve the tensions of our hurried lives or does it add another dimension of obligation when being happy or achieving mastery over one's emotional life becomes a new duty and gold standard? Is it realistic to reduce psychology to the positives or is this as limited an approach as a psychology that concentrates on negatives only? Positive psychologists and therapists argue that they are simply trying to even out the score by rebalancing our negative thoughts and habits with positive ones. But this raises other spectres. Do we want our thoughts and habits to be interfered with in this manner? There is something intrinsically disconcerting about the idea of mind control. It conjures up images of social and emotional engineering and of religious persecution. The lines of an old Germanic folk song, which was banned by the Nazis, spring to mind. It was written to bring comfort to those suffering under torture during times of religious persecution:

> *My thoughts are free, they stay deep inside me.*
> *They run through my mind like shadows at night-time.*
> *No hunter can shoot them, no person can loot them.*
> *Whatever will be, my thoughts remain free.*

Such sentiments are reassuring and uplifting, for they remind us that to be in charge of our own states of mind is an inalienable right. No one can rob us of this most precious and fundamental freedom. Should we give in to the pressure of conformity and let our minds be re-educated to think nothing but positive thoughts? Can it really make scientific sense to single out upbeat experiences when all the evidence is that people struggle and suffer many disappointments and troubles over a life time and need to process and understand these? Few people are fooled for long by false smiles or fake expressions of positive sentiments. We experience them as superficial. Being able to face despair and darkness is an asset not a failing. Before we decide to gamble on happiness we would do well to wonder whether life is better when happiness is favoured.

To be or not to be that is the question

Hamlet's soliloquy and Camus' affirmation that the only serious philosophical problem is whether life is worth living (Camus, 1942/2006) go to the heart of the matter. If life is not worth living then suicide may be the most sensible solution to all our problems. But Camus goes on to show that life, though futile, probably does hold considerable worth if we are prepared to take hardship and suffering in our stride as part of the process of finding meaning. It is, he suggests, the assumption that life should be happy that is the cowardly stance and it is this that may lead us towards suicide when it becomes evident that happiness is not attainable. Frankl (1946/1964) held a similar view and showed how meaning could be created from even the harshest of conditions.

Positive psychologists come up with a different answer: their claim is that we can make life worth living by cultivating a positive attitude. If we opt for happiness and well being, we can reorganize our lives around this and make life worthwhile by achieving it. It is an interesting sleight of hand and a circular argument which fails to address the philosophical issue of whether life is worth living *per se* and whether positiveness may imply self-deception and a turning away from reality. It only makes sense if we accept the idea that the human mind is a programmable black box, whose task it is to help us pass the time as pleasantly as possible. If this were so then surely it would be a good thing to improve our moods by fiddling with the settings. It would make sense to take mind altering drugs or to aim for maximum happiness by psychological methods. But it would beg the question of whether such tweaking is desirable or whether it interferes with our capacity for independent thinking, which many people value and which may be our best possession.

We know from experiments that bliss is much overrated and that even in an abstract manner people do not aspire to feeling good at any cost. The philosopher Nagel has shown that people prefer their own careworn lives to the mindless contentment they might obtain if in a post accident situation they found themselves in a coma allowing them to drift into an endless carefree existence. Most people would not choose to be happy fools, devoid of freedom or intelligence (Nagel, 1986).

Nozick's 'experience machine' (Nozick, 1974) is another example of the same kind of experiment. Nozick found that people who were asked whether they would like to be hooked up to a machine which would provide them with the most pleasurable experiences in the world generally did not elect to be given this privilege for more than a couple of hours. They might indeed quite like to enjoy their favourite pastime for a bit but would prefer to intersperse this with other, more creative activities. This is partially because people recognize that the addictive and senseless aspects of such an experience remove its desirability. We want consciousness, not unconscious satisfaction.

People have known this for centuries. Plato argued the very same point in his *Gorgias* (Plato, 405BC/1998), where Socrates asked the question of Callicles whether giving in to an impulse is always the best thing:

Tell me now whether a man who has an itch and can scratch to his heart's content, scratch his whole life long, can also live happily. (493d)

Callicles replied that no, in order to be happy some impulses need to be curbed and that scratching the itch is not all life is about. The question is then which impulses we curb, how and to what extent. Curbing impulses is not a pleasant prospect and we may well try to get away with giving in to them whenever we can. We like to daydream and indulge ourselves against our better knowing: we postpone the moral life in favour of the easy life all too often. And this is where positive psychology corners the market, in promising a moral life which is also pleasant.

Positive psychology

The main authors of this movement are people like Seligman and his concept of authentic happiness (Seligman, 2002), Diener and his notion of subjective well being (Diener, 2000; Diener and Suh, 2000) and before that Veenhoven (1984), who has the merit of having surveyed various countries and classes of society to draw conclusions about the state of happiness in various parts of the world. All these authors have wonderful intentions of improving the human condition and are well worth reading. Their books are certainly more inspiring than many other psychology books and go some way to counterbalance psychologists' preoccupation with pathology. But at the end of their rhetoric we are left with the same old human quandaries and there is a possibility that their strong desire to make things better can only make things worse by making us expect more than is reasonable. Any system that doesn't face the negatives of life and fails to integrate them is doomed to making a big mistake.

And yet this new branch of psychology has some important contributions to make in providing us with information and research on aspects of human living that other approaches have missed out. Take for instance Seligman's investigation of signature strengths, which can help us to inventorize a person's virtues and character strengths, putting the emphasis on potential instead of on character flaws and pathology, as standard personality inventories tend to do. If we want to systematize psychology, we might as well do it in a positive way and help individuals articulate what they are best at in order to maximize these strengths. The values that Seligman describes (2002) sound familiar. He speaks of:

- Wisdom
- Courage
- Love
- Justice
- Temperance
- Transcendence

These concepts can be found in many philosophical and pastoral systems and introducing them into psychology seems like a good thing. But there is also a real danger of reducing philosophical thinking to its bare bones and cheapening the ideas in the process. Concepts that are complex and deserve debate and in depth reflection get minimized and used in an instrumentalist fashion. They become narrowly defined and turned into a manualized commodity for mass consumption. Is this the way to teach people how to live their lives better? Or is this another example of using the latest technology to simplify our lives only to find that we have missed out the essentials? Building high rise apartment blocks that use the latest technology but still provide second rate living conditions is not progress. Helping people to get access to a place they can truly call home and that is worth investing in and looking after and where they can cultivate their own garden is far more worthwhile. In this case this would mean teaching people to think about living rather than telling them how to do it.

When positive psychologists condense complex acts of existence into formulaic concepts they save us from having to make the effort of thinking for ourselves since we can now rely on an ethics of sound-bites. They lend us short cuts to insight and understanding which, though highly marketable and attractive, are no more than false promises of psychological and philosophical accomplishment that are of little consequence. It is as if we are given a canvas of life that can be painted by numbers. Is this the way to find happiness? Apparently yes.

Things that work

Seligman's research (Seligman, 2002) into the exercise of signature strengths delivers some interesting though predictable findings. For instance he submitted as many as 500 people to an experiment, consisting of one simple week-long web-based exercise (so that no human hands were involved) which taught them new well being skills. Then he tested their state of well being repeatedly for the next six months. The outcome was remarkable.

He found that three exercises worked consistently well, producing lasting reductions in depression and lasting increases in happiness. These three effective exercises were old familiar therapeutic stalwarts:

1 *The three blessings exercise*, which consists of writing down three things that went well for you today and why they went well.
2 *The gratitude visit*, which requires the writing of a gratitude testimonial to someone who has been good to you. This testimonial has to be delivered personally to the person one is grateful to.
3 *The use of your signature strengths in a new way*, which is about using the personal abilities you have already recognized in a more creative manner.

All these exercises increased people's self-reported happiness. There is no doubt that if such exercises are woven into a well conducted therapy they may enhance a person's progress. Essentially they consist of validating people's experience and helping them to validate themselves by making them more aware of their own impact on self and others.

Another guru of positive psychology, Ed Diener (2000), prefers to speak of subjective well being. His argument is that happiness is a relative phenomenon but that we can assess quite simply whether a person is or is not experiencing a state of subjective well being. He uses an instrument called the 'Satisfaction with Life Scale' (Diener, 2007) to measure subjective well being and especially a person's evaluation of their whole life. He generously encourages people who visit his website to use the instrument, which is therefore copied below in full. So would we trust a simple measure like Diener's Satisfaction with Life Scale at the start and end point of therapy in order to assess the necessity and effectiveness of the therapy? As a very simple test, Diener's short questionnaire lends itself to this purpose.

The Satisfaction with Life Scale
By Ed Diener, Ph.D

_____1 In most ways my life is close to my ideal.
_____2 The conditions of my life are excellent.
_____3 I am satisfied with life.
_____4 So far I have gotten the important things I want in life.
_____5 If I could live my life over, I would change almost nothing.

Diener asks people to rate themselves from one to seven on each of these statements, with seven being the highest and one the lowest score. A very simple calculation will tell you where you rate on life satisfaction, with a score of 35 being complete satisfaction and a score of five total dissatisfaction. An average score of 20 or more would indicate moderate well being. While I have little doubt that the scale reveals something about people's lives and that it can be useful, it clearly does not give us any real idea of why people rate themselves in this way.

I recently experimented with it in a workshop of around 100 people in St Petersburg, Russia, and found that the three people who scored less than ten were two foreign girls who were studying in Russia and who were feeling extremely homesick on that dark, cold and snowy November day at the Bechterev Institute. The third person was a woman from Chechnya whose family had been massacred and who herself worked with war victims. It certainly indicated their dissatisfaction effectively, but when talking more with each, it became clear that they felt very differently. The first two were fairly hopeful about what the future might bring for them as soon as their year abroad was over, but the other was understandably disgusted and disenchanted with the state of the world and burnt out with the effort of coping. However she had a deep sense of meaning in her life task of helping others and also of letting the world know just how terrible the tragedy of her home country was.

The same dissatisfaction with life can therefore hide many different motivations and outcomes and what matters is more how the person is processing it. I can certainly recognize this when I apply the test to myself. I can easily score myself close to the maximum on the scale when I am in a buoyant state of mind and rate the constant troubles and hard work of my daily existence in an optimistic and bullish fashion. My subjective appraisal is much less positive as soon as even a small problem occupies my attention. Temporarily

I may even come across as negative and dissatisfied if I am asked to complete the test when someone has just treated me unfairly or several unpleasant things have happened and the day is not going right for me, leaving me feeling mournful and discouraged. It is only if I can explain this complex understanding of my life to myself or another and debate it with them that it truly comes to life and begins to make sense. It is then also that I begin to see how I am handling my adversity and my burdens. A questionnaire does not capture the complexity of a person's evaluation and interviewing a psychotherapy client for the first time, probing for the more hidden evaluations and motivations that lie behind their state of mind, brings out a more nuanced understanding of where they are at. Of course one can appreciate the beauty of the instrument in providing measurable and comparable results, but to base our understanding of life satisfaction on it is, I fear, quite misleading.

Other approaches considering good living

The work of another positive psychologist, Mihaly Csikszentmihalyi (1990), takes a more complex approach to the idea of mood and happiness. He favours the psychology of optimal rather than positive experience. His notion of 'Flow' is defined as that experience that makes us feel on top form, where we are 'in the flow' and fully engaged. The flow state is an optimal state of intrinsic motivation where the person is fully immersed in what he or she is doing. This is a feeling everyone has at times, characterized by a sense of great freedom, enjoyment, fulfillment and skill – and during which temporal concerns (time, food, ego-self, etc.) are typically ignored (Csikszentmihalyi, 2007). Flow, whether in creative arts, athletic competition, engaging work, or spiritual practice, is a deep and uniquely human motivation to excel, exceed and triumph over limitation. Many people refer to it as being in the zone. This is not so much about being happy as about being fully and optimally engaged. This seems more productive because it means that we are prepared to deal with challenges and difficulties rather than expecting an easy time. The concept of flow has now been adopted by many positive psychologists, including Seligman.

These ideas are powerfully attractive to many since they promise a better world and a happier life. It is therefore not surprising that they are used in some religious sects as part of evangelical practice, since they bear the same hallmark of positive and wishful thinking. What is more remarkable is that they are also used in the meditative practices of Tibetan Buddhism. We find duplicate ideas in the recent publications of the Dalai Lama, for instance, who in his exile has restyled himself as a Western guru, still representing a long line of traditional Tibetan Buddhists, but increasingly media savvied and au fait with the astutely harnessed mantras of positive psychology. His instructions for life, which are published in a number of bestselling books as well as on the Internet, propose elements of the happiness science that are easily recognizable. They are the product of his collaboration with the positive psychologist Cutler. Here are some of his ideas as summarized on a website devoted to his teaching on happiness (Cutler, 2007):

> *The Art of Happiness is based on a few basic premises:*
>
> 1 *The purpose of life is happiness*
> 2 *Happiness is determined more by the state of one's mind than by one's external conditions, circumstances, or event – at least once one's basic survival needs are met.*
> 3 *Happiness can be achieved through the systematic training of our hearts and minds, through reshaping our attitudes and outlook.*
> 4 *The key to happiness is in our own hands.*

The process of achieving this is described on the website and in his co-authored book (Dalai Lama and Cutler, 1998). It reads remarkably like positive psychology:

- Take into account that great love and great achievements involve great risk
- When you lose, don't lose the lesson
- Follow the 3 Rs:

  1 Respect for self
  2 Respect for others
  3 Responsibility for your actions

- Not getting what you want is sometimes a wonderful stroke of luck
- Learn the rules so you know how to break them properly
- Don't let a little dispute injure a great relationship
- When you realize you've made a mistake take immediate steps to correct it
- Spend some time alone each day
- Open arms to change but don't let go of your values
- Remember that sometimes silence is the best answer
- Live a good honourable life and enjoy it again when you get older and think back
- A loving atmosphere in your home is the foundation for life
- In disagreements with loved ones deal only with the current situation not the past
- Share your knowledge. It is a way to achieve immortality
- Be gentle with the earth
- Once a year, go some place you have never been before.

How familiar this commonsensical advice sounds! Whether this is the depth at which human living should be rooted is another matter.

Media interest

Because of the growing interest in these matters there have recently been some interesting attempts in the media to grapple with the same issues. Most of these have been based on some elements of positive psychology in one shape or form. I will briefly describe two television programmes that bravely tackled the issues of morality and happiness. The first was a programme on Channel Four and the second one was a BBC programme. In 2005 the journalist Jon Snow commissioned a large study of modern beliefs (Snow, 2005). He wanted to find out whether British people still live by the old commandments or whether their rules have changed. Online pollsters YouGov organized two big surveys and ultimately 40,000 people from all over the UK took part. The vote led to a new top ten of commandments, which was aired in a programme on Channel 4 in February 2005.

New Ten Commandments

 1 Try your best
 2 Be true to yourself
 3 Enjoy life
 4 Appreciate what you have
 5 Respect your parents
 6 Protect your family
 7 Never be violent
 8 Look after the vulnerable
 9 Protect the environment
10 Protect and nurture children

This is a very interesting list, which is remarkably humanistic and 100 per cent secular. It is worth mentioning the next five that came up since they contain some of the old Ten Commandments which have disappeared from the top ten:

11 Do not steal
12 Be honest
13 Do not kill
14 Take responsibility for your actions
15 Treat others as you would want them to treat you

So what does such a list tell us about the way in which our society has evolved over the past decades and indeed centuries? It is remarkable in that some aspects of our values seem to have disappeared entirely off the face of the planet. The top four are quite positivistic and somewhat ego-centric. There is nothing about love, though there are several items about care and protection.

There is no mention of God or transcendence. There is no real sense of long-term aspirations. There is no reference to the struggle of life and no emphasis on the need for prayer, self-reflection or spiritual practice. The list is still in the biblically familiar prescriptive mode however. While we have moved away from reference to an authoritarian voice that commands us we have not achieved a more evenly balanced system that relies on personal reflection. All of these commandments are still about action, though the emphasis on the importance of personal well being is completely new. Society has clearly become more self-centred and more preoccupied with enjoying life. It is as if people know the formula of happiness that psychologists have come up with, i.e.:

Pleasure + engagement + meaning = happiness

They know they have to do something actively and in a committed way to make the most of life. Whether we have quite got the right way of doing so is a different matter. Perhaps we are betting a bit too hard on the pursuit of happiness and well being.

This was far more obvious from the second British television programme, which actually boldly focused on happiness. It was called 'Making Slough Happy' and aimed to come up with a package of activities and attitudes that would achieve maximum happiness for the greatest number of people, even for people who felt rather low. In fact the programme addressed itself to making Slough, a city apparently associated in the minds of many with misery, more happy. To meet this challenge the team put together a happiness manifesto which they taught a number of people to apply consistently over several weeks. The manifesto had been written by some well-being specialists, including the psychologist, Richard Stevens, and the psychotherapist, Brett Kahr. The Happiness Manifesto (bbc.co.uk/lifestyle, 2006; Hoggard, 2005) was based on positive psychology research and each of the activities recommended had been shown to increase happiness scores significantly. This is what participants were presented with and were encouraged to follow.

Happiness manifesto

1 **Get physical.** Exercise for half an hour three times a week.
2 **Count your blessings.** At the end of each day, reflect on five things you're grateful for.
3 **Talk time.** Have an hour-long uninterrupted conversation with a partner or a friend each week.
4 **Plant something.** Even if it's a window box or pot plant. Keep it alive!
5 **Cut your TV viewing by half.**
6 **Smile at and/or say hello to a stranger.** Do this at least once each day.
7 **Phone a friend.** Make contact with at least one lost friend or relation.
8 **Have a good laugh at least once a day.**

9 **Every day make sure you give yourself a treat.** Take time to really enjoy this.

10 **Daily kindness.** Do an extra good turn for someone each day.

Clearly the programme of change envisaged was based on making participants engage in the kinds of concrete and positive actions that have been shown to give a person a sense of self-improvement and subjective well being. Each of these activities was based on hard research evidence. Not only were the programme makers well intentioned, they were also able to show that most participants, who committed to this programme for a few weeks, did actually increase their happiness scores. How could they not? These actions are all designed to engage us more with others, with ourselves and with nature in a constructive manner. They are undoubtedly good, even excellent habits to cultivate and participants were helped enthusiastically by the team to apply these ideas in practice.

The questions that were studiously ignored is why people generally give up on such things and why, even when they do them, they may not get any benefit. It is possible to do all these things in a mindless or dutiful fashion without the spirit it is meant to spark off. In this case the exercises would become an irritating chore rather than a pleasure. Many people object to living their lives by rote or to having artificial emotions imposed on them, even when they are told this will work for them. In the programme in question it worked wonders, partially because the programme animators put such enthusiasm into the exercise and partially because people derived a great deal of excitement from participating in a televised experiment. It would be more impressive if the temporary increase in happiness quotients that was achieved could indeed be maintained a year after the end of the programme.

While such a programme of activities may indeed be useful for people who need to focus more positively, it was not designed to help them deal with the ups and downs of life. Interestingly there was a person in the programme who was experiencing a bereavement during the filming and who therefore did not feel able to fully engage with the project anymore. Her predicament brought a dose of realism to the procedures and it was only because one of the consultants acknowledged her position and attended to her in a personal way that her rather more real engagement with life issues was taken into account and valued. She was not showing a smiley face like some of the others, but she seemed human and genuine. In fact this seemed the most poignant part of the programme, when suddenly the need to deal with life in a real way came to the fore. No attention was paid otherwise either in the manifesto or in the programme to personal loss, conflict, difficulty, tragedy or suffering. The assumption throughout was that if I make myself happier then everything will get better and brighter. I don't think one could fool too many people about this for too long. For someone who went through the human potential movement of the 1960s and 1970s and got fed up with its unreasonably positivistic and humanistic outlook this approach evoked the old battle fatigue: yet again it was all about building on positives rather than looking at hardship and loss and recognizing human frailty. Positive psychology is just a bit too one sided and too sugar coated to have much of a future in the longer term. In the interim it will appeal greatly to many who hope for utopia.

Following the science of happiness

It is not surprising that we see this revival of the quest for happiness, since our world wants ease and pleasure. But this is hardly a new state of affairs. At various points in history people have made the pursuit of happiness their number one goal in this way. There is an inbuilt human desire for overcoming the troubles of everyday existence and easing the pain once and for all. As we have seen there are various responses to this: a hedonistic, pleasure driven, feel good response or a eudaemonic, good living, virtue based one. With our current Western hedonistic outlook, it is not surprising that the pursuit of happiness is top of the agenda. Considering the technological nature of our world it is even less surprising that we are now seeking to establish an entire science around this pursuit of happiness. But as we follow this route are we sure it is happiness we are after?

If we look at the happiness distribution maps we soon observe that this 'happy state' is most widely spread in economically successful countries. They appear to measure people's satisfaction with quality of life rather than a more morally or emotionally defined form of well being. This looks awfully like we are measuring people's smugness with being well off. Unfortunately since we can now measure such states and call them life satisfaction we can use these data as a weapon in political and economic battles. Politicians, health economists and journalists are finding the science of happiness very useful. If we can promise people a short cut to well being, we do not only save on healthcare costs, but we will have satisfied customers and voters all the way. We have found the ultimate goal of consumer society: we no longer content ourselves with wealth and health, we now also feel entitled to happiness and emotional well being.

But are these questionnaires and self reports reliable or are they really just measuring the extent to which people assign positive values to their current life circumstances? Are those people who come out on top simply more self-satisfied? If this is so, we should be cautious with these measures, for the things we attribute the highest value to may be contradictory with a thoughtful and careful existence that leads to meaning and truth and purpose. Not all who call themselves happy lead admirable lives. If we based our judgment of who looks best on similar criteria, by asking people whether they were satisfied with their appearance, we would get a similarly biased and bizarre result.

We certainly would not want to measure beauty by self-appraisal. We know only too well that those who are satisfied with their own appearance might not be the same people who exhibit true beauty. Many of us would wish to avoid such self-proclaimed beautiful people, finding them vain, insufferably ego-centric and lacking in true comeliness. True loveliness is not skin deep and cannot be captured by a survey. And so it is with happiness too. What are we really measuring when we ask people to score themselves for happiness? Perhaps we are tracking a self-congratulatory moral conceit, rather than a worthwhile state of mind? Who says that we ought to make ourselves happier anyway? Happiness is really not where it is at. It is not as if a veneer of hap-piness is going to solve the complex problems of our difficult lives, with their discontents, anxieties, boredom, depression and other miseries. Dumbing down into cheerfulness is not the answer to our problems. Of course we can teach people to think more constructively about their lives and doing so will always be an essential part of any psychotherapy. However if we equate the experience of constructive thinking with that of positive thinking, we are jumping the gun. Constructing life anew requires dealing with negatives as much as with positives.

Critique of the science of happiness

The single minded pursuit of positives makes us into one dimensional card-board characters. Plastered smiles are no substitute for coming to terms with the depth of life. Turning therapists into merchants of happiness who peddle their goods to all who want to pay good money for a slice of paradise is a trav-esty of the profession. Therapy has never been about providing short cuts and rapid results, cutting corners or pulling the wool over our clients' eyes. We may be slightly tantalized and curious about what is on offer, but we will soon recognize the same old wish for wonders and miracles that led people to buy snake oil. Beware of the adders in the grass of the happiness industry with their promises of a brave new world of sublime and enduring well being on the other side of our fence.

Fortunately clients themselves understand the difference between a cos-metic change of heart and a real breakthrough into new understanding. They do not like being patronized or fobbed off with superficial methods that leave them stranded in dysfunctional lives. They have too many axes to grind, grudges to clear, losses to lessen and negatives to sort out before the idea of achieving any sort of contentment strikes them as realistic. The idea of fobbing them off with nothing more than a handful of happiness skills is preposterous.

The limits of positive psychology are therefore the same as the limits of psychopharmacology. Of course we can improve a person's mood by chem-ical intervention as well as by positive suggestion. We can explain well being and happiness as a phenomenon mainly related to neurotransmitters and in particular to the transmission of dopamine in the meso-limbic pathway. We know we can create pleasure in people by electric stimulation of certain parts of their brain, for instance in the mid forebrain bundle of the hypothalamus or the cingulate gyrus. We can also obtain results by using drugs, most directly and easily by injecting opiates such as morphine. But what we achieve is highly a-specific and artificial and temporary. The problems we create by habituating people to such interventions are potentially greater than the relief obtained. Every intervention has a price tag and as a rule of thumb a change achieved by personal learning, insight and integration is more effective and enduring than a change obtained by suggestion or prescription. The dramatic difference true understanding makes in neuropsychological terms is that in processing experiences through understanding them we engage the neo-cortex and the prefrontal lobes and thus the knowledge obtained will therefore be filtered and honed into wisdom that can be generalized to other areas of existence.

Artificially enhanced pleasure or happiness has the opposite effect: it acts as an addictive spur but makes people less confident in their own capacity to tackle life unaided. We would not want to inject new principles into a person's life that might ultimately debilitate their personal creativity rather than stimulate it. What we want for people is greater courage and resilience to improve their capacity for dealing with adversity, not a greater desire to escape from it.

We should also be watchful about singling out certain aspects of a person's strengths and magnifying these, without tutoring a person in self-evaluation, teaching them to probe the whole range of their feelings and scrutinizing the wider context of their experience. I have argued above that virtue-ability or morability is crucial in our new global village with its wide diversity and virtual availability of such a wide range of experiences and products. This is so, because we are exposed to such a wide range of sources of information that we are at the mercy of exploitation. To be taught how to maximize certain strengths without also being taught how to think about our lives and the values we want to live by could be disastrous. We have to be able to increase our own judgment together with the number of choices available to us, for otherwise we fall prey to potential abuse.

Tim LeBon, author of the book *Wise Therapy* (LeBon, 2000), also a philosopher and psychotherapist who is trained in the existential approach, has similar reservations about positive psychology (LeBon, 2007). Familiar with the philosophical debate on authenticity he has spotted immediately that there is something fishy about an approach that is supposed to lead to authentic happiness but which consists of a series of clever manipulations that he recognizes as self-deception rather than authenticity. If a person is led to focus exclusively on what they are good at and on what will make them happy, how are they going to be authentic also, i.e. aware of the dangers, limitations and negatives? LeBon, on his website, makes a tongue in cheek point about the irony of coaching people to favour certain traits rather than allowing a person to develop in a more wholesome and self-reflective manner. He points out it may lead to some strengths getting out of hand if they are not carefully balanced against others:

> Which is why many ancient philosophers (e.g. Socrates, Plato and Aristotle) argued that you needed all the virtues to be virtuous. The really dangerous criminal is not the completely non-virtuous person. Personally, I'd prefer terrorists not to be self-controlled, brave or socially intelligent. (LeBon, 2007)

Therefore the concept of 'authentic happiness' leaves much to be desired. It is a relative and ill defined phenomenon which is open to exploitation and manipulation. More recent texts on the subject have begun to shed some light on the limitations of such methods and they define positive psychology as a discipline that looks for optimal functioning and which gathers together all those who are as interested in health as in illness (Linley and Joseph, 2004). This immediately leads to a questioning of the narrow philosophical frame, and from there to a more broadly based existential approach. For instance Bretherton and Ørner (2004), argue that positive psychology is really an optimistic version of an existential approach and they suggest that positive psychology has a lot to learn from a more balanced philosophy of existence.

The dangers of a comfort society

But why should we want an optimistic version of an approach that seeks the truth about existence? Why do we want to make things look better than they are? Our whole civilization implicitly encourages such behaviour by being centred on the idea that we should avoid effort and pain as much as possible. We come to expect protection from challenging experiences as if it were a birthright. This is a huge problem which has far reaching ramifications and implications throughout our society including on decisions around bioethics, genetics, medicine, the environment and euthanasia. We are quick to pre-empt problems and most decisions these days are made with the idea of greater ease and happiness in mind. This may be a big mistake. A Japanese biotechnologist puts it like this:

> The more we pursue the preventive reduction of pain, the more we lose the chance to transform the basic structure of our way of thinking and being, and the more we are deprived of opportunities to know precious truths indispensable to our meaningful life. Preventive reduction of pain means preventive reduction of the possibility of 'the arrival of the other' (the words of Emmanuel Levinas). It leads us to a situation where all of us live in a state of the living dead. (Morioko, 2003)

Closer to home Oliver James (2007) has described this post-modern tendency towards complacency as 'affluenza'. This stands for the obsession with more and more achievement and possessions that keep us on the treadmill of our western lives. It seems as if we have become caught up in an irresistible compulsion to acquire increasing amounts of goods and pleasures in a desperate attempt to achieve control over our lives and our destinies. We appear to fear discomfort and labour more than anything and will do all we can to eradicate pain from our daily existence. The purpose of most of our technological advances (think of cars, computers, kitchen equipment, but also of medical science) is to stop us suffering or better still to give us greater comfort and protection. It is nearly impossible to object to this and put it in question. Arguing against progress is not easily done and will invariably lead to ridicule and opposition. The human search for progressively more control over the threats to existence is hardly a new phenomenon since many ancient philosophies illustrate the same quest. Minimizing pain and maximizing pleasure is a goal we can all unite behind. We have seen this throughout history for instance in Epicureanism, Stoicism, Utilitarianism, and also in Behaviourism or Humanism: all seek the greatest happiness for the greatest number of people.

What is different now is that we actually have the science and technology to put behind this project. So it is not surprising that the social sciences in tune with this mood of protectionism and collective hedonism promise the elusive goal of happiness for all as if it were achievable. We may well ask what happened to the role of the social sciences in critiquing society. And what has happened to our philosophers that they remain quiet? Perhaps we should take more seriously the dystopias drawn so vividly by Huxley's *Brave New World* (Huxley, 1932/2003), George Orwell's *1984* (Orwell, 1949), or more recently Garland's *The Beach* (Garland, 1997), which all show grim images of what happens when a society tries to eliminate pain and hardship to create utopia, but ends up in a nightmare of oppressive well being.

The closest we recently got to such misplaced ideals in real life was with Nazism. Contrary to how we remember it now, Nazism set out as an exuberant and enthusiastic ideology which had as its goal the creation of an intensely controlled society in which all negative influences would be eliminated so that positives could thrive. It was in blindly following a misplaced ideal of healthy, wealthy and happy people, who could rise to such great heights that extreme solutions were sought. The consequence of such perfectionism was that it appeared desirable to eliminate those who were seen as obstructing this wonderful progress: Jews, gypsies, immigrants, the mentally ill and dangerous intellectuals all had to be eliminated. Shocking as it seems now, there were many people who believed this was necessary. We remember the Holocaust, but we often forget the human experiment it represented. It failed predictably and spectacularly because in terms of political power Germany became a threat to other nations, who fought back. But did they truly perceive the underlying threat it represented in human terms? Or have we forgotten already that we can only achieve outstanding conditions of happiness for the privileged few at the cost of much misery, oppression and death for the many? It is easy to forget and when we are on the privileged side of the fence we may not notice when our society is wrong footed and rotten. Communist experiments in the USSR, China and Cuba were also experienced by many as positive and important, for they too set out with great ideals. Again initially good intentions backfired leading to a high cost in human lives and in freedom.

As soon as you try to impose a certain way of life, even one you are convinced will lead to the greatest happiness for the greatest number of people, you end up with a dictatorship, in which you have to eliminate or discipline those who stand in your way. If we bear this in mind we may well wince rather than applaud when we see scientists propose experimental and revolutionary methods to make us all happy. Levin's book *The Stepford Wives* (Levin, 1972), which was brought to the cinema twice, is a shocking representation of a science fictional universe where women are turned into perfect robots miming marital devotion and apple pie contentment. Far from this creating a Garden of Eden it instead creates a frightening dystopia for all concerned as the women ultimately falter into frightening zombie like creatures. In the shape of accomplished and beautiful housewives these women conjure up complete inhumanity and horror as their lives are nothing but a picture of absolute meaninglessness, idle smiles and soulless vacancy. The lesson is that creating a smooth and utopian way of life, which only allows for pleasantness and positive feelings, invariably leads to disaster. The unwelcome reality is that eliminating the negatives only strengthens the dark side. Negativity not dealt with or expressed accumulates till it explodes back into our lives in a different guise. The complexity and variability of the world will eventually out. So, how is it that we still strive for a state of affairs that is untenable and that can only lead to us being materially, mentally and emotionally taken over by wishful thinking, stranding ourselves in an existential desert?

Hoping for Utopia

We never seem to learn. It is quite simply utterly irresistible when the promise of the good life is suddenly on offer. How we cheer when politicians and economists appear to take the emotional needs of people seriously at long last. How fascinating to see Lord Richard Layard championing positive psychology in his book *Happiness, Lessons from a new Science* (Layard, 2005) and to find that he is actually listened to by those in power and that happiness for all has become a feasible election promise. And of course we cannot disagree with an influx of capital towards mental health. It is a fantastic achievement when a government is willing to train many more therapists in short-term well being based therapy. Yet therapists panic when this happens. They know their profession might be about to be diluted.

One would be forgiven for falling for the bribe though: who would not vote for the politician promising a new utopian state with happier citizens? How can we disagree with the extra millions spent on mental health care? Surely this is progress, rather than a threat? Yet, Layard's book shows a simplistic approach to human existence, which depicts the optimism of an economist with a plan to improve people's lives. It is devoid of the clutter and chaos that are so pervasive in the real lives of those who come for help. People like Layard more or less assume that the well being of a nation could be easily and significantly enhanced by increasing people's ability to be happy. Though his book prides itself in being 'evidence-based' and advocates cognitive behavioural therapy as a sure-fire way to help people overcome depression and achieve greater well being, the evidence it is based on is not only flimsy but misleading and biased.

For instance Layard quotes a piece of research that shows that of the 750 actors and actresses who have ever been nominated for Oscars, those that went on to actually get an Oscar lived on average four years longer than the losers (Redelmeier and Singh, 2001). He swiftly concludes from this that 'such was the gain in morale from winning' (Layard, 2005: 24). Of course this conclusion does not follow at all. Such a correlation could hide numerous causes and reasons and could very well be the reverse of what is suggested, i.e., it may be that those who were more vital and lively were more likely to win than those who were less vital. Even if he were right in his conclusion it is still a remarkably odd cause for optimism, for all it would mean is that such rare experiences as winning an Oscar are the best way of achieving longevity: not exactly a recipe that we can duplicate very easily, since by definition the pleasure of the experience is entirely based on its rarity and exceptional victory over others.

Interestingly Layard nearly puts his finger on this problem himself when quoting the research that shows how people value their income in comparison to that of others, rather than by how much they actually earn, so that they would prefer to earn 50,000 dollars, while others earn 25,000 dollars, rather than 100,000 dollars while others earn 250,000 dollars (Solnick and Hemenway, 1998). Clearly the latter position is less favourable, since the value is less than half of what others earn and people would pick this up immediately, as monetary value is measured in relative quantity. He seems surprised to note that in terms of holidays people do not apply the same standard and if given the choice between two weeks holiday when others have one week, or four weeks holiday when others have eight weeks, they do not hesitate and prefer the four (ibidem). This is also a perfectly obvious choice, since holidays are measured in personal quality and actual length of time off; therefore the more you have of them the better, regardless of what is allocated to others. Of course this presumes that a holiday is valued, which on the whole it is since it affords us not happiness, or money, but time to do what we want. This would indicate that freedom is the greater value, since more freedom is afforded to me also if I earn relatively more than others. But of course this obvious conclusion is not drawn.

The myth of paradise lost

Most of us have secret fantasies about a state of safety and never ending good experiences, in a place where resources do not run out and we get everything we need and want. There are many examples of such mythical places and they are mostly promised to us after our death, providing we have lived our lives in the right way. In the old Germanic religion the warrior is promised eternal life in Walhalla. Nirvana is a close equivalent in a Buddhist worldview, though this actually refers to a state you achieve through the right way of living, acting and thinking. In many other religions there are similar images of the after life, where everlasting glory and peace will be found in heaven for those who have been virtuous and horrible punishments will await in hell for those who have sinned. But some have conjured up images of a heavenly life created as part of society on earth as well. Thomas Moore's description of Utopia is the elusive image of a place on earth that we might come to build one day. The same is true for that South American paragon of riches and wonders, El Dorado, the city built of gold. The Garden of Eden, a picture of a presumed glorious past, continues to inspire many with a vision of a lost paradise to yearn for. Of course, looking forward rather than backwards, we may yearn for a different kind of Promised Land: a country of milk and honey where happiness will flow. Homer similarly spoke of the Land of the Lotus Eaters, where endless ease and bliss could be had by the lucky few.

But alongside these omnipresent idyllic fantasies, others have consistently tried to get the hang of the difficulties of life instead. This is not a second rate solution to our desire for a better world, but in my view, a wholly more realistic one. Kierkegaard wrote poignantly about the fall from Paradise as one of the best things that ever happened to mankind (Kierkegaard, 1843/1974). He argued that even though it seemed a tragedy, it was actually the *sine qua non* of consciousness. It was only after having been expelled from Paradise that conscious awareness became possible for the first time. In Paradise we were spoiled and protected, idle and ignorant. Once outside of Paradise we were confronted with the necessity of survival, and coincidentally with our ability to get a hold of our own lives. Kierkegaard argued that man rejected the wholeness and happiness of Eden in order to explore his destiny to its darkest and inmost depths. He pointed out that the tree of life was placed in Paradise, quite deliberately, not just as the root of all evil, but as the source of all knowledge. To eat the apple of knowledge is to opt for curiosity and discovery and to step into a life more interesting, though much harsher than that inside the magic circle of over protection and ignorant bliss. It is clear that the return to Eden is not the objective and indeed is not possible and not desirable. To understand the contrast of good and evil and in the process to discover the secrets of living with consciousness and in awareness of the differences between us is more valuable than the innocent delights of Paradise. Once we know what we know we cannot un-know it. We cannot turn back the clock. Consciousness is precious and should not be given up so lightly, in exchange for pleasures that only lead to living in a passive daze. Even though we have to work by the sweat of our brow, struggling with original sin and the trials and tribulations of existence, it is all worth it in order to make the most of our human capacity for consciousness, knowledge, understanding and labour.

The fact is that when we get down to the business of living without expecting comforts and ease and without special pleading to be exempt from the hard work that this entails, we discover our capacity for transcending troubles. But this capacity is often not very well honed. For in the secular world we are encouraged to float and enjoy rather than learn how to live. Most people are so lost when they have to deal with hardship that they are grasping at straws or teeter on the edge of disaster. How do we learn to deal with life?

A Sisyphean task

And here we return to Camus, whose premise it was that life was essentially meaningless. To him human living was a Sisyphean task, where we are continuously pushing our boulder up a hill only to find that when we get anywhere near the top the dreaded thing rolls all the way down again and we have to start from scratch. It is logical, considering the life events people suffer and the troubles they experience, that they become discouraged and conclude that life is not worth living.

It is this that provides us with the most challenging question: not whether existence can be made happy but whether we can stop allowing it to seem futile. According to Camus (1942/2006) rolling the stone up the hill and seeing it come down again is actually what challenges us to live to the full, not in a cosy state of happiness, but with the ability to struggle. There is plenty of learning and interest along the way as we roll the stone up the hill, again and again. We can live a good life even when times are tough. This is not so because there is a God in heaven who approves of our hard work. It is only because the work of our everyday life is in itself worthwhile, not in spite of all the effort and hardship, but precisely because of it. It is the struggle for the heights that makes it right. For Camus the only sin against life is to want to make it easier and less difficult for in doing so we remove the grandeur and tragedy that make life what it is. The very contrast between difficulty and relief is what makes our effort stand out and ultimately valuable.

This is an unpopular view, though one that Nietzsche held as well. He said:

Happiness and unhappiness are twins that grow up together. (1882/1974: 270)

We cannot have happiness without being prepared for unhappiness too. Not many people have arrived at such a Dionysian perspective. It is quite clear by now that it is more usual to believe that ultimately only happiness can make life worth living and that a good life is identical with a happy life. Yet we have seen that:

> ... *if we accept that happiness is paramount in life, things like love, friendship, meaningful activity, freedom, human development, or the appreciation of true beauty are merely instrumentally valuable for us. They become denigrated as things that lead us to happiness rather than being valued in their own right. In other words, they are no longer good as ends but they merely serve us as means to the only thing that is good as an end, namely happiness. (Brulde, 2007)*

The only way to avoid this predicament is to stop looking for happiness and learn to live instead. It will be clear by now that this means facing up to both happiness and unhappiness. So let's move on to look at the obstacles we need to learn to take in our stride on the rugged path of life.

Chapter 4

Predictable Difficulties:
Everyday Challenges

For I have known them all already, known them all-
Have known the evenings, mornings, afternoons,
I have measured out my life with coffee spoons;

(T.S. Eliot, The Love Song of J. Alfred Prufrock: 13)

It is pretty clear now that life is not essentially about happiness. Daily living is usually a fairly treacherous and tricky obstacle course, where many sorrows, joys and other mixed emotions are encountered. To live is to practise a curious and unpredictable sport which consists of facing up to new difficulties at every corner and where seemingly unfair events test our stamina and determination continuously. In this game of life we are exposed to inevitable losses and disappointments, which we have to deal with in order to clear the way to make the most of remaining options and opportunities. The trick is to enjoy this intricate process by mastering it rather than feeling at its mercy or despair about it. It is no good presenting this sport as simple fun and games, putting a romantic gloss over it and making it seem like a pleasant outing. On the whole life is a pain and not a picnic. Anyway even picnics carry their fair share of troubles when ants get onto the blanket you are sitting on or wasps compete for the jam and butter. It is unhelpful to idealize life and present it in the guise of a positive experience where those who are disenchanted are spoil sports or lacking in moral fibre. Theorizing about life is all very well but we need to take our cues from the everyday practice of living if we are really to come to grips with the complexities of human existence. We better take a look at what we can learn from the practice of psychotherapy and counselling. For it is here more than anywhere else that ordinary people discuss their daily troubles and that creative solutions have to be found, rather than either dismissing people as having mental illnesses or inventing a utopian standard of happiness for all. Psychotherapists are confronted constantly with the quest for security, health, wealth and happiness that people are on and they are wiser than most to the daily quandaries and long-term battles that people have to wage in the process.

Difficulties are part of everyday life

In the recent past the problems that drove people to seek professional help have usually been considered as pathological and as proof of some intrinsic internal weakness on their part. Since Foucault (1965) and Szasz (1961) challenged this notion, it has become increasingly obvious that pathology is often only the long-term consequence of our predictable problems in living. Mental illness, except for when it has a physical origin (as for instance with autism, dementia or brain injury), results from failing to understand how to effectively tackle existential and relational problems. Yet difficulties are a fact of life. We are inevitably faced with a range of obstacles and dangers on a daily basis. Of course some people are stronger than others and there is no doubt that some of us are more vulnerable to faltering into confusion or despair than others. Few of us are a deft hand at all of life's challenges. All of us are occasionally faced with exceptional trials and tribulations that require special skills and extraordinary persistence to come to grips with. Some events will so disappoint and distress us that we suddenly feel out of kilter. They will detract from the quietude of the easy or cosy life we think we would like to enjoy. Experienced therapists and counsellors learn to recognize the predictable limitations and problems of human living that are universally present and they also develop a flair for the catastrophic life events that can rock a person's life and self-esteem to the core. Interestingly they do not learn much about this in their training, since training tends to focus on normal human development or on specific aspects of psychopathology. The range of existential issues that clients bring is fairly steady and persistent however (see also van Deurzen and Arnold-Baker, 2005).

Facing the basics

This is quite simply because there are a number of existential challenges that all human beings have to face, because they are an inevitable part of the human condition. Quite often people come for therapy to find a way of dealing with one of these challenges. As Jaspers pointed out we all have to suffer in small and big ways, we all have to labour and earn a living, we all end up feeling guilty by unintentionally failing to live up to our own or other people's expectations, we are all subject to chance and we all die sooner or later and therefore have to live with the temporary nature of life which exposes us to inevitable losses (Jaspers, 1951). Yet, we do not really like to admit this and we spend a lot of time trying to pretend that we can be exempt from these unpleasant aspects of the human condition. It seems to us that we have failed when we encounter one of these limits of human living.

> *The ultimate situations – death, chance, guilt and the uncertainty of the world – confront me with the reality of failure. What do I do in the face of this absolute failure, which if I am honest I cannot fail to recognise? (Jaspers, 1951: 22)*

When faced with failure some of us carry on regardless, trying to prove we are impervious to negative assessments, disappointments and deprivation, but others flounder and despair and feel like giving up. Some people come to see a psychotherapist, a counsellor, or perhaps even a philosophical consultant at this point. They may or may not wish to pathologize their own distress and they may or may not want to blame it on someone else or on circumstances. But it is important to remember that they inevitably bring more than just the presenting difficulty and that their predicament shows up a whole way of being. Laing noted that what people bring into psychotherapy is never more or less than the totality of their being.

> *... no matter how circumscribed or diffuse the initial complaint may be, one knows that the patient is bringing into the treatment situation, whether intentionally or unintentionally, his existence, his whole being-in-his-world. (Laing, 1960: 25)*

Existential therapists take the view that interventions should be made from a background of understanding the whole of a person's existence. To do so requires us to have a grasp of the wider sphere of the totality of human existence. It is never enough to come just from the bias of one theoretical framework or, even worse, from the one-dimensional perspective of psychopathology. It isn't what is wrong with the person that should be the focus of our work but rather what is right with them for wanting to learn to deal better with their problems. The focus should therefore be shifted slowly from the issue at hand to the wider perspective of their life. As therapists we need to help people remember and reconnect with what it is that they want to achieve in getting through the current constriction. The objective of happiness, i.e. of the simple release of tensions, is not sufficient. Happiness is a mood, not a project or an end goal. To help others to think clearly about worthwhile life objectives we need at least some minimal philosophical understanding of the human condition. As a bare minimum therapists should have a working knowledge of the predictable difficulties and predicaments that people frequently present in therapy. Rather than categorizing people's individual traits or disorders, as is done in psychology, philosophical counsellors or existential consultants need to be capable of recognizing the many varied forms of human worries that will be presented by clients, hour after hour.

First, we need to make distinctions between those who come with chronic problems and those who come with acute problems related to a particular crisis or instance of change in their lives. Acute problems may be clarified with a narrow focus, whereas chronic ones will need to be lit with a wider beam. Secondly we need to consider what personal resources and talents each person brings for dealing with their difficulties. It is astonishing how many human problems disappear like snow before the sun by simply reminding people of their strengths and abilities. Reminded of their past and present successes they rally to the task and resolve thorny issues with alacrity. Thirdly it is helpful to have some framework for one's understanding. It can help to consider the various dimensions of existence with which the person is presently struggling. A systematic inventory of how a person manages each aspect of their lives can give a foundation from which to tackle any troubles (van Deurzen, 1988/2002; van Deurzen and Arnold-Baker, 2005). Fourthly it is useful to ask what the other side of the coin of a person's difficulties may be. Experiences come in opposites and we need to wonder where the opposite polarity is hidden. Finding it will throw light on the issue at hand and may hold the key to the solutions clients are struggling to find. Every weakness has a hidden strength inside of it. Every strength carries vulnerability.

But most importantly a person's worries need to be kept in a philosophical perspective. There are many difficulties that are familiar and foreseeable and it is good practice for therapists to acquaint themselves with most of these, whilst remaining open to the multiple forms and individual and surprising variations on these common themes that will emerge. In this chapter I shall present to you some of these predictable difficulties in human living without claiming this to be a complete or exhaustive list. I am sure that most therapists and counsellors will recognize them as well as being reminded of other variants of these that they have encountered over the years. It is not by chance that the difficulties presented here all start with the letter 'D', since the prefix 'de-' refers to the removal or absence of something: it indicates a lack, an undoing, a de-motion. It would seem that human problems are most often about such loss or lack of something. I have long considered that dictionaries and the systematic thesaurus are pretty good inventories of human experience that can give the *DSM* or *ICD* inventories that clinical psychologists and psychiatrists refer to a run for their money. I shall briefly sketch out some of the ordinary losses and lacks that affect human beings on all four dimensions of human existence. I have described these dimensions in much further detail elsewhere (van Deurzen-Smith, 1997; van Deurzen, 1988/2002; van Deurzen and Arnold-Baker, 2005). They are simply the physical, social, personal or spiritual spheres of human living which can provide us with a simple scheme for organizing our understanding of what has gone wrong. Of course, in reality

Figure 4.1   Dimensions of existence

these spheres and world dimensions overlap, interact and flow together as do the troubles that visit us in each. The descriptions that follow are a bird's eye view and schematic sketch of the complexity of human reality and its inevitable troubles and plagues.

Physical dimension

The bottom line of human existence is the physical dimension. This is the dimension of our relation to the material world, where we interact with the world of objects and physical things. It is primarily our bodies and their sensory experience that provide the medium of interaction on this dimension. At the physical level we encounter lots of challenges that may ruin our well being. To look at just a few: some of us encounter deficits or defects in life from an early age. All of us have to deal with later deficiencies. Disease comes to all of us sooner or later and we are all doomed to manage our own desires: not always an easy job. Dependence is the starting point for all human beings and we learn to become independent and interdependent in later life. Ultimately we all meet the threat of death and our demise is the only possible outcome of our physical existence. Lets put a bit more detail on it.

1 Deficit

To experience physical deficit is necessary. As a small child you feel deficient all the time, but this is not the same as feeling that we cannot overcome our deficiency. There is no doubt that some people come into the world with major deficits, including physical deformities that mark them out as different. Learning to take on board our peculiar ways of physical existence is a major challenge at the best of times. People tend to find deficiencies the harder to deal with as they perceive themselves as not fitting in with others. Deficiency may be purely physical, as in the person born with a hole in the heart or with a major facial or bodily deformity like a hare lip or a port wine stain. It may be acquired later in life through illness, accident, neglect, abuse or aging and it may then have far reaching consequences for the person's actual survival and sense of fundamental security. There is an enormous challenge in working with people who are struggling with deficits and it helps to have one of one's own, as most of us do.

My work with Elsa, who had had a double mastectomy after breast cancer had ravaged her, was initially entirely focused on her sense of physical deformity. She had a deep hatred of what she considered her female failure. She needed to work her way through her disgust and horror of her new self to a gradual acceptance of the streamlined new shape that now was hers. Ultimately she learnt to value her scars and her flat chest which reminded her of being like a little girl again and she found great strength in reclaiming her new status and even refusing reconstruction. There are many examples of people who learn to bear defects in this manner and who come to prize them as part of their individuality. We all love to see people overcome physical defects in extraordinary ways. There is heroism in this. Such people inspire us. Taking on board a physical problem with zest conjures up true vitality. It may even be that we cannot be truly physically aware until we have achieved this.

2 Disease

Beyond defect and deficiency is the experience of disease and its concomitant experience of pain and suffering. It is certainly not only in cases of terminal illness (Yalom, 1980) that disease brings a challenge that can help us appreciate life in a new way. Mental illness is a different experience altogether (Bracken, 2002; Laing, 1960, 1967; Szasz, 1961), but no matter how we think of it, feeling out of one's mind makes one feel out of one's body too. Therefore it is usually best to begin by retrieving physical security, safety and shelter before anything else.

Connie had recently had a recurrence of her ovarian cancer and had been told that the cancer was now in her lungs and her bone marrow as well. While she was certain that she wanted to continue to fight for her survival and was doing everything she possibly could to do so, she was quite realistic about the likelihood that she would die within the year. She wanted to set priorities for the little bit of life that was left to her, but in doing so constantly had to heed the needs of those around her as well as attending to the needs and limitations of her body. This meant she could not go on the world tour she had promised herself for instance and we had to work hard at overcoming this setback in creative ways, since it had meant a lot to her in principle to travel the world. As many existential philosophers have pointed out the limitations that we discover in our existence can set a framework for our experience and thus make it more intense, rather than destroy our lives. Connie found this out for herself when she used the limit of her mobility to get closer to people rather than let it distance her. For instance she asked her niece and nephew to share the pictures of their world travels with her and so made a stronger relationship with them. But it can never be a foregone conclusion that new limitations will lead to revelations and depth. Frequently to achieve this we have to be prepared to clear our minds and do a lot of hard work. It is a struggle worth going through though, for every limitation is a potential discovery of a new dimension of your life.

3 Desire

Desire is central. We are not much without it. But there are many more forms of desire than sexual desire. Desires reveal to us what we most want and most aspire to. They set us in the direction of what we crave but is still out of reach. They can lead to constant dissatisfaction and frustration or spur us on to constructive action. Obtaining what one wants and becoming addicted to it is as dangerous as not obtaining what one wants and becoming obsessed with it. The process of craving and constant dissatisfaction is a familiar one in Buddhism: in fact it is seen as the foundation of all of our suffering. The Buddhist solution to the problem is to turn away from desire, which is not so dissimilar to the solution proposed by many of the Hellenistic philosophers, who often searched for ways to suppress or minimize their desires as well (Nussbaum, 1994). Desire can be a positive force if it is tamed. Nietzsche's will to power is primarily about desire and one's willingness to act on it. Sartre saw desire as the counterpart to people's fundamental nothingness.

> The existence of desire as a human fact is sufficient to prove that human reality is a lack. (Sartre, 1943/1956: 87)

Working with desire is not about trying to eliminate or control it but rather to see it as a spur to action. To be driven by our desires is to go on a riding to nowhere. To eliminate our desires is to dampen our spirits. To learn to master the force of our desires is to be in harmony with life.

4 Dependence

In following the path of desire a little further we come to dependence. We are dependent on what we desire and need. The child is dependent on the parent and learns to become independent gradually. But our independence is always relative to our need for others and so we have to learn to be interdependent: to give and take, need and be needed. The nothingness or lack at the centre of human beings makes us not only reach out for people but also for things that we can become dependent on. Many people become enslaved to things or others. There is no doubt that managing the capacity for physical autonomy is crucial to our survival. There are many ways in which we may lose this capacity and when we do so, we need to seek to take small steps towards some self-sufficiency.

When I saw Eric, he had been in primal therapy for five years and he had become so regressed that he had given up his job two years previously and was living off benefits and his savings, which were dwindling fast. He felt like a child who could not work for his own living. He felt helpless. He hoped that existential therapy would be more bracing and might encourage his autonomy and in this he was probably right. He still had a tendency to lean on me and he wanted to be given the religious texts of existential therapy and follow the dogma that would make everything right for him. But he thrived on the challenge to find his own authority instead. Rekindling his desire to earn his own living and make himself physically, materially safe again was the crux of the work we did together. Eric had to train the muscles of his will power and in fact literally the muscles of his arms and legs to overcome the strange akrasia, apathy and wishful thinking that had kept him back for so long. He felt much relief in exercising his own will, walking again and then striking out on his own.

5 Disembodiment or disassociation

Perhaps it is particularly in schizoid individuals that the sense of disembodiment occurs. Laing (1961) observed how some people never find a secure way of owning their own bodies. Somehow they are not introduced to selfhood even in this basic sense. Life circumstances prevent them from finding their own centre. The body is the instrument through which we live in the world and achieve personhood and autonomy. Without a good practical sense of being in the world in a physical fashion there is very little chance that we can go forwards. Incorporation is the *sine qua non* of feeling real and the body experienced in mastered movement is the secret of a secure self.

> A movement is learned when the body has understood it, that is, when it has incorporated it into its 'world', and to move one's body is to aim at things through it; it is to allow oneself to respond to their call, which is made upon it independently of any representation. (Merleau Ponty 1945/1962: 139)

For some people such directness of embodied relating to the world is too dangerous or taboo. People who have experienced abuse or neglect may have learnt to dissociate from their bodily experience in order to make their pain less real. The body is experienced as an object rather than as a subject: it becomes like a thing that others can observe and manipulate.

> *Thus we flee from anguish by attempting to apprehend ourselves from without as an other or as a thing. (Sartre, 1943/1956: 43)*

To enable a person to feel real again we have to begin by helping them to reclaim their bodily existence. With each client attention needs to be paid to their experience of being a body in space, for that is where our consciousness of ourselves begins.

> *The body is what consciousness is, it is not even anything except body. The rest is nothingness and silence. (Sartre, 1943/1956: 434)*

To feel real we have to be prepared to feel pain. Avoidance of pain leads to unreality. People who self harm often do so to make themselves feel again and bring back some reality. Perhaps self harm is the necessary counterpart to a culture based on maximum pleasure and happiness.

6 Death

If our consciousness starts with the body, it also ends with it. Death is the unavoidable spectre of our lives: the border of our existence. It marks the limit, the frontier and the frame within which we operate. Fear of death is a major motivation in emotional problems. The confrontation with the end of our possibilities haunts us. Death is when everything we have been suddenly comes to nothing. And none of us can avoid this moment ultimately. Death is the one thing we are sure of in life. It comes to us all. By the very fact of being born we are condemned to dying. We are all on the way towards the end. We spend much of our lives hiding from that certainty. Until people recognize the reality of their own mortality it is difficult for them to be truly alive. Facing up to the reality of death leads to an acceptance of our inevitable incompleteness. We are always not yet what we can be. It is only in death that our life is completed and comes to its culmination. Until death we are incomplete and have potential.

> *Everydayness is precisely that Being which is 'between' birth and death. (Heidegger, 1927/1962: 233)*

Death had been something that Helen had feared for many years. She had avoided going to her mother's funeral by pretending to have a nervous breakdown and she had been deeply ashamed of her cowardice. She felt unable to get out of the house at all after this. She became depressed and it was her GP who referred her for therapy, with the message that she had not been able to mourn for her mother properly. She came for psychotherapy because she did not know what else to do but she did not believe her mother's death meant a lot to her at all. Helen needed to weep for herself rather than just for her mother. She realized that her mother had always been as anxious about losing things and people as she was. Her mother had encouraged her to live in fear, as she had herself. Helen quickly felt that she was much sadder about her mother's constricted lifestyle than about her actual death. This constricted lifestyle, she knew all too well, was similar to her own and she soon figured that it was designed to ward off the sort of dangers that had led to her mother's death. Now Helen cried for the lack of life and courage that had been her mother's tragedy. She became eager, though still scared, to change her own *modus operandi* and to strike out a little further, show some temerity, take some risks and stop avoiding death. Two years later, when her aunt died, Helen had reached a very different attitude towards life and death and she was able not only to go to the funeral but to sit through a night's vigil with her uncle by her aunt's coffin. This experience moved her deeply and she felt a profound sense of redemption afterwards. She was now able to claim her life in dramatic new ways, because she had realized that it might soon be too late and that she would die anyway whatever she would do with her life, so she might as well make the most of what she had before it was too late. This is what she did to very good effect and she made new connections and relationships with others, finding confidence and joy.

Social dimension

Being with others in the right way is hugely important to make our lives work. The extent to which we are able to relate to others in the right manner determines what we get out of life. There are many fundamental elements of social relations that can become problematic and there are lots of predictable problems that we have to learn to deal with.

7 Difference

In spite of our shared human condition, sooner or later we discover that we are in some ways different to other people. We may be proud of our difference if it is experienced as specialness or superiority, but many of us experience our difference as negative or inferior and end up feeling discriminated against. We may feel excluded from groups we want to belong to or we may become bullied and ridiculed and end up feeling worthless. Such a sense of personal inferiority or exclusion undermines any feeling of having a right to be who we are. Yet, ironically separateness is an important part of becoming an individual. In principle and in some ways all of us are different to everyone else. We have to learn to live our difference in ways that are neither offensive to the other nor destructive to ourselves.

People need to know they belong and are respected by the groups around them. All of us need a sense of kinship with our fellow human beings. One of the challenges of finding our own place in the world is to create the right distance in relation to other people, neither too far nor too close. When clients bring issues of difference to psychotherapy they do so in order to discover some of the ways in which their variance from the norm can become an asset rather than a setback, an advantage rather than a disadvantage. Some people pretend to be more different from others than they actually are. Difference in this sense can be used as a way of saying: stay away from me, I am not like you and I may be dangerous to know. The experience of dissimilarity creates anxiety because it creates barriers. It is impossible not to feel anxious when we suddenly realize that we are distinct from others and that we stand out: alone. This experience is inevitable and according to Heidegger necessary to claim our selfhood.

> *Anxiety individualizes. This individualization brings Dasein back from its falling, and makes manifest to it that authenticity and inauthenticity are possibilities of its Being. (Heidegge, 1927/1962: 191)*

To claim our capacity for authentic and inauthentic being is to claim freedom.

8 Discord

When difference leads to conflict, such problems with others can spoil all of our experience. Some people seem to be predisposed to have consistent difficulties in getting on with fellow human beings, feeling out of sorts with them and rubbing them the wrong way. People who are labelled as having Asperger syndrome, borderline personality disorder, or narcissistic or sociopathic disorders may all end up spending much of their time in disharmony with those around them. Their difficulties need to be understood in terms of their different ways of perceiving and interacting with the world so that they can reconnect and come into safe harbour. They may need to learn how to respect others and avoid overt conflict.

On the other hand, with people who avoid aggression and discord an active encouragement of entering into disagreement may be a positive step forward. Disharmony is inevitable in life, given that we are all in some sense in competition with each other and potentially dominated and oppressed by the other's judgment on us. Sartre described it so clearly:

> *The Other looks at me and as such he holds the secret of my being, he knows what I am. Thus the profound meaning of my being is outside of me, imprisoned in an absence. The Other has the advantage over me. (Sartre, 1943/1956: 363)*

9 Dominance

Contending with the challenges of dominance and submission in human relations is hard to do. Some of us find it so hard that we would rather withdraw from others altogether. We all know people who try to push us around, outsmart us, take advantage of us and dominate us in a variety of ways. Some of us are good at getting what we want, some of us are not so good at it. Dominance is really about territory. We defend our territory or push others off it. But some go beyond this into trying to expand their territory at the expense of others. Issues around dominance are rife. Much of life is upsetting because of this. But the reality is that we have to learn to get on together. Many feel they are selected specifically for bullying or singled out for rough treatment by others and feel helpless about it. In close relationships this becomes an even more important issue, since people have to find mutually satisfactory ways of getting along. Sartre described the process of loving another as a process of possession, making for a dramatic image of what goes on in a relationship.

> *Thus the lover does not desire to possess the beloved as one possesses a thing; he demands a special type of appropriation. He wants to possess a freedom as a freedom. (Sartre, 1943/1956: 367)*

It may be that we really do want to continue to be free whilst belonging to another. But most of us want to learn to be ourselves and safe whilst also with each other. It is a relief then to discover, as Sartre did in his later work, that besides competitive relationships there are also relationships of cooperation and mutuality (Sartre, 1960b) where we give generously to each other and achieve more than we would alone.

10 Dishonesty

In this negotiation with others some amount of dishonesty seems to creep into the proceedings, especially in public life. Honesty is essential for closeness and intimacy for there can be no trust without it. But those who try to live life in an honest way in relation to all their interactions may come out worse than those who lie. This raises real moral questions and there is quite an art in learning to be truthful without being blunt or without making oneself too vulnerable to attack. We do not know whether we can respect ourselves if we tell little white lies about trivial things, like pretending to like people we actually dislike for the sake of peace. Negotiations with others are seldom conducted without some bad faith or pretence. Those who can appear most confident tend to attract the most resources. Dishonest representations of self and the creation of a persona which is acted with poise are part of the relational strategies which not everyone finds comfortable or correct. Yet much of our secular world thrives on such patterns of interaction and all of us have to come to terms with this and determine our own attitude. Making reflection on truth and reality the cornerstone of our interactions can be a hard choice, but it provides a solid ground on which to build. The successes obtained by dishonesty are short term and lead to disenchantment in the long run for in the end they alienate us from others and ourselves.

11 Disengagement

A more extreme form of disconnecting from human relationships is that of disengagement. When we disengage, we keep others at a distance, withdrawing and removing ourselves from the dangers that social relationships bring. Most people will know the feeling of mistrusting others and will have times when they do not want to take the risk of getting close. When this strategy is habitually used however a complete state of social isolation can ensue. This leads to a lack of positive connections with the world, which in turn engenders apathy and boredom. Disengagement is the ultimate evasion of the human condition. Without engagement we cannot be fully human. Yet, we find over and over again that those people who disengage do so because they feel there is no place for them in the world where they can be safe. They are often people who value their individuality and do not find it easy to go along with the crowd. Strangely enough it is those who can just go along with the herd who will get most engaged in life, even though their engagement may stay at surface level and their success may be ephemeral. They will still find themselves accepted and happy to carry on being who they are. Those who ask themselves the question 'who am I?', and who do not find a simple answer to it, may resonate with Merleau Ponty and consider that their identity is a personal but also a universal issue that cannot be so easily settled:

> *My life seems absolutely individual and absolutely universal to me.* *(Merleau Ponty, 1964: 94)*

If we find others incapable of appreciating our individuality we may well withdraw into our shell, incapable of making those universal connections as well.

12 Destruction

There seems to be in many of us, and perhaps in all of us, an active desire to destroy the very same things, situations or people that we love. As Nietzsche argued, the self is always busy comparing itself to others and overpowering others and failing this it may seek to destroy them.

> *The Self is always listening and seeking: it compares, subdues, conquers, destroys. (Nietzsche, 1883/1933: 62)*

Some people become destructive because they feel it is their only way to maintain themselves against the overwhelming force of others. For other people it is more when things get too easy that they seem to want to make them a little more difficult again, lest they be bored. Once a cycle of destruction is embarked on it is easily taken beyond what is socially acceptable. As psychotherapists we sometimes work with people who have committed violent criminal acts. Although toughness is required in the face of such behaviour, we also need to be capable of a special kind of attentiveness and indulgence if we are to understand what has really happened. People who have been violent are often ready to be violent again and their only hope of breaking the cycle is to finally find a better way of expressing themselves. We need to be tough on the aggression and soft on the person inside who is trying to address the fear that has not found its voice yet. It helps to remember that in the last analysis what people destroy when they become destructive is always their own lives and their own opportunities. If we accept the notion that self is only a relation and not a substantive entity, then destruction is always also self-destruction and this can be a key to its resolution as well.

> Things are structures – frameworks – the stars of our life: they gravitate around us. Yet there is a secret bond between us and them. (Merleau Ponty, 1968: 220)

Personal dimension

Our physical and social interactions determine ultimately how we form a picture of ourselves. Awareness of difficulties often starts at this level, for it is when we cannot get a strong sense of identity or when it gets challenged that we know we are in trouble. All of us have to face predictable difficulties in relation to our personal being.

13 Dilemma

Most clients who come for existential therapy present with some sort of dilemma. A dilemma is a choice point where you know you have to make a decision but you feel paralysed in doing so for fear of the consequences. It literally feels as if you will be damned if you do and damned if you don't. People always experience their dilemma in a very personal and harrowing manner, even though universal tragedies are always played out in them. But this is not obvious when we are stuck with our own little problem and we easily get isolated with our worries. Our dilemmas affect us deeply. They are the edge of our lives, against which we become aware of ourselves as troubled. They immobilize us temporarily and this makes us doubt who we are, for to be a person is to be in movement and feel confident in the choices we make. In other words to be trapped in a dilemma means to experience the situation as a crisis of identity. When we are caught between several courses of action we may have an acute sense of the loss each choice that we make will involve, but we have lost track of the direction we want to go in and the gains we may achieve. Some dilemmas are actually trilemmas, or quadrilemmas, where multiple seemingly contradictory options are available and it becomes impossible to know where to turn. Some dilemmas are clustered together and form a more complex dilemma in which each component needs to be sorted out separately before the whole riddle can be solved. The trick in these situations is to get to the root of the problem and clear the way for the final decisive cutting of the Gordian knot. Exploring the ins and outs of the dilemma and the actions taken and not taken in relation to it will usually separate essential from non essential issues, making it clearer to the person how things stand and what matters most. Providing real clarity about the situation will lead to the person suddenly realizing there is a natural, organic solution. Providing the dilemma is elucidated plentifully and completely a decision will emerge in the same way in which snow melts in front of the sun and plants turn to the light.

All dilemmas take time to understand and come to terms with. These are important moments of our lives when we determine what sort of person we are opting to become. Do we want freedom from what we have now or commitment to something beyond our horizon? What are our expectations and concerns? How will we cope with our inevitable losses, one way or another? It helps to have some insight into the resilience of our character: how much are we capable of coping with? We need to mind both sides of the equation: that which needs to be done and that which is possible. We have to ride the paradox between these. Our sense of self will be strengthened in the process.

> *Personhood is a synthesis of possibility and necessity. Its continued existence is like breathing (respiration), which is an inhaling and exhaling. (Kierkegaard, 1855/1941: 40)*

Sometimes dilemmas are unsolvable and we have to learn to live with the contradictions and tensions that are a vital part of life and can become a source of energy.

14 Deceit or self-deception

This is perhaps the single, most tricky human tendency to hinder our progress. Deception and self-deception stand in the way of us seeing our life clearly and mask the very truth that is our best guide. How come we all try to fool ourselves or other people about the actual facts of life, hampering the process of clear decision making? It seems impossible for people to see things just as they are. We are all guilty of some pretence. Sometimes we pretend that things are not what they seem, at other times we pretend that they are something that they actually are not. Sartre's notion of bad faith has much to contribute in this respect (Sartre, 1943/1956). But it was Heidegger who recognized that self-deception is a pervasive and necessary evil, even though he did not use the term. Heidegger (1927/1962) described human existence as a continuous struggle with the tendency to fall in with other people's expectations of us. He showed how the other in many ways is always our self, so that we present the world to ourselves as determined by others who only exist in our own minds. We live in this mythical universe in what he called an inauthentic or disowned fashion, following other people's prescriptions and opinions. Heidegger saw this struggle with veracity as the fundamental battle to become a real human being. As long as we cover up rather than face what is there we are only partially in charge of our own lives, but often this is all we feel capable of. The more we stand for truth and face things, and ourselves, as they actually are, the more engaged with life we can get. But this requires courage.

How much reality each person is able and willing to bear has got to be their own judgment. How much reality each therapist can bear is another matter. There is much partial honesty in psychotherapy. It is so much easier to provide clients with pre-packaged solutions than to truly face the impediments and hardship they are contending with. Therapists can project an image of knowing more than they do, so that they don't have to face the client's distress too closely and can keep their personal illusions of grandeur in tact. This does not give the client confidence in their therapist. An agoraphobic client might think the therapist naïve for not acknowledging that cars are deadly machines for instance. Are we prepared to face the client's true fear and find the courage to tackle it at the root, rather than dismiss it as their problem? Similarly convincing a person prematurely that it will not be the end of her world if she fails an exam or misses a particular family event may be counterproductive and highly constrictive: perhaps we could call it a kind of con. This is not to say that the con will not work, but if it does it will have worked as a manipulation of the client rather than by the person finding her own truth and her own strength to understand, face up and cope. Finding out exactly what it is that makes the person feel distraught and how they fear their world may be destroyed is a more honest way forward. Finding out whether being destroyed in this way might also have some advantages is to be direct and take a step towards truth. But how tempting it is to foreclose such explorations and instead reframe the client's universe in some more positive way. Of course such spin almost always involves some level of deception and self-deception on the part of the therapist and the client. Such sweet lies may sometimes be a good thing, because they may afford us temporary relief and a moment of happiness, but ultimately they are shown up as the pretence they really are. Dishonesty forms a new barrier against life. The pressure to be happy might actually stop us from getting to know ourselves or getting better at life.

> *Why does man not see things? He is himself standing in the way: he conceals things. (Nietzsche, 1881/1987: 438)*

This is precisely the reason that people come for help: because they stand in the way of seeing themselves clearly. As therapists we owe people a clearer vision and as much truth as they can bear. Truth is often as much about life as about the person. A lack of understanding of the world is at the root of as much trouble as a lack of self-knowledge. Helping clients to become more realistic about life and the world around them as they get to know themselves is a vital part of the therapeutic task.

15 Disappointment or disillusionment

One of the things that happens as soon as we look for truth in ourselves and around us is that we get disappointed. Life is not easy and it may overwhelm us with its losses and disenchantments. When we feel disillusioned nothing seems possible and worthwhile anymore. The world has lost its attractiveness and everything has become blank and bland. We feel defeated. No wonder people withdraw from the world after they have tried to achieve something and have failed. Now they are not so keen to try again, for fear of failing once more. Sometimes there may be a sense of disgust with the absurdity that has resulted. Sometimes we may feel totally depressed or dejected. Such experiences lead to what Nietzsche called the experience of resentment, which consists of leading one's life as if one has been deprived and not been treated fairly.

When Christopher came to see me he had had three unhappy relationships in a row. He had withdrawn from social life in disgust and after having given up first on dating, then on shopping, and then on going to work, he was now struggling with severe sociophobia. Indeed his dread of going out in public was so great that he avoided social situations altogether fearing that they could only bring further humiliation. It soon became clear though, to both him and me, that the phobia was not some illness but a disillusionment followed by a decision that other people were not to be trusted. Chris was afraid of reaching out to others for fear of further disenchantment, disaster or defeat. He needed help to discover a new courage in himself that would enable him to engage with others again on his own terms rather than on the frightened terms of someone trying to please and avoid disappointment. He realized quickly that it was himself he had lost faith in and that it was time to have the courage of his own convictions rather than trying to please and appease others. He enjoyed recognizing what his own convictions actually were. This was a question of enabling him to recover his enthusiasm for activities that pleased him and that he could do by himself, like fishing and playing golf. Doing these he gradually got himself over the phobia without focusing on it as a problem. It was not hard to notice that he actually got on fine with non threatening people around him, like the caretaker at the golf course and the fellow fishermen he liked to chat with. The hardest bit was to pluck up the courage to move into the company of those whose judgment he feared. He needed to brace himself quite a few times in order to include such others in his life again, especially women. It was courage that cured him, he said.

> But there is something in me that I call courage: it has always destroyed every discouragement in me ... For courage is the best destroyer – courage that attacks: for in every attack there is a triumphant shout. (Nietzsche, 1883/1933: 177)

16 Distress

But if we have lost all courage as a result of trauma and crisis we may run out of courage for a while. Not everything that happens to us can be immediately absorbed and digested. Distress often coincides with a feeling of weakness for our ability to cope has imploded. We have been pushed beyond our limit and need to ease up on ourselves for a while. Stress is the opposite since it is a sense of coping with so much that we may soon explode. It can be dealt with in a philosophical manner, by looking at priorities and assumptions about work and putting the idea of labour and achievement in perspective. Distress cannot be dealt with that easily, since it indicates that we have already gone beyond our capacity for coping, so that reason alone won't save us anymore. It usually involves physical symptoms as well as emotional and mental upheavals. These days we tend to call it PTSD, post-traumatic stress disorder. People who have encountered experiences of disaster, accident or war are shocked and disorientated. Their world has broken down and with it their sense of safety. It does not help that people who come for help with PTSD are often involved in court-cases to get redress. This can complicate things considerably when it means the person has to document their distress and hold on to it in order to get compensation. This is not a good basis for philosophical work. The flashbacks, insomnia and catastrophic fantasies or fears that distressed people experience indicate that they need protection and release before they can come to understand what has happened. Their equilibrium is disturbed and has to be re-balanced. This is best done by re-establishing a safe life in which they can fully take charge of things themselves.

When I worked with Ian, whose father had been murdered in an attack on their home in which he was also injured, his lack of safety stood out beyond all else. It was clear that Ian was lacking in the kind of basic sense of safety that we normally take for granted. He feared that his own mental health was at risk and for the first few weeks we worked in the volatile atmosphere of his instability and self doubt. He was terrified that he might flip into acute states of panic and he was frightened of meeting his own death like his father. Images of horror haunted him. He needed basic assistance in finding inner strength to repair his trust in a world where such events are fortunately rare.

Support networks and positive input from music and film were essential in getting him back into a more peaceful frame of mind. Stopping him from disintegration meant stopping the haemorrhage of feelings and fantasies that were driving him crazy. He found his own methods for doing so, instead of following a particular prescription. As Ian emerged and gained strength we began a vigorous process of re-evaluation of the values that he felt had killed his father and which he needed to safeguard himself against. It was only in recognizing he could create a different world to live in than the one that had led to disaster that his confidence returned. But his capacity for dread would never return to his previous level of 'devil may care'.

17 Dread

Anxiety, or Angst as Kierkegaard (1844/1980) named it, is an experience that helps us stay alive. Dread in the face of real or imagined danger is one of the most fundamental human experiences. It is the reality of existential anxiety, which reminds us that life is not essentially a safe place. As many authors have recognized, to some extent anxiety or dread is desirable and energizes people. Facing the depth of existence can give us new perspective on the truth of a life that is never beyond challenges or pain.

> *Anxiety makes manifest in Dasein its Being towards its own most potentiality-for-being-that is, its Being-free for the freedom of choosing itself and taking hold of itself. (Heidegger, 1927/1962: 188)*

Anxiety accompanies the experience of freedom and responsibility. It also announces the possibility of our individuality, as Heidegger suggested. In a negative sense this can be undermining, if we do not feel up to the challenge. In a positive sense the rush of adrenaline that comes with anxiety makes you aware that you are in fact alive. There is something to be done and you are the one who has to do it. Of course there is such a thing as paralysing anxiety or panic, and when this gets generalized it may turn into something debilitating like anxiety disorder or phobia: a blocking of one's capacity to function. Understanding anxiety as a sign of life and potential liberation means that we have to find ways to be the author of our own anxiety rather than letting it overwhelm us.

Finding the maximum point of anxiety leads to uncovering our values. We are most anxious about that which matters most. When we know what makes us anxious we know what our original project is. We can only experience wild anxiety or panic when we are out of touch with the meaning of our anxiety. Then anxiety circles around in senseless ways, never connecting to either understanding or action and we falter and fail. Contained anxiety or mastered anxiety is a source of great energy. The goal is therefore neither to fall headlong into high anxiety, nor to become immune, but rather to be capable of an optimal level of anxiety that leaves one free to live and soar.

However I will say that this is an adventure that every human being must go through. To learn to be anxious in order that he may not perish either by never having been in anxiety or by succumbing in anxiety. Whoever has learned to be anxious in the right way has learned the ultimate. (Kierkegaard, 1844/1980: 155)

18 Despondency or depression

If we refuse anxiety we may fall into the other trap in ourselves which is that of despondency or depression. This often happens to people who have found anxiety or dread too overwhelming and who have withdrawn from the risks of life altogether. Despondency is often referred to as depression in psychological circles. In phenomenological terms it is a very personal state of mind: a feeling of deflation, a sense that there is a lack of something, outside or inside oneself, and usually in both at once. It is the low point of the emotional cycle (van Deurzen, 1998a, 1988/2002) and comes from giving up and letting go of one's aspirations and hopes. It leads to the feeling that everything will press one further down and lead to further deprivation. Despondency is a very insidious way of being and usually responds well to taking a renewed interest in one's own well being and to paying attention to what it is still possible to be. Yet, we need to take heed of the depression that can come from internal factors such as malnutrition or genetic predisposition, as well as from our life experiences, such as bereavement and losses of various kinds. The time it takes to overcome despondency varies enormously from person to person and according to the significance of what has been lost. It also depends on the resources we still have available to us and on the help we can get in finding meaningful explanations for what has happened to us. Language and understanding are subtle instruments that are crucial in judiciously gaining a new perspective on our decompressed, deflated existence. They help us get a new perspective.

A lucid view of the darkest situation is already, in itself, an act of optimism. Indeed, it implies that this situation is thinkable; that is to say, we have not lost our way in it as though in a dark forest, and we can on the contrary detach ourselves from it, at least in mind, and keep it under observation; we can therefore go beyond it and resolve what to do against it, even if our decisions are desperate. (Sartre, 1965: 289)

Spiritual dimension

Ultimately all of the problems discussed are grafted onto a deeper structure: that of the worldviews we have. Our interpretations of the misery we endure or the happiness we are after are modulated importantly by the way in which we conceive of them. Human beings create meanings and values that provide a sense of coherence in their lives. The spiritual dimension is therefore about our relationship to the ideas we form and our clarity of our view of life is what makes all the difference between a life merely suffered or a life in which we act with determination and purpose.

19 Disorientation

Whilst our beliefs and values normally provide us with a clear sense of direction, we can easily lose track of these. Disorientation is the state of having lost our sense of direction so that we feel in limbo or simply confused. If no purpose to life can be found and no sense of destiny is felt then it is difficult to resolve to do anything at all. Heidegger refers to this state of being as one of dispersion when we let ourselves be taken over by the world. We lose our connection to our own intentions and have no sense of authorship. We stop knowing where we are, who we are and what we want. We have to collect and recollect ourselves out of this dispersion to become capable of defining ourselves and recovering the knowledge of what we want to become.

> *If Dasein is to be able to get brought back from this lostness of failing to hear itself, and if this is to be done through itself, then it must first be able to find itself. (Heidegger, 1927/1962: 271)*
>
> *So if it wants to come to itself it must first pull itself together from the dispersion and disconnectedness of the very things that have 'come to pass'. (ibid.: 389–390)*

When Gail came to therapy she was quite lost: her mind was preoccupied with so many problems that she had lost track of the road ahead. She had raised four children and had struggled to look after two aging and confused parents as well. When her husband left her shortly after her parents' death she felt she was losing it altogether. She had no idea of where she wanted to go in her life. Her disorientation came from having no one left to help any longer and not knowing how to help herself. Gail's search for a new purpose turned into a search for an old purpose, which had been forgotten under a heap of chores and responsibilities, well conducted and to be proud of. She rediscovered goals she had not thought of for ages and relished the initially hesitant idea that her new life could be a liberation and an opening towards adventure rather than a duty and a chore for others. Her new sense of destiny soon gave her direction like never before.

20 Decadence

What stops many of us from finding our destination is that we are out of touch with what is worthwhile in life. In a society where so many old holy cows have died and where the sexual and gender revolutions have changed morality, we are at a loss to define our own principles. We easily slide into decadence. The technological revolution affords us such comforts from our armchairs that we slip into consumerist luxuriating and lose track of what matters at the end of the day. And often we feel we need it, for life is a mad rush and we need some distraction to get out of our rut. But imperceptibly we go down the slippery slope.

All around us a malaise is spreading, as values and meaning get sucked into a black hole. We experience life as absurd and the world as corrupt. Society is dissolving. Scepticism rules. Some of us cannot tolerate this nihilism and pervasive sense of dissolution. Many people who turn to psychotherapy feel there is nothing of any significance in the world and that their actions will not make any difference whatsoever. If anything is allowed or possible, nothing leads to satisfaction or a real experience of meaningful achievement anymore. Existential desolation and decadence are rife. The search for happiness is sometimes an impulse to look for something better and so it may be the start of a new departure, but it may still be the wrong quest.

Kevin came to therapy because he had lost his taste for life. He had been a member of a rock-band and had travelled worldwide with his four friends and a back-up team, living a frenzied life, travelling from town to town, hotel to hotel, in a constant daze of alcohol and drugs and getting up to all sorts of things he wished he had not done. He still supposed it had been worth doing, but felt it had eroded his self-respect and his ability to find meaning in an ordinary, sober, nine-to-five kind of life. The contract had run out and several of his mates had quit and there had been little alternative but to find something else to do, since there was no one who wanted to extend his recording contract anymore. Kevin had had some trouble kicking the cocaine habit, but the worst thing was to quit smoking and drinking. He just did not have the motivation for it. It was an uphill struggle to keep questioning his nihilism, but therapy consisted of some very hard discussions and gradually Kevin did get a new picture of what might be possible or desirable for him. We talked a lot about hedonism and the secret of a well-lived life and such discussions gave Kevin a feeling of hope that something else might be possible. Eventually he took the initiative of dropping the habits that kept him chained to his hide-away life. He decided that he did not want to end his life with a liver complaint and smelling like an ashtray. He took up a creative career as a picture framer and started carving out a new life for himself. The struggle to establish the meaning that made it worth his while doing so was as hard as climbing up a very large mountain. He kept slipping back and needing a helping hand. He wanted no empathy or pity, for that would have dented his self-esteem. He had had enough self-indulgence to last a life time, he said.

21 Delusion

Liberating yourself from decadence is easier than liberating yourself from delusions. If you have flipped into beliefs that are ungrounded it is difficult to find a sure foothold again. It is only when life becomes impossible that people find refuge in a world of their own. Why should we reality test when reality has got out of focus and holds no promise for us? But now we become the target for wishful (or nightmarish) thinking and we may get lost in the utopian or cataclysmic fantasies that are not recognizable to others. Delusion is a form of extreme self-deception coupled with a lack of reality. But we should not be so quick to dismiss it as mental illness. Many forms of dogmatism are a form of shared delusion. Some people make a fine art of living a deluded life and somehow convincing others of the realism of their delusions. The question is whether we are still capable of doubt and rethinking or whether we are once and for all committed to our chimeras.

22 Doubt

Doubt indeed is a great redeemer. As Descartes suggested, doubt is the foundation of all knowledge. Doubt is the best place to start thinking again instead of assuming we already know. There can be no real understanding or wisdom without doubt. Yet, doubt is a most uncomfortable experience. Losing what we once took for granted and having to think anew about all that seemed steady is no easy option. It leaves us homeless and lost.

> *In anxiety one feels 'uncanny'. Here the peculiar indefiniteness of that which Dasein finds itself alongside in anxiety, comes proximally to expression: the 'nothing and nowhere'. But here 'uncanniness' also means 'not-being-at-home'. (Heidegger, 1927/1962: 188)*

Heidegger's term for this was *Unheimlichkeit*: literally not being at home. It means to be ill at ease, uneasy, unsettled and not cosily at home, but in doubt. Heidegger actually believed that this experience of being uneasy and in doubt was fundamental and necessary for us to be human.

> *From an existential-ontological point of view, the 'not-at-home' must be conceived as the more primordial phenomenon. (Heidegger, 1927/1962: 189)*

Therefore doubt should never be too quickly overcome and can be a precious background to a continuous process of searching for the well-lived life.

23 Debt

Doubt, if experienced with awareness, can become articulated into a sense that one is in debt to life. This sense of being indebted to life is the experience of existential guilt: the sensation of having fallen short in some way, or indeed of having wronged someone, or oneself by not doing what one is capable of doing. Decadence, which is a kind of self-indulgence, can lead to the experience of existential guilt after doubt has set in. As soon as people become sensitive to their sense of debt a new departure on the road to life becomes possible. Heidegger took the view that human beings are fundamentally in debt to life and that to live well we first have to become aware of this.

> This implies, however, that Being-guilty does not first result from an indebtedness [Verschuldung], but that, on the contrary, indebtedness becomes possible only 'on the basis' of a primordial Being-guilty. (Heidegger, 1927/1962: 284)

We never live up to our potential, for life always holds out more hope and possibility than we can realize. If we are all guilty or rather lacking and guilt is an indication of our capacity then guilt is a good thing, not something to be avoided.

24 Despair

With so many things to go wrong and so many responsibilities, it is no wonder that we often feel overwhelmed and fall into a deep state of despair. If we lose sight of our own capability and the opportunities that life affords us, we may drift into a spiritual alienation or emptiness that leaves us sore and unsure. There are all kinds of reasons for this and when disasters happen in our lives we can be excused for failing to remain upbeat or optimistic about the meaning of life. Making sense of our lives is what is necessary at those times, rather than a blind pursuit of pleasure or happiness. As long as we can make sense of our lives and ourselves we can manage again. When the meaning slips away the road to despair is open. The desolation or soullessness that we may experience as a result makes life seem futile and its distractions and pleasures banal and absurd.

Yet this may be a good thing in the long run, for it stops us following the easy path and forces us to think again. Kierkegaard claimed therefore that despair, though a bad thing, wasn't a bad thing if it encouraged us to rediscover ourselves and live a life of truth.

> Is despair an excellence or a defect? Purely dialectically, it is both. (Kierkegaard, 1855/1941: 14)

To be truly human we have to be willing to be open to the contradictions of life and we have to be willing to suffer all these troubles along the way. We can live without these things occasionally, but it is through living whilst facing these things that life becomes true and good.

> Noone is born devoid of spirit, and no matter how many go to their death with this spiritlessness as the one and only outcome of their lives, it is not the fault of life. (Kierkegaard, 1855/1941: 102)

PHYSICAL	SOCIAL	PERSONAL	SPIRITUAL
deficit	difference	dilemma	disorientation
disease	discord	deception (self)	decadence
desire	dominance	disappointment	delusion
dependence	dishonesty	distress	doubt
disembodiment	disengagement	dread	debt
death	destruction	despondency	despair

Figure 4.2 Everyday difficulties

Conclusion

Figure 4.2 summarizes the points that have been discussed in this chapter. They are not an exhaustive list of all the difficulties of living, but merely a sketch of some of these. Is it credible in the face of such hardship and constant challenge to merely hope for happiness? Or do we have to find better ways to live, allowing us to be equal to the challenges so that we can stop fearing them? Mastery over our own fate is not to be found in a place of ease, but in a consistent attitude of understanding and learning, according to our own lights, experience and talents.

Chapter 5

Life Crisis: Triumph over Trauma

*I described my spiritual condition to myself in this way:
my life is some kind of stupid and practical joke
that someone is playing on me.*

(Tolstoy, Confessions: 2)

If the ordinary everyday troubles weren't enough to stop us being happy, just to make sure we do not get complacent, we occasionally get confronted with disaster. Sudden crises upset the balance of the lives we so carefully protect and shelter from fate. While we can learn to deal with the repeated trivial challenges that are an inexorable part of our daily existence we don't get to practise weathering these cataclysmic storms. They break out unexpectedly and threaten to mow us down all together. We can never be fully prepared for the occasional acute calamity. These require an entirely different mentality, especially when they strike at the heart of our existence. Heading off and overcoming crisis is not an easy part of human life and the mark of accomplishment is whether we manage to absorb, digest and transcend our catastrophes successfully, distilling some learning from them in the process.

Transitions and transformations are an intrinsic part of normal human evolution and without them life stagnates. But not all transitions are smooth and those that hit us hardest are the ones we did not choose and that come to us uninvited as upheavals and disruptions of the very structure of our lives. While such crises eventually may lead to catharsis and new beginnings, initially they often lead to confusion and chaos and we rarely welcome them with open arms. They drain all contentment from our veins and leave us feeling as if there will never be a moment of peace or contentment again. Nevertheless our success and progress in living are commensurate with the extent of our flexibility in crisis rather than with the extent to which we have managed to remain exempt from adversity and challenge. Happiness is not the measure of our existence at those times: resilience is.

Some crises are so profound however that they shake us out of our security and make us experience life as disastrous. Some catastrophes are so cutting that they leave us in acute pain and lead to experiences of trauma that take us years or even decades to abate and absorb. The short sharp shocks of existence have a way of flattening us initially, but eventually they spur us on to greater heights. Crisis and catharsis are often closely connected to each other and, though unwelcome, sudden blows wake us up from our slumbers, rudely reminding us of realities we might not otherwise want to think about.

About d-, c- and e-words

As we have seen in the previous chapter our dealings with ordinary daily difficulties are frequently expressed in d-words. We will now see that acute states and the important acts they require of us are remarkably often referred to by c-words: change, crisis, conflict, confusion, challenge, catastrophe, catharsis, chaos, courage, confidence, communication, connection, crystallization. We will also encounter experiences of emergence and renewal, which are often introduced by e-words. This is obviously due to the Latin and Greek roots of our language, reminding us that 'de-', which always indicates the removal of something, stands for severance and loss, whereas 'co' or 'con' means bringing together or closing in, whereas 'cat' from the Greek stands for what goes down into and through something. Similarly anything that starts with 'e' refers to something that goes out and escapes or soars. Language has its own existential categories and paying attention to this can help us to orientate ourselves within the field of human existence.

Crisis experiences then are stressful or traumatic moments when we are cut off from what is habitual and safe. They are unstable moments of change when any outcome may be possible. As such they are a test to our stamina and endurance. They are critical times that are hard to bear and none of us elect to have them in preference over quiet times of peace and continuity. Yet we often learn more in moments of disaster and catastrophe than at other times in our lives. The process of our transformation and learning coincides with experiences of loss, anxiety, sorrow and confusion and we have to learn to transmute these into something good. All great lives are riddled with crises and new beginnings. We cannot choose to live smoothly all the time and a life entirely without pain and adversity is not an option. The difference between a life lived well and a life lived in resentment and regret is the extent to which we bounce back and face our defeats with lucidity and courage. Sometimes though, when life is particularly hard, it is best to give in for a while and have the graciousness to let go or even give up momentarily. Hitting rock bottom can be the best way forward, since in the depth of ourselves we will find a new and more solid foundation on which to begin building a worthwhile and meaningful future. It can be a relief to let go of the pretence that we are in control all the time and some respite from the effort of seeming happy can feel like liberation. It is ultimately only in plumbing the depths of life and of ourselves that we discover the roots of reality. But that does not mean we should let ourselves slump into disaster and offer ourselves for martyrdom or victimhood. It is a case of knowing how to be light on our feet in defeat and despair and understand when and how to emerge and surface again. And this is of course where therapy comes on the scene. So how can therapists work with moments of crisis and help clients reshape their lives in the crucible of disaster? Is the quest for happiness a good guide during those times?

Crisis as a new beginning

There are times in a person's life when everything is turned upside down and nothing stays standing. Something happens, either internally or externally, though usually both, to upset the status quo and disturb the previous balance of their everyday existence. These are critical times when everything is altered and looks different. Everything is up for grabs. The Chinese diagram of crisis, which is often said to be composed of two symbols, meaning danger and opportunity, is actually composed of two symbols meaning danger and crucial point (*wei ji*). This is only turned into an opportunity if the situation takes a turn for the better (*zhuan ji*). In the state of turmoil generated by the cataclysm that has struck us, at first confusion reigns because much of what we took for granted is unravelled and undone. In the middle of that disruption and commotion we have to make new beginnings, even though we feel on shaky ground. Crisis is usually a time when loss and gain occur alongside each other, but the emphasis is initially mostly on the mayhem and the pain and the disturbance. What seemed previously unassailable and certain is now suddenly in the balance. What was solid is dissolved and put in question by oneself, by others and seemingly by fate itself. Stability and equilibrium have been shaken and are about to be altered for ever. From order chaos will ensue and it is up to us to try and fight this, attempting to re-establish the previous status quo to the best of our abilities or to relinquish the old order and pass into an interim state before creating the new. Going for the new means to flirt with danger and possibly not succeed, for there is always a chance that we shall fail to cross over into the safe territory on the other side. Holding on to the old may mean that we do not adjust and will suffer more from the crisis than is necessary, as the defunct habits and values will not be revived and will slowly crumble and desert us however hard we try to hang on. It is quite possibly the hesitation between the two states that plunges people into disaster.

Therefore the single most important asset in a crisis is that of having the courage to face the situation and to establish what our best options are to get through it all. If we can be determined and confident in negotiating our transitions we will gain at least as much as we lose and we may find that our crisis turns out to be the beginning of a breakthrough into a whole new and better phase of life.

How does crisis come about?

One fine day we may be struck by lightning. Out of the blue unexpected developments suddenly change everything we take for granted. Frequently we do not think we are responsible for this state of affairs. We have not called for it in any way, but we cannot dodge it and have to take it on board and find a way to accommodate all the implications. At times like these it may seem as if the universe is cruel or, worse, indifferent to our plight. We may feel that life is nothing but a sick cosmic joke at our expense.

People come to therapy in these acute states of sudden shock, still reel-ing from the blow. The last thing on their mind is that of creative transfor-mation. They just want the pain to stop. There might have been a sudden bereavement, or an illness or an accident in their lives. It may be the loss of a job or a spouse, or a parent, or a child, or a lover that has shaken their universe. It may also be that they have been exposed to a natural disaster or a catastrophic event brought about through human intervention as happens in wars or revolutions or assaults or accidents. Crisis is a time when we are exposed to extraordinary amounts of stress and distress and no matter what the cause of the crisis is we need to acknowledge the pressure on us and change our habits to accommodate it. This kind of flexibility in living is an important asset for minor life events as well as for the big crises and whilst learnt in times of special hardship they can be applied to daily life as well. When Holmes and Rahe (1967) did their work on stressful life events they included many ordinary or smaller occurrences. They showed how these cluster together when experienced in close proximity to each other, accu-mulating into a higher stress quotient, potentially leading to disastrous consequences and illness in the person experiencing them. Strangely some of these may be fairly ordinary situations or even apparently happy events such as a move or a marriage or a pregnancy, showing up the relative value of happiness once again. Sometimes crisis is brought about by the very same event that was longed and yearned for and that was supposed to be entirely joyful.

Holmes and Rahe listed the number of life change units each event carried and found that a score of 300 points or more would lead to an 80 per cent risk of physical or emotional illness. A score between 200 and 300 was shown to lead to a 50 per cent risk. Figure 5.1, taken from the Holmes and Rahe website, indicates the values they accorded to each life event (Holmes and Rahe, 1967).

Read each of the events listed below, and check the box next to any event which has occurred in your life in the last two years. There are no right or wrong answers. The aim is just to identify which of these events you have experienced lately.

Life Events	Life Crisis Units		Life Events	Life Crisis Units	
Death of spouse	100	❏	Son or daughter leaving home	29	❏
Divorce	73	❏	Trouble with in-laws	29	❏
Marital separation	65	❏	Outstanding personal achievement	28	❏
Jail term	63	❏	Wife begins or stops work	26	❏
Death of close family member	63	❏	Begin or end school	26	❏
Personal injury or illness	53	❏	Change in living conditions	25	❏
Marriage	50	❏	Revision in personal habits	24	❏
Fired at work	47	❏	Trouble with boss	23	❏
Marital reconciliation	45	❏	Change in work hours or conditions	20	❏
Retirement	45	❏	Change in residence	20	❏
Change in health of a family member	44	❏	Change in schools	20	❏
Pregnancy	40	❏	Change in recreation	19	❏
Sex difficulties	39	❏	Change in church activities	19	❏
Gain of new family member	39	❏	Change in social activities	18	❏
Business readjustment	39	❏	Mortgage or loan less than $30,000	17	❏
Change in financial state	38	❏	Change in sleeping habits	16	❏
Death of close friend	37	❏	Change in number of family get-togethers	15	❏
Change to different line of work	36	❏	Change in eating habits	15	❏
Change in number of arguments with spouse	35	❏	Vacation	13	❏
Mortgage over $100,000	31	❏	Christmas alone	12	❏
Foreclosure of mortgage or loan	30	❏	Minor violations of the law	11	❏
Change in responsibilities at work	29	❏			
Reset			**Your score is:**		
Source: Holmes and Rahe (1967).					

Figure 5.1   The Holmes-Rahe Scale

Of course the assignment of values and points depends on the individual context, for each of these events will have a different impact on us according to the context and particular meaning that is attached to each experience. A scale like this can only give a general indication of how events will affect the average person and in practice this will vary with each specific occasion. It also depends on the level of resilience in an individual as to how hard they will be hit and how well they will respond. We know only too well from psychotherapeutic practice that stressful events are borne very differently by different people. The table is also surprising in its omission of the sort of items that show up as predictors of suicide, such as violent break-ups, court appearances, self-harm, alcoholism or drug abuse and similar long-term life situations. On the other hand we must not forget that sometimes stress is a stimulant as Hans Selye's work has shown (Selye, 1974/1991, 1978). Indeed a certain amount of stress is essential for good functioning. Life without stress or troubles is like a system without energy, a motor without fuel, a current without differential. Tension is good for us when handled in the right way. Overprotection is not a good recipe for a well lived life.

Nevertheless the question of how much crisis anyone can take is an important one. A fairly recent study by Spurrell and MacFarlane (1992), based on work done in relation to communities that have been hit by disasters, investigated the ways in which people actually cope with stressful events. It found that cognitive intrusion was the most important factor standing in the way of a person's ability to manage. In other words it is the processing of the experience and the impact of the disaster that are of prime importance. If a person can manage to assimilate the crisis and make it meaningful in some way then it can be emotionally integrated and thus overcome. If it is not dealt with in this manner it will remain a cognitive intrusion in the person's life subsequently and potentially for a long time to come. This is a reminder of the Zeigarnick effect (Zeigarnick, 1967) which was quoted by Lewin (1999) as indicative of the fact that we remember unfinished tasks much better than finished tasks. This is nature's way of reminding us to complete our existential chores and to learn from the traumatic experiences in our lives rather than suppress them or try to forget them. It is not just a matter of habituation or coping. It is a matter of processing problems, which means understanding and absorbing them: weaving them into a meaningful fabric of life. It does not mean to turn them over in our minds as a problem, to worry about them vacantly or obsessively, or to create a state of victimhood and resentment in ourselves. It is possible to do more harm than good by prodding and probing the person in crisis, tipping them into a state of desperate unhappiness and passivity.

Affirming existential crisis

The crisis has to be mined and exploited and made useful if it is not to continue to be experienced as an occasion for terror, self pity or helplessness. We have already seen the role existential anxiety can play in finding the energy to tackle the new challenge. It is not a rare occurrence that people who are struck down by fate eventually begin to wonder whether they themselves brought the crisis about in some subtle way because they needed a change so badly. But it is usually only with hindsight that people can acknowledge that it helped them to recover new energy and even motivation and excitement in living. There may of course be guilt attached to the realization that one has prompted or been part of a series of events that have escalated and led to catastrophic consequences or that others did not come out as well as one did personally. But underneath the guilt may also lurk a certain dose of satisfaction, relief or even pride in having effected an ultimate change for the better or having been through a cataclysm. Quite often there is secret relief at one's release from a previous pattern that had become like a prison.

Terry was a client who had been married to Helen, a woman ten years older than himself, for just over a decade. In spite of considering his marriage to be blissful and regardless of the fact that he and his wife often declared themselves very happy together, he had suddenly found himself, unthinkingly, courting and then making love to a young secretary in his office. She was eligible, appealing and flirtatious. Never having thought of himself as attractive, he had been stunned that she was at all interested in him. An apparently irrational thought had obsessed him: 'I must not miss this opportunity which may never come along again. No matter what will happen I must not count the cost. This is my last chance of real excitement and true enjoyment.' In the circumstances it did not take long for him to give in to the girl's advances. He did not just have his one night stand but went home to his wife enthusiastically flaunting his success with the other woman, crediting his new attractiveness to their marital happiness and claiming it to be a testimony to his love for his wife. Unsurprisingly his wife, Helen, experienced this as the ultimate offence and provocation and she felt deeply hurt and let down. She was so upset that she shouted at him to leave the house straight away and never darken her door again. Terry did not argue with her, but obeyed her command willingly. He was totally bewildered and promptly left his home with no more than a suitcase and chequebook. In confusion and with a deep sense of doom and gloom he went on a solitary trip to Spain where he had always longed to go with his wife Helen. He stayed there for several months, hiding away in a hotel, using up the meagre savings in his personal bank account on hotel bills and alcoholic drinks. He was well aware that he was not enjoying his desperate escapade and that he had probably got himself fired from his job as well as from his marriage by now. Eventually the hotel manager, seeing him become increasingly bedraggled, advised him to go to hospital. They kept him overnight and diagnosed symptoms of malnutrition and depression and advised him to return to England to consult his doctor, which he promptly did. He was then referred for counselling.

When he started in counselling he was still dazed and he had mixed feelings about waking up from his self-induced crisis. He was reluctant to come out of the stupor he now lived in, for he had found some refuge and safety in the no-man's-land of alcohol and loneliness. He had taken up residence in a town 100 miles away from his marital home and had not been in touch with his wife at all. He was terrified of facing the music, he said. He was working in a badly paid job, at a level far below his professional status, and he did not think he deserved any better. He claimed that this would be the score from now on. It seemed that he got a perverse satisfaction in claiming this humble station in life. He admitted this freely and could recognize that it had been a relief to pull out all the stops from what had been a tedious and predictable, though supposedly happy, life. At least he had proven to himself he could survive with very little, no matter what. He liked the idea that this was his modest form of heroism and rebellion, even though it had nearly destroyed him.

The long road towards recovery started with him putting events into this kind of perspective and acknowledging and articulating why he had done what he had done. It was only by taking responsibility for his actions, rather than seeing them as just having happened to him, that he began to get a grip again. He got a real hold of life when he discovered that his provocation and affront of his wife had been half intended, in all its naivety and all its cruelty. It was the only way he had found to establish his independence of a wife who had organized his every moment and his every thought. He had shown her what he was capable of at last. Of course having an affair was not enough; in fact it was almost immaterial. The important act had been to flaunt it at his wife, in order to differentiate himself from her and call her attention to his new found confidence and freedom, which he knew full well she would have trouble allowing and tolerating. He could even see that he had had the desired effect in spades, for he had indeed succeeded in breaking the tight bonds between them. He had finally escaped from the narrow circle of homely happiness that had confounded him for so long.

The tragedy was that he had done this without awareness or explanations and that he had broken both their hearts in the process. This however had not been his intention, since he had genuinely assumed that their relationship could bear this affront. He had never really seen his wife as a person, but only as an extension of himself, and vice versa. His despair and guilt were huge and his self punishing tendency was fierce, but nevertheless he began to understand that he had also felt a great relief at escaping from the contented marriage. The debacle had given him freedom and space and time to think, no matter how destructively. Once he could accept that the crisis had been necessary, he could begin to find his way through it. It took quite a while before he felt prepared to get in touch with his wife and strong enough to work things out with her. He would, he thought, have been unable to do so if he had not broken away like this, disrupting the ordered life that once was his. In the long run his crisis and turmoil in finding himself were the best thing he ever did, he said. Sadly he did not succeed in convincing his wife of this idea when he finally did get in touch with her for he found her living with somebody else, even younger than him, quite under her influence. She was unwilling or unable to talk things through with him and in the end this confirmed for him that he had done right by pulling out when he did. He felt sorry for her new partner.

Crisis as a test of one's capacity to cope

There are many people who test themselves in this kind of manner until, playing with fire, they themselves, directly or indirectly, set off the blaze that destroys some part of their life. It is usually hard to trace the true origin of crises. Usually they happen at the crossroads of many intersecting points of pressure. If we could trace this network of catastrophic influences and events we could make sense of them properly without attributing blame. It is difficult to know whether or not to insist that an individual takes responsibility for the actions that have hurt them and other people, since their part in events is usually limited. But there are certainly disasters that have their roots in hidden actions or past neglects and that are never shown up as such. There are many skeletons in people's cupboards and many inner volcanoes waiting to explode. Once one crisis has been set off, others will often follow. This may connect to the superstitious belief that bad luck comes in threes. It is true that life sometimes falls apart like a house of cards or collapses like a row of dominos: everything is interlinked and when one element in the structure topples over the rest tends to follow soon after. One can liken this to the ripples created by the stone thrown in the water, spreading wider and wider and creating new circles of perturbance around them all the time. Because of this a crisis usually touches more than one person at once and each individual reaction may touch off further crises or ripples in its wake. This will continue until the force of action and reaction has been bent or contained in some way or until the energy behind it has fizzled out and the knock-on effect slows down.

I have observed this kind of sequential pattern both in my own life and in the lives of my clients and have learnt to distinguish between the events that are preventable and those that have to run their course. Depending on the magnitude of the crisis, the after effects can last for months or years, in some cases even decades or generations. Such a period of instability goes on until a new equilibrium has been established, but of course some of the people involved in the crisis may have an investment in keeping the situation unbalanced.

To bring about a crisis one has to transgress the established order in some way and this can happen violently or more gently with a number of smaller unbalancing acts. To stick through the crisis with a cool head and calm in the face of feelings that rock us requires temerity and determination, courage and self-confidence. These have to be reiterated daily since they will get sapped constantly. Of course there are no short cuts in this process: the sooner we learn to acknowledge and understand what is going on and how we can ride the storm the better the outcome.

On the whole going through crisis is a lonely experience since being in crisis is to be out of synch with the ordinary and cut off from those around you. In crisis you are outside the established order and chaos reigns for a while. Of course not all crises are unwelcome and whether they are welcome or not, initially crises can best be weathered by going with the flow and letting ourselves float downstream for a while. Not everyone will want to get out of the storm by tying themselves to the mast, nor by steering back into quiet waters at the earliest opportunity. Some people learn to welcome crisis as a sign of new opportunities. Some people even learn to enjoy them and see them as occasions to test their character and become more flexible, tougher and stronger. Some people never emerge in one piece and feel trampled and traumatized ever after. To get out of crisis we need to find a safe harbour to shelter in until the worst of the upheaval dies down. Then we need to find new ground on which to prepare to start building again. We need to learn from the past and establish new rules, routines and regulations and stick to them consistently.

The different levels of crisis

Crisis and trauma can affect us at lots of different levels. It is helpful to distinguish between crises that are the consequence of our own actions and crises that are visited upon us by others or by fate. At the same time we can separate out crises and trauma affecting us in a mainly physical way from crises and trauma affecting us in a relational manner. Putting these four dimensions together we arrive at the following diagram (Figure 5.2), which shows numerous potential sources of trauma, distress and life crisis. Some are imposed by nature from outside, some originate in our own actions or those of others. All these things will revolutionize our lives and destroy the safety we had up to the point where catastrophe hit us.

Most of these events speak for themselves and can be lethal. Everyone will understand immediately that the person who survives such incidents will be shocked to the core. The way in which specific events touch each of us varies enormously though and in order to help another person get safely through such experiences it helps to think in a structured way about crisis and its effect on a person's life. Most crises affect us in a variety of ways.

Physical crisis and physical implications of crisis

Physical crises are those that affect our bodily safety. They may be brought about by physical illness, either our own or that of another, or they may be

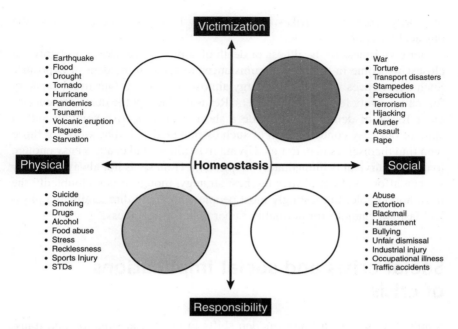

Figure 5.2   Source of trauma

brought about by other physical causes. In Figure 5.2 we see a list of the natural events that can shake us to the core, if not kill us outright, such as floods and droughts and hurricanes and tsunamis. Dealing with those should be primarily about re-establishing physical safety, before any other intervention is called for. The same is true with assaults, wars, accidents and illness. Without physical care and the securing of our safe haven, nothing else will do. Only in the aftermath of such physical events do the emotional aspects come to the fore: the lack of trust in the world, in other people or in nature that has resulted leaves a person exposed and open or frightened and closed. True trauma almost always has a physical component (Bracken, 2002).

Any crisis that involves a physical element is costly and onerous. There are frequently physical implications in other forms of crisis and transition, for every traumatic event has its practical consequences and leads to changes in material circumstances. People may lose their house, an office, or their right to other physical spaces as things break down around them. Stress may bring on physical symptoms or make one accident prone. Crises frequently involve geographical changes and moves of all sorts. Many forms of crisis have implications of financial loss or the diminishment of physical security of one sort or another. The physical comforts we lose when relationships end may have much more of an impact than others fathom. Our sense of self as it is experienced in its physical reality is altered significantly in more ways than we realize ordinarily when crisis strikes. We can easily be unbalanced as we lose the physical basis of our safety.

Our own illness or the illness or death of someone we love is probably the closest we come in ordinary circumstances to such an incident of exposure. Such experiences will sap our energy almost completely. Our usual capacity for taking safety for granted founders. Refusal to accept the death sentence or other forms of denial may provide a short-term protective solution and in spite of our easy condemnation of such ostrich tactics, it may work for those who find themselves in extremis. Giving in to illness and death is easy enough to do, but survival is immediately in question. Honesty is not always a luxury we can afford and not always the best strategy, though it is undoubtedly the most honourable. Interestingly most people who are in dire straits in a physical fashion clamour for normality rather than for happiness.

Social crisis and social implications of crisis

Similarly crises often imply sudden shifts in our social situation and transform our position in the world with others. Social crises like wars or revolutions will affect our position in the world in extreme ways: undermining all previously taken for granted structures that secure us. But any loss of position, job, status or role, even in times of peace, can impact greatly on our sense of who we are. We may find that each of these has knock-on effects. When we lose a partner we are not just lonely but suddenly a single person rather than one half of a couple. When losing a child our status of parent may also be questioned. Our social identity crumbles together with the loss we suffer and weakens our capacity for coping. Loss of role can be equally poignant when linked to a positive outcome, when retiring or when children leave home for instance. All of these situations can be made worse by the fact that they take place in a public context and may lead to social pressures on us to deal with things in a certain manner. Others, who are not themselves going through the same changes and who are smugly ensconced in the safety of familiarity, will berate us or counsel us and often against our will. We get unwelcome warnings of what will happen to us if we were to make the wrong decisions. People admonish us and suddenly feel the right to treat us as if we are morally inferior or feeble. What would they do themselves if they suddenly found themselves in a similar situation? They can think themselves exempt, for they are careful and would not take the risks we have taken, until their life changes and they find that their presumption of superior inner balance has been rash and mistaken.

It is extraordinary how much people pretend that conflicts and difficulties in life can be avoided and are somehow a mark of failure. We have a crying lack of social tradition in supporting each other in the ways in which we can face up and deal with conflict and crisis effectively and robustly. Couples for instance expect their marital lives to be smoother than is reasonable in the best of circumstances and find themselves taken aback when they have to deal with predictable but yet unexpected problems between them, let alone with crises.

When people are exposed to bad behaviour in schools or in offices there is an initial tendency to turn a blind eye to what is happening. We are just not prepared for such things. Bullying thrives in those conditions, as people do not want to be besmirched by the violence involved and will turn away from it, even if it is done in their presence. We look the other way and resent the whistle blower who calls the problem to our attention. And yet, this passive tolerance of bad behaviour is the source of much misfortune and nastiness in the world. Though many have observed this difficulty, there is still a long way to go in remedying it. A saying attributed to Edmund Burke, but which does not actually appear in his writing, sums it up nicely:

> *The only thing necessary for the triumph of evil, is for good men to do nothing.*

It is hard for us to take responsibility for things that do not directly seem to concern us and if we can keep our life peaceful we tend to turn away from the source of unhappiness we see around us. Yet, reality shows that the more we are willing to address the troubles that do not directly concern us but indirectly are part of our universe, the better we make our own world too. We instinctively know that tolerating evil taints us. As Martin Luther King claimed:

> *He who passively accepts evil is as much involved in it as he who helps to perpetrate it. (King, 1963)*

When we do try to take a stand we may of course pay the immediate price of getting hurt. We may even become a victim rather than a bystander or a perpetrator. So why should we take responsibility? Perhaps this throws some light on the problem of happiness as well. The problem is that we want to be offered safety and happiness as a passive and enduring state rather than being prepared to earn it, over and over again. But to keep earning it is the only way to find anything remotely like it.

Personal crisis and personal implications of crisis

The reality is that even if we avoid physical and social crises, we cannot avoid the occasional personal crisis. A personal crisis is generally triggered by experiences of personal failure. It is typically tipped off by the loss of a project that was dear to us, failure at an exam, interview, or test, or by a fiasco of some other sort. We have fallen short in relation to our own expectations or in relation to another person and see ourselves as insufficient in some way. We have been told off or are questioned about the very essence of our character or our being. We suddenly seem to be faulty or defective. Any of this can trigger a questioning of our identity. Of course any of this can also be caused by loss of any kind, after the break-up of a relationship, death, or disaster in any context. The emotions triggered are strong. Guilt, shame, humiliation, resentment, jealousy, desire, fear, regret are all customary companions to our personal defeats. We are numbed or flummoxed and quite overwhelmed. The only way out of our predicament is to find a new way to tackle the situation and to recover a sense of our own capacity for facing the worst and to do well out of it. If we do this we may carry forward some credit to our name, a sense of our strength, of our courage and our stamina. If we are resilient we can think of ourselves as survivors and this may be a welcome and unexpected gain that will stand us in good stead for the rest of our lives.

Spiritual crisis and spiritual dimensions of crisis

But personal crisis, or indeed crisis of any sort, can be even more far reaching and profound when it touches the very essence of our being and is experienced as a dark night of the soul. Such a spiritual crisis may confront us with a sudden loss of faith in everything we used to believe in. Spiritual crisis shakes us to our foundation and questions the meaning of life. Someone in the midst of a spiritual crisis will typically not doubt the world, or others or themselves, but the very possibility of life making sense.

People often come to counselling or therapy in the midst of a spiritual crisis, when their trust in life itself is bruised or shaken. The need to find meaning again is excruciating and yet they are deeply suspicious of the easy solutions or predictable soothing that a novice counsellor may threaten to offer. They need to tough it out and test their own stamina and they also need to check out the truth and limits of life's conditions for themselves. Such crises season a person and they should not be dealt with lightly but taken deeply seriously. Such individual moments of soul searching are too precious to waste and they are what lead us to a deeper and more complete understanding of the human condition. To be in spiritual crisis is to stand out of oneself. It is literally to come to that place that Heidegger called ec-stasy: where nothing can be taken for granted and we have to stand outside of ourselves instead of hiding on the inside. Such a standing out affects the past, present and future. There is no place to hide. The only stance that will do is to stand up and be counted. In

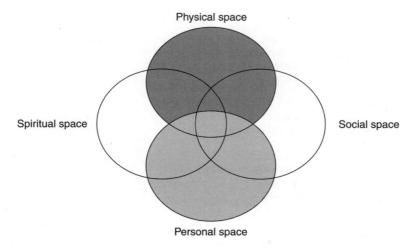

Figure 5.3   Existential space

this process we will learn to manage our existential space better and make more room for ourselves and those things that truly matter.

Existential space and crisis

While we feel a sense of self in all the different spaces of our lives it is where they overlap and come together that we recognize ourselves as centred human beings with most intensity and strength. Before we achieve this we need to go through many stages and it is often in our crises that we are forced to rediscover different aspects of ourselves. As we face the desert of aloneness and the doubts that leave us wondering whether our lives are worth it, we intensify our grip on life and renew our commitment to making it somehow, whatever the price. We may often feel as if we are going to break when all we have to do is learn to bend. The crisis may start with a certain amount of excitement as the newness of the situation appeals with its promise of revival. We come to experiment with this and express new longings and yearning, until the exhilaration of the situation leads us into an exposure which requires a new level of explanation of ourselves. When we come to the focal point where the ecdysis occurs, much energy is required to deal with the sheer quantity of the challenge that faces us. This is where we uproot ourselves from the comforts of the past situation once and for all and find ourselves excluded from what we once knew and took for granted as our home. In this exiled position we emerge out of ourselves and give ourselves over to new explorations, forced upon us at first but gradually also wanted and enjoyed more and more. Now we can start expanding again, in the freedom of our new lives. And finally our

• Growing interest in something new	Excitement
• Trying out a new way to be	Experimentation
• Acknowledgement of situation	Expression
• Developing one's commitment to this	Exhilaration
• Public declaration (Discovery)	Exposure
• Challenge	Explanation
• Crisis	Ecdysis
• Chaos: living several lives	Exhaustion
• Giving up past beliefs and aspirations	Extraction
• Letting go	Extinction
• Realizing there is no way back	Exclusion
• Integrating pain and understanding past	Emergence
• Creating new opportunities	Exploration
• Making a new commitment	Extension
• Living life anew	Expansion
• Success	Ecstasy

Figure 5.4 Cycle of crisis

efforts are crowned with success and ecstasy, so much longed for, now arrived, though it will have taken a large toll to arrive at and will continue to require much persistance (Tantam and van Deurzen, 2001).

This success and ecstasy, so hard earned, will not of course last long. Going for broke or going for crisis after crisis may seem attractive to some who are desperate or bored but is no guarantee of happiness. Crisis management saps our energy. People who are in a position of constant fire-fighting will burn out fast. The process of dealing with crisis requires us to be resolute and this takes energy and commitment. If we remain tense in this process we may wear out and it is important to learn the art of being receptive and yielding when appropriate. Sometimes we need to be resigned to our lot and accept what is coming to us, not because we necessarily deserve it but because it is inevitable and part of the way things are. Going with the flow as much as possible and trusting the laws of life help us to get it right when we can no longer decide exactly what it is we can do by ourselves.

It can also help to have a model of transformation and to remember that there are seasons in our lives. Images of salamanders standing the heat of the fire or phoenixes rising from their ashes have inspired many. Others have found more succour in thinking of themselves as caterpillars or larvae ready to turn into butterflies. In essence these are images of crossovers between one state and another, where the new state is worth the hardship that has to be endured. They provide people with a model of human development and transformation that they can relate to when they are in need. They are all images of existential re-birth.

Similarly the image of a snake shedding a skin is often quoted by those who are itching to provoke a crisis that will lead to liberation. People who do so will often feel like rebels but can end up wondering why they did invite the wrath of fate upon themselves. They defy more than they deny, as Camus said in his book *The Rebel* (Camus, 1954). And it could be said that some crises are brought about to stave off other crises. Ultimately the struggle through crisis is always a struggle for survival and a claim for a new way of life. When the rebel claims the right to life he or she has to be willing to pay the ultimate price of death.

> *It is only in the anticipation of death that resoluteness, as Dasein's authentic truth, has reached the authentic certainty which belongs to it. (Heidegger, 1927/1962: 350).*

The moment of vision (Augenblick) that Heidegger describes as the point at which we suddenly see past, present and future come together is not unlike kairos, the special moment of crisis where all is known and possible and we see our way through the obstacles ahead of us. In Jaspers' terms crisis is a limit situation, where everything is in question, everything is in flux. Everything is split, everything is in opposites. As Master Eckhart said: "if you want the kernel you must break the shell." Crisis is when our shell is broken and we can show what is inside of us.

How to learn from crisis

But we have to move beyond our crises and learn to live again with normality. As Rollo May (1983) pointed out: decision precedes knowledge and insight and so we have to act until our crisis subsides and then comes the time to understand and know what has happened, after we have settled into a new secure pattern. Sometimes our past decisions and actions may seem questionable, especially if they were taken at a time of upheaval. Time for reflection is crucial, lest we want to repeat the mistakes of the past. As we learn and live we come to life ever more fully. We become more real and tough and yet more smooth in our capacity to deal with the realities of the human world and of life itself. Overcoming the losses and trauma suffered is by no means an easy matter. Grief may linger longer than any of the other consequences of our rites of passage. It is our task to master our grief and take it to heart.

William Worden (2002) reconsidered the tasks that a grieving person has to accomplish before the depth of their experience can be reflected on and made sense of. These four critical tasks they have to accomplish are:

Task 1   To accept the reality of the loss.

Task 2   To work through the pain of grief.

Task 3   To adjust to an environment in which the deceased (or lost object) is missing.

Task 4   To emotionally relocate the deceased (or object) and move on with life.

This is just as true when the crisis is not about the loss of a loved one. Whatever we have lost we have to readjust to a world devoid of that which we valued. Now we have to make ethical decisions and take a new direction. We are at a point in life where we have to envisage a change and let go, but we can also remember our losses in such a way that they point us in the right direction. We can shape a new world to the image of what we have come to think of as good and right. We choose the legacies of the past and cut our losses. In engaging in this process we have to ask ourselves how we wish to solve our moral dilemmas and what kind of world we are creating for ourselves and for others. This means our own actions and decisions and motivations have to be monitored and sometimes questioned.

On the whole people who are in crisis or transition after trauma wish to get out of the state of alarm they find themselves in. They may therefore rush into the wrong solutions: going for what seems easiest or most comforting. But if we want to ensure that our crisis will count and that it will turn out to have been a defining moment, we need to dare hold out for more than settling down as soon as possible. We need to be unafraid to opt for the hard work of progress at this point. This is the only way in which we can ensure that our next crisis will not be a mere repeat of the last one. Faced with repeated crises as is the case for instance in domestic violence, it may be tempting to go for a minimal solution, a brokering of peace in which there is no guarantee of a better future.

But what is needed instead is that we include an element of challenge in the change we are proposing. Those who limp from crisis to crisis may be doing so in search of intensity. If people keep pushing their lives to the edge in a destructive or self-destructive fashion they have not discovered more creative, positive or constructive ways to get the glow and intensity of the life that they crave. It is often hard to understand such behaviour. Living with someone who lives from crisis to crisis is an exhausting and painful experience. It may be experienced as a constant state of torture. Pain resists all meaning. Pain deconstructs the world, focusing attention intensely on the here and now. Pain stops the world. It interrupts the flow of existence and focuses us around the distress of the body or of our self. In torture all of the complexity of our identity, our loyalties and values are broken down. Only the body and its suffering remain. All else is forgotten.

Baumeister understood this well:

> Traumas and victimizations tend to contradict a person's broadest fundamental beliefs about self and world. The world no longer seems a safe, benevolent, or fair place, and the person may question whether he or she is a good enough person to deserve a decent fate. Victims may say that their world has been shattered. The resultant meaning vacuum may take years to repair. (Baumeister, 1991:246)

The irony is that much pain is inflicted by people who seek to have their own pain lessened in some way. Punishment and escalation establish a dreadful cycle of violence in which everyone loses dignity, safety and meaning. Restoration, restitution and release are far better options.

Transcending trauma

Transformation of our trauma in a creative way requires us to go beyond the wrongs done to us and not to oppose or avenge, but to transcend our pain and injustice. This does not mean to forgive and forget, but rather to understand, comprehend what has happened and go beyond it in some way. Such transformative moments are the most potent ones in therapy, when a person gets a real inkling for the first time of the way in which they can make their suffering count and get it to work for them rather than against them. When we are shattered by life we have to make room for these sacred moments where we reach the depth of existence and transform what is wrong into something that is set right, not just for us but for others as well. How this should be done and what the meaning of our crisis and trauma can be is never clear initially. We have to mine the situation for its significance. This is certainly one of the functions of psychotherapy: finding a safe place to face up to the implications of the dangerous and difficult situations we have found ourselves in. We can however become mesmerized by the mimetic immortality we experience at these moments and overly enchanted with our own suffering. Therapists need to make sure things are kept in perspective.

Transcendence of crises and trauma is a large part of psychotherapy. As therapists we deal with the misery most effectively by addressing it squarely rather than by trying to either deny it or remove it altogether from a person's life. Happiness hardly comes into it. Hardship is overcome by the satisfaction of having borne it, rather than by a flight into contentment. Though as we have seen, it is important to re-establish our capacity for both safety and challenge.

How to triumph over trauma?

So what can we conclude about triumph over trauma? There are a number of things that are useful to remember:

- The person who goes through crisis and trauma needs to accept the shattering of their life and let go of the old structures. They need to find a new inner coherence and integrity. This is best done by discovering and affirming why what has happened did indeed happen and why they acted as they acted.
- Making peace with mistakes and finding pride in facing the inevitable moves the trauma towards meaning. It is better to stand by the changes

that have occurred and to find a place of acceptance where there are no regrets.

- As soon as an inner balance has been found we can rebuild a new sense of community with others. We all need to be connected with the social world and in our crisis we have probably disconnected from it. Now we need to link back to the continuity of respect we can receive from our peers, elders and offspring.

- We need to find also, as soon as possible, some sort of public forum in which we can speak about what has happened to us and get validation from others for having handled ourselves the best way possible.

- Loving something or someone and commit one's life to this cause also gives a sense of greater overcoming. Of course this someone or something may have been destroyed in the crisis. In letting ourselves inherit the legacy we have earned we have the beginnings of a new start in life.

- Such love and commitment require effort and work and in such a labour of love we learn to stand the pain whilst drawing energy and motivation from it.

- In this process we learn to recognize that living the hard way without too much hiding and with a willingness for love and labour, tolerating the hardships of life, makes one a better or at least a more realistic and certainly a stronger person. Many a person triumphing over trauma and hardship feels purified and strengthened by their experience, learning to value the scars it leaves and the tightening of the personality it affords.

- Faith in the power of life is another asset in the process of survival. Overcoming trauma generates a new sense of confidence in oneself, others and life, believing that if this could be overcome than anything can.

- There is new room for hope and a feeling that there will be a time for setting the record straight and having one's comeback or one's well deserved break. To trust in the natural ups and downs will eventually turn our fortunes if we are on the right path and do not give in to despair.

- Time changes things and while it does not necessarily heal, it does grind on and provides a long-term slow force of justice.

- Many people who transcend grave problems find an ultimate meaning and purpose that goes well beyond the norm. They discover for themselves that life is preoccupied in both perpetuating itself and in transcending itself. But transcendence often requires loss and we need to be prepared for things sometimes to come to a cruel and sudden end. There may indeed be some truth in Simone de Beauvoir's idea that:

It is not in giving life but in risking life that man is raised above the animal.
(Simone de Beauvoir, 1972)

Overcoming trauma and crisis can be summed up by reprieving the diagram from the previous chapter with specific ideas about the tasks that need to be attended to at each level (see Figure 5.5).

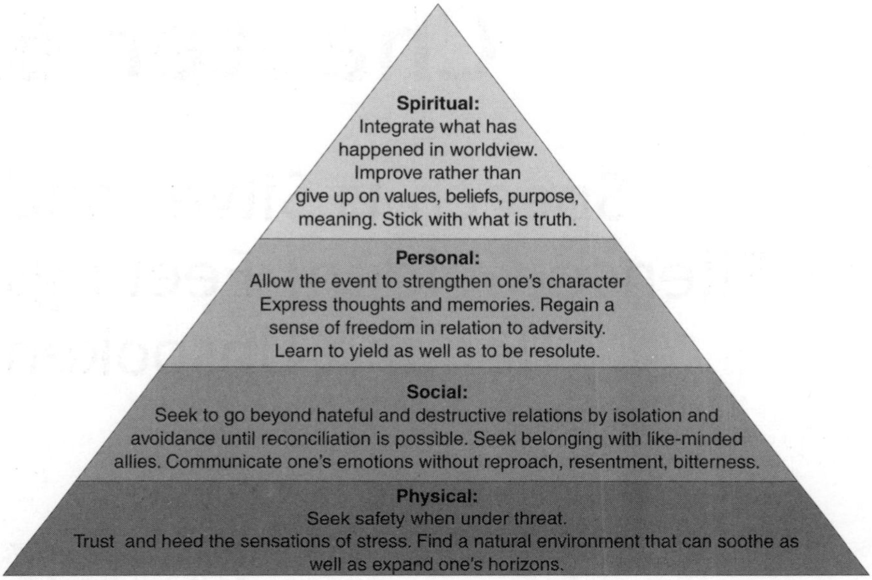

Spiritual:
Integrate what has
happened in worldview.
Improve rather than
give up on values, beliefs, purpose,
meaning. Stick with what is truth.

Personal:
Allow the event to strengthen one's character
Express thoughts and memories. Regain a
sense of freedom in relation to adversity.
Learn to yield as well as to be resolute.

Social:
Seek to go beyond hateful and destructive relations by isolation and
avoidance until reconciliation is possible. Seek belonging with like-minded
allies. Communicate one's emotions without reproach, resentment, bitterness.

Physical:
Seek safety when under threat.
Trust and heed the sensations of stress. Find a natural environment that can soothe as
well as expand one's horizons.

Figure 5.5   Overcoming trauma

In the final analysis, overcoming trauma and crisis is about transformation, transmutation and transcendence. We need to go beyond our troubles and turn them into something worthwhile, becoming a better person in some way. In other words: we have to find a way to put our suffering to good use. Yet, even then we are not out of the woods. We may live a new and better life, but there will be new problems on the horizon and other crises and daily troubles will visit us. No wonder we find life a little trying and tiresome at times and that we tend to turn away from reality and create fanciful fantasies to escape into instead. So, how do we prevent a naïve harking back to a quest for happiness? We now need to consider the role of therapy in dealing with the whole range of such feelings.

Chapter 6

Speech is Silver and Silence Golden: Feelings Remain Unspoken

*Dig within. There lies the well-spring of good:
ever dig, and it will ever flow*

Marcus Aurelius, Meditations: 59

There is so much to do if we are to live a good and full life. It would be that much easier if all we had to do was to pursue a single minded quest for happiness. We would not need to worry about the complexities of therapy if problems and crises could be resolved purely by aiming for positives. Since we know that therapy has to do a lot more than simply making people feel happy, we need to consider what it is realistic to expect of therapists at all. If therapy is not about happiness, is it always a wise choice for those who are feeling lost? Or do therapists sometimes make things worse, by interfering with a person's natural process of coming to terms with their distress? Do they mollycoddle people who should just get on with it? Or is therapy on the contrary too harsh and too demanding? Is understanding and transcendence really possible or is it only reserved for the elite? Do therapists sometimes steer people in the wrong direction? Should they direct people at all or should they be non-directive? Or better still, how can therapists steer a clear path between being non-directive and directive? How can we develop a form of therapy that is direct and that enables clients to find their own direction? How can we establish therapy on the basis of a search for competent living? How do we know when to stop talking with clients and let them get on with their life? Should we keep them focusing on feelings quite so much? If happiness is overrated, may that be true of other feelings, like anger and fear and sadness too? If happiness is not all that desirable, what happens to love?

Should we suppress our feelings and deny them, or express them and emphasize them? It is time we reconsider the tasks of therapy in light of our findings.

Talking therapy

Psychotherapy is about talking your way out of difficulties or confusion. Speech is its central medium. Or is it? Sometimes it seems as if speech was given to man to disguise his thoughts rather than to express them, as Talleyrand once remarked. Most of us are only too aware of the mixed blessing of communication, which gets us into trouble sooner or later. When we have to represent our thoughts and experiences in words and gestures the possibility for misrepresentation and misunderstanding, deliberate or involuntary, is immediately introduced. Derrida said:

communication is always miscommunication. (Derrida, 1967/1978)

The difference, or the gap between what we intend to say and what the other hears, is enormous. There is no such thing as absolute communication or total understanding. We cannot expect our words to carry certainty or precision. As linguists have shown it is this very differential between what we mean and what we say on the one hand and between what is said and what is heard by the other on the other hand that makes communication possible at all. If we could be totally exact in expressing our subjective understanding of the world, we would end up in a solipsistic universe from where we could not reach each other. The divide between us is bridged by the false assumption of understanding and by the wishful notion that the other is the same as ourselves.

Issues of miscommunication and misunderstanding are as pertinent to psychotherapists and counsellors as to linguists and philosophers. In talking to clients in order to puzzle out what their experience of the world really is we cannot afford the usual fuzziness of a 'you know what I mean' banality of understanding. We have to learn to be precise and careful when we help clients discover what their true meanings are. Only if we are meticulous can they have an accurate awareness of what they think and mean and feel. Then they can amend and correct their worldview, in accordance with what they come to see as the true objectives of their lives. In this process we start at a disadvantage, for the clients that come to psychotherapy frequently mistrust the communicative process between people as they have often felt misunderstood and hard done by in the past. Yet they come to talk to a stranger in order to try and make sense of what has previously been chaotic. They reluctantly put their trust in the act of communication that has previously led to so many disappointments. They want to be more confident of their own ability to communicate and they want to be much more lucid in their self knowledge and their understanding of the world, so that they can convey their meanings better to themselves and others. Elucidation is therefore the first port of call of therapy: clarification of what is the case and of how the person experiences the world. Of course this does not just involve a clarification of their own point of view, their meanings and desires, but also some recognition of the context in which they live and further more of the limits and possibilities and realities of life. This will help them to work out their problems in living, by reflecting upon them and communicating about their own experience of being alive and feeling lost. Frequently it also means challenging their utopian views of happiness.

Method

Of course this process occurs mainly in a dialogue between the client and the therapist and the quality of the encounter between them defines the extent to which real light can be shown on the troubles the client is dealing with and the dilemmas they are contending with. This involves a philosophical search for understanding and I have long argued that psychotherapists and therapeutic counsellors would do well to take heed of the philosophical dimensions of their work and of their own role as moral arbiters in human dilemmas (van Deurzen, 1997, 1988a, b). But besides this philosophical, intellectual understanding we also need full awareness of the personal, emotional, moral and spiritual facets of human living and we need to have a method for following the compass of a person's inner experience in helping them direct themselves in the vastness of human living. Before I go any further with this, I shall set the scene by declaring my own bias and background as these sharply determine my outlook on the issues in question.

Background

Although I am a counselling psychologist and a psychotherapist, I remain a philosopher by conviction and Plato and Socrates were my earliest tutors of dialogic questioning and of the fundamental attitude of wonder that makes philosophy and thinking about the human predicament possible. Undoubtedly existential thinkers like Husserl, Jaspers and Heidegger, Sartre, de Beauvoir and Merleau Ponty, Marcel and Camus have been an important source of insight too, as were philosophers like Kierkegaard, Nietzsche, Rousseau, Pascal and Spinoza and even Hegel, Kant and Locke, from all of whom I learnt much. At first I was somewhat shy about speaking of philosophy with clients. I tried to fit into the psychotherapeutic mould and this was easy enough since as part of my philosophy training I read lots of Freud and Lacan, who at that time were central figures in the French philosophy departments where I did my training, along with authors like Barthes, Deleuze, Guattari, Foucault and Irigaray. Some of my early clients in mental hospitals were themselves arm-chair philosophers and wanted to learn or hold forth. But on the whole my supervisors did not think it a good thing to have philosophical arguments with clients or patients. To suggest that they were capable of working out their own position in life was enough to raise people's eyebrows. Working in a thera-peutic environment meant that one's credentials and motivations were con-stantly under scrutiny and in question. In spite of my deeply held and vigorously defended belief that philosophy was a good basis for the work I did, I soon accepted that I was missing the psychological knowledge and psy-chotherapeutic training to adequately deal with the personal, emotional and relational issues that would inevitably come up and so, reluctantly, I acquired further training.

I have written about this process in my book *Paradox and Passion in Psychotherapy* (van Deurzen, 1998a), where I describe the crisis that led me to realize that some further study was in order. This happened as a result of the philosophical and psychotherapeutic large group discussions I used to lead once a week in the psychiatric hospital. These discussions were held in relation to the articles that patients were encouraged to write for the internal newsletter and they often carried deep emotional charges that were riddled with heavy existential questions. The discussions frequently brought about complex dynamic processes between people and I realized that I should be able to handle these a lot better than I was initially equipped to do. Indeed it taught me that understanding human interaction and human emotion is as important as understanding ethics, politics or logic.

Philosophy or psychology?

All the while I have argued with the narrowness of psychological thinking and rebelled, sometimes too vociferously, against the reductionism of psychologi-cal or psychotherapeutic interpretations of reality. I have continued to define myself as a philosopher rather than as a psychologist and found great support in the work of Karl Jaspers (1951, 1963, 1964), Martin Buber (1923/1970, 1929/1947), Ludwig Binswanger (1946, 1963), Rollo May (1969b; May et al., 1958) and Medard Boss (1957, 1979), who have all been able to build bridges between philosophical thinking and therapeutic practice. The discovery of R.D. Laing's (1960, 1961, 1967), Cooper's (1967) and Esterson's (Laing and Esterson, 1964) work was a revelation for me in the early seventies. They made the obvious connections between existential philosophy and psychotherapy in questioning the simplistic labelling of human pain and developing a new atten-tiveness to human suffering that made philosophical intervention possible and relevant. When reaching out to people in crisis and in deep distress and in helping them to disclose the full intensity of their suffering all these people showed how to uncover the most extreme contradictions of human existence. Their work brings a sharpness and poignancy to philosophical thinking whilst retrieving the sense of the nobility of the human struggle that is so essential to the suffering individual. How can you find clarity about yourself and about life unless you are treated as a thinking human being instead of being reduced to a case of mental illness in a psychiatric ward? People in that position do not seek happiness, but only the human dignity and recognition that their wrestling with demons is relevant to us all. There were moments in the early days of my practice that being with people on the edge of life and seeing the world through their eyes was almost too much to take, because I was acutely aware of the poignancy of their experience to my own life. I learnt that there were much more distant places in being alive than I had ever dreamt of. I lived in the middle of several psychiatric hospitals for quite a number of years in France in the early seventies and befriended many people who had been to hell and back and were happy to tell me their story.

I learnt to respect the lessons of experience and found that listening to what others had been through and how it had coloured their view of the world was essential to even begin to create a dialogue with them about their position. I found that I had a role to play in guiding patients when reclaiming their right to dignity and well being, as well as in sharpening their ability to think and talk about their predicament. At the same time I had much to learn myself, for instance in being silent and listening attentively before I could encompass and comprehend the full significance of their preoccupations. Argument alone was not enough: it was good, but not enough. Speech was silver and silence was golden, providing that the silence was filled with previously communicated and shared meanings and that it was used for reflection and contemplation, leading on to some new formulations and further communication.

On the whole, what it meant to do philosophy in a psychiatric environment was to have discussions with people who had been labelled mentally ill, whether they had been in institutions for many years, usually with chronic schizophrenia, autism or manic-depressive disorders, or whether they had just recently been referred with an acute problem. I remember how I began to hold regular private conversations with some of the patients in the hospital of Saint-Alban in the Massif Central, a special hospital dominating a mountain village in the department of the Lozère. I used the excuse of my role in running the weekly magazine meetings, for which I prepared in the hospital library. Here I would meet up with some people twice weekly amongst a wonderful collection of books, which lent a special atmosphere of learning, counteracting the more medical atmosphere of the usual consulting rooms or the wards. I found that these people were fascinated to discuss their difficulties in philosophical terms, even though they were not used to doing so. Their life in the margins of society often coincided with a natural inclination to philosophize. They had invariably developed their own theories in order to make their personal predicament meaningful to themselves and they liked to give voice to them. Quite often they tried to teach me about the diagnoses they had been given or about the interpretations that had been made to them in the past by psychoanalysts, psychiatrists or psychologists. Just as often they were dismissive of these interpretations and had thought of better explanations themselves. For a long time I was protected from being dismissed by them as yet another medical or psychological authority, because of my status as an outsider. Being a foreigner and a philosopher would in itself have lent sufficient credibility, being a rather fragile young female made me even less of a threat.

Jacques and an ethics of vengefulness

I had some memorable discussions with Jacques, a 34 year old widower, or murderer, depending on how you looked at it. Jacques was a man who had killed his wife and had pleaded insanity, now regretting the life sentence in hospital that this had led to. We debated good and evil. His view was that his wife who had not understood him and who had been unfaithful had been evil, and he, who had been long suffering and naively caring, had been good. Yet, when he stabbed her to death with a knife when finding her in his bed with another man, he had done an evil deed and she had been an innocent and good victim. At his trial he had claimed that he had to cleanse the world of evil-doing women like her and when asked whether he would do the same again he had truthfully answered affirmatively. Even after the fact he was still persuaded of the rightness of his action and the immense wickedness of his dead wife. He would discuss the female nurses as if they were all potential Jezebels and it was clear that he still believed that it would be a good thing to cull any women who were too sexually provocative. It was a mercy that I came across as a sensible, married and overly serious woman.

No one had ever discussed his ideology with him in a truly searching or incisive manner, as everyone had always assumed he was psychotic and would not be able to hold a rational conversation. I suspected it was also because doctors and psychologists are not generally speaking at ease with such argumentation and they fear they will be tripped up if they engage with such discourse too much. Philosophizing is dangerous and a tendency to philos-ophize could be seen by some as a sign of schizophrenia. No one wants to be drawn too deeply into the dangerous, dark and murky universe of the madman: keeping one's distance is much safer. It is true that Jacques did see himself as the representative of God on earth and it was easy to be put off by his tone of apparent arrogance and intolerance. In addition to this he looked the part as well, dark and stern, with long black hair, a credible incarnation of evil. However it was clear that he considered it his personal task to protect the world from evil female manipulations. But he also craved the challenge of being made to define his terms and in having to declare and reconsider his convictions. The conversation would quickly turn into a hard-edged philosophical debate about the existence of God and the role of human conscience. He was pleased to be made to think about societal structures and the individual right to life. He was particularly keen to discuss issues of power and of dominance and submission. I don't know how one could have had such talks with him if one weren't trained in philosophy and did not know Hegel and Marx, Rousseau, Hobbes, Machiavelli, Sartre, Fanon and Foucault. Jacques, amongst other things, was very well read, having had considerable time in prison and hospital to further his education.

While he would keep up his side of the argument very well and strongly, it was obvious that he easily felt under threat when questions were fired at him. It became increasingly evident that he was much more vulnerable than dangerous and terrified of not being able to protect his own right to live. When I pointed this out to him he told me somewhat reluctantly that there was abundant proof that he was under constant threat. His father, after beating him regularly until he was about seven, had left him and his mother to fend for themselves. She earned her living through prostitution and was unable to protect him from her male entourage, who sometimes abused him, or even from other kids, who tended to bully him. She was herself regularly beaten by her customers and her employer. She would pass the punishment on to him and beat him at least as hard as his father had once done. He concluded that his mother was a dangerous woman and he had left her when he was sixteen, hardly ever visiting her since. He had still given women in general the benefit of the doubt and had high hopes in the affection of the girl he made his wife. He had wanted her to be a sort of other worldly angel and saviour when he fell in love with her and he managed to blind himself to her actual character until well after the wedding. When her proneness to flirt with other men had become blindingly obvious he began to beat her, not, he claimed, out of jealousy, but because he wanted to stop her leading these men on. This he believed was a reasonable and good thing to do, for he had to correct her and protect the sensitivities of fellow men that she was leading on and harming. Unfortunately his corrections had not been well received and had not helped since she protested and fought back, speaking to him with a foul mouth. He gradually settled into the conviction that women were dangerous creatures who tantalised men and led them to losing their self-control. They were unreliable and fickle and if you loved them they were your downfall. God had after all put women in his paradise to test men. Eve had seduced Adam and this had led to the Fall. He figured his father had similarly failed the test when confronted with his mother's evil doing. No wonder he beat her when he discovered she was prostituting herself. His father had been right to do so and he had been right to leave her when he did, because he had come to the conclusion that she was a lost cause. Jacques decided that similarly his wife was a constant challenge to his own ability to stand up to female taunting and he had been determined that for his part he would meet this challenge and keep his wife under control. When she finally flaunted her wantonness at him by defiantly sleeping with one of his friends, right under his eyes, he felt certain that he had to act decisively. He had to set an example to other women and not merely leave her to do more harm to other men. He stabbed her 20 times, in cold blood, to set an example and to avenge and prevent the wrongs women did to mankind.

It is not easy to speak to someone so engrossed in his worldview and so absorbed in the bitterness of an existence crushed, warped and forlorn. One can open oneself to the suffering that the person is speaking of or one can be silent and respect the point of view exhibited. One can argue and try to convince the other of the error in their thinking. One can appeal to their empathy and pity for their victim. It is tempting to try and show the person how they are generalizing from exceptional suffering and are not making room for the possibility of different experiences that would contradict their own. In practice though such argumentation quickly grinds to a halt as the source of the other person's insight runs dry. It is with some people as if their ability to encompass the world and its workings is not fully developed as they have not been given adequate resources to start with. Jacques' prospects of getting out of psychiatric hospital were very slim indeed. His worldview had become distorted accordingly. His experience had proven the destructive wickedness of women, for even though he had killed the woman who was evil, she had made his life into a hell even after her death, as now he had not only lost his freedom but any hope of succeeding in life or having any sort of self-esteem or position in the world ever again. So she had had the better of him after all.

In working with Jacques I became acutely aware of my own bias: my philosophy of life was a lot more constructive than Jacques' and I found it hard to work with his, for my mind was made up from the start that he was in the wrong. For instance I believed in love and in happiness, which he curiously did not. At first I just wanted him to fold and abandon his view of the world, since I was so sure that it was defective. My missionary zeal wanted him to discover goodness and happiness. Then I became aware that I had to make room for a different quality of being in the world, which I could not understand by thinking in philosophical terms only. I had to learn about human distress and stress and how these influence our ability to think and act. I had to learn about human development and the cultural, social and familial effects on a person's inner sense of security. I also had to learn about possible biological and genetic influences on a person's tendency to be optimistic or pessimistic, extrovert or introvert, active or passive. Helping Jacques would not be such a straightforward matter as having a philosophical dialogue with him. I never did change his life for the better, but he helped me in changing mine by teaching me something about the limits of verbal exchanges and of the individual human horizon.

Boris and the barrier of silence

While Jacques was difficult to argue with, it was much worse with Boris, who did not speak at all. He was in his late forties when I first met him and he had been in the hospital since he was a young autistic child. He communicated by barking like a dog and was bent over with his head nearly at hip level most of the time. He was gruff and scruffy and quite scary to be around. He was always dressed in blue overalls. Nurses informed me that he had been known to speak occasionally when taken on a holiday by the seaside and it became my personal challenge to get him to talk in the hospital. Boris played the piano and I started to show an interest in his piano playing by standing by him, watching him play at the social centre of the hospital where I was based. At first he was highly suspicious of me, but he soon began to tolerate me, then one day volunteered to teach me some notes to play. This game developed into me having regular piano 'lessons' with him, during which he sometimes grunted noises that seemed like words. It seemed to me that a miracle was happening: Boris almost smiled at me sometimes. I desperately wanted him to be happy. We did not get anywhere near philosophical dialogue and the end of our work was marked in a dramatic fashion. One day I was prevented from coming to our regular piano session by an urgent admission which I had been asked to attend. I had been unable to get a message to Boris and he waited for me for over an hour in the piano room. When I eventually did turn up he jumped out at me from the doorway and punched me violently in the jaw. After this he stood and stared at me silently, with fierce eyes, fulminating with reproach and hatred. He spat at me too. I understood his habitual silence and usual refusal to speak for the first time as the potent protest it represented. His violent gesture had been no less powerful than any words might have been and I had to take notice. It took me quite a while to get over the shock of the experience and it was surprisingly difficult to actually understand and forgive the assault. Realizing how let down he must have felt by my absence and how it must have confirmed the unreliability of human interaction, I made an extra effort to rally round.

Boris would not resume the piano playing, but did listen carefully to my apologies and explanations. He respected my acknowledgement of my disrespect of him and was clearly much relieved to be forgiven for the physical assault, which left me with a few bruises, not only on the chin but also in my professional pride. It was obvious that he had expected retaliation. There was, I discovered, a long line of previous assaults like this on staff members, always followed by injections and restraint. Since I did not report the attack, none of this happened this time. I felt more ashamed of having provoked the attack than angry with him for assaulting me. I told him that I understood that he had wanted me to know how hurt he was by me not turning up. I told him why I had not honoured our arrangement. As I spoke I realized that the slimness of my excuses did not balance with the intensity of his hurt. Not taking the trouble to tell him that I would not be able to turn up was a bad mistake. He was totally silent the whole time I spoke. He grunted a rather more audible good-bye to me than was usual for him and from that moment he usually barked a distinct hello at me whenever I saw him. Perhaps he had learnt something from me owning up to my mistake. Perhaps my non-communication and subsequent acknowledgement of his pain taught him something about the need to bridge the silence between people by verbal communication. If so, much more would have been needed to help him to cross that bridge to the other side, for his grunted hellos were the closest thing to verbal expression I ever heard from him. Still, in his own silent way he remained a loyal and friendly presence to me for the entire time of my work in the hospital and he sometimes surreptitiously touched my hand in a gesture of gratitude, which would melt my heart and the thought of which still has the capacity to move me to tears all these years later. I considered him a trustworthy, though silent friend and was sorry not to be able to do more for him. Yet, in his own characteristic way, Boris taught me about some of the things that matter in life, like decency, respect, honesty, loyalty and kindness. As far as I am concerned these things beat happiness by a long shot.

It also taught me again that the rules of human interchange are complex and do not always follow the rational patterns we would like to think of as standard. An exploration of human inconsistency and eccentricity is an important part of learning to be in dialogue. Some of every dialogue happens in silence and in gesture. Some of it happens in structural exchanges, which are preverbal or situational. Simple facts of being present or absent, open or closed to a person, friendly or unfriendly, cold or warm, have a tremendous impact on the exchange between two people. The hierarchical set-up and the functions people hold or the roles they play with each other equally determine the impact of their interactions. Much that happens in dialogue has already happened before any words have been spoken.

Dialogue or silence?

In some ways dialogue is a bit like education: it merely brings out what is already there in the situation, in the person and in between people, it does not start from a clean slate. When dialogue does not take this background into account and purports to be able to ride over established codes, or to run against expectations, norms, or rituals or silent agreements of any kind, the words will not be trusted, nor will they be taken seriously. Words can hide misunderstandings, they can also create them, they can mislead as well as lead to truth. Silence can be a powerful intervention. It can lead to thought and comprehension, or it can lead to doubt and isolation. The most important part of a good rendering of a piece of music is the silences in between the notes, musicians tell us. But those silences have to be managed to perfection, exactly as intended: not too little and not too much. An important part of a speech is the pauses that I leave in between the sentences. But when do I stop and when do I start? When I stop speaking, I leave room for the other. In the space I leave open you can get ready to speak yourself or you can turn away from me and turn me down. When the monologue has errors or holes in it, you can bust it right open or plant seeds of disagreement in the holes. If I lecture my clients about morality or about pathology, I leave them no space for thoughts of their own, unless I become so boring that they switch off and create a silence in which they can harness their protest. Talking can be a barrier to dialogue.

Elsewhere (van Deurzen, 1998a) I have spoken about the difference between monologue, duologue, which is a monologue that two people share, and dialogue, which is a talking through problems together until we come closer to understanding. The gift of the gab is not the same as the gift of dialogue. Dialogue is as much about listening to another as it is about speech. Psychotherapists and counsellors have written many books about good listening, especially about listening to body language and to the hidden or unconscious messages that are being conveyed. Listening in dialogue is not about argumentation but about proceeding together to a deeper comprehension of what still remains hidden. It is, as such, a cooperative effort.

Those who speak a lot might sometimes be mindless and thoughtless. It is harder to attend to hidden and deep meanings of what is said, when so much is being said that speech takes over the process of one's thinking and observing of the world. There has to be enough silence to make room for thought. Those who are speechless might have deep thoughts. Silence can be the sign of wisdom, but it can also be the sign of alienation or the sign of anger, or of confusion. Speech and silence can both be used or abused.

Thomas Mann in *The Magic Mountain* (1924/1996) took the view that speech was civilization itself. He said that a word, even the most contradictory word, preserves contact and that it is silence which isolates. It is true that we need to use words to remain in contact with people, even though our clumsiness of expression or our misunderstanding of what is said to us may compromise the contact.

It is also true that speech needs to be examined for its full potential impact and often it is not subjected to this treatment. As I have given several examples of the limitations of a philosophical dialogue with psychiatric patients, let me now give you an example of a psychotherapeutic experience where philosophical thinking and dialogue became immensely important. A number of elements that would otherwise have remained hidden underneath assumptions of pathology were only drawn out of the client's experience because the silence of the therapeutic relationship was broken by much needed philosophical challenging.

Nathalie and her son

Nathalie was the client of someone whose therapeutic practice I supervised. She was a lady in her forties with a son of 17. Nathalie was in psychotherapy because of her agoraphobia, which for a while had kept her completely house-bound, as she would have severe panic attacks as soon as she ventured out-doors. Her phobia had much subsided and she was coming to therapy sessions unaccompanied by the time that a new development struck her down with a fresh attack of anxiety. This time it was generalized anxiety and it was clearly triggered by a specific event.

Nathalie's son, Jason, had been involved in a nasty series of bullying events, which involved a boy, Adam, who used to be his friend when they were younger. The school had disciplined Jason and his friends who were seen to be ganging up on Adam after Adam's parents complained to the school. None of this made any difference and the boys had carried on pestering Adam until Adam was found hanging in his room, having left a letter in which he stated that his life was not worth living. His death thus appeared to be directly related to the bullying. Nathalie's son Jason was almost certainly involved in this and he had been questioned by the police. He had denied any responsibility, as had his friends. They had been let off the hook. Then, just a couple of days after attending Adam's funeral, Jason broke down and told his mother that he and his friends had repeatedly taunted Adam and had threatened to torture him even further if he told on them again. It was clear to Jason that Adam's suicide had been directly motivated by the gang's threats. Jason was only a peripheral member of the gang but he knew that three of the other boys had actually attacked Adam on his way home from school the day that he killed himself. The same boys had now threatened him with similar violence if he told the police of what he knew had gone on. The police in fact were already aware of these events, but as Adam's death was a clear case of suicide had left the school to discipline the boys. Jason had not however told the truth when questioned and he felt dreadfully guilty and in a quandary over how to act.

Nathalie was frozen with horror to discover that her son had been involved in acts that had led to another boy's death. She had known Adam all his life and felt a tremendous sense of responsibility for what had happened to him. She became frantic with dread. She could not speak up because it would harm Jason and the other boys. She could not remain silent because that would be condoning what she saw as criminal behaviour. In fact she could not face the idea that her son was part of a gang capable of such behaviour. Paralysed with anxiety she fell back into her old symptoms and remained ensconced in her house, cancelling her therapy sessions several times. When she finally did come back to therapy, she avoided telling her therapist what had happened to make her so upset. She merely said it wasn't safe to go out since Adam, a friend of Jason's, had died. This seemed a mysterious statement that the therapist at first left unchallenged. In fact the therapist, faced with Nathalie's erratic behaviour and mysterious and secretive withholding, took the view that the anxiety seemed to have taken a psychotic turn. We discussed this opinion and she realized how dismissive such a diagnosis was. The therapist could easily see that Nathalie's statement was hiding more than it revealed and that she needed to get to the bottom of its meaning before jumping to conclusions. She decided to enquire directly into the connection between Adam's death and Nathalie's safety. Now the truth began to emerge. It took quite a lot of discussion and questioning before Nathalie could explain the complexity of the dilemma she found herself in.

What Nathalie was experiencing was intense existential anxiety. She was aware of the dangers of living and at the same time aware of her own responsibility in confronting these dangers. Her previous attitude of hiding away from danger until it became impossible to be safe anywhere was still with her, but she could no longer give in to it. Here she was being offered an opportunity to live bravely and speak up and yet she was once again trying to evade the challenge. Now she had a choice to either encourage Jason to speak up and perhaps be punished, or to remain silent and cover up what had really happened. She knew evasion was not really an option as it led to renewed paralysis not just in her but in her son as well. Before long she accepted that to discuss her dilemma openly with the therapist would be a step in the right direction. She told her therapist that she was only able to do this when she saw that her therapist would not pathologize or diminish her experience.

It was clear that Nathalie was inexperienced at solving moral dilemmas because she had previously denied and avoided them. But it now became possible to help her see that the avoidance of such challenges placed her in a cul-de-sac from where she could see no way forward. Facing this challenge bravely was the only way to go to retrieve her freedom of movement. She knew that overcoming her agoraphobia had required her to face her fear and go out to do the very things she dreaded most. She knew therefore that facing these problems in living would equally make her stronger and that with this new strength she would stand the best chance of finding a solution to her predicament.

She agreed to look at the issues directly. She thought at first that she was mainly concerned about Jason. She worried that his chances of succeeding in his exams would be wrecked if he owned up to the part he had played in Adam's drama. She acknowledged that this seemed a catastrophe to her, because Jason was usually so clever and made her proud of him. His successes made up for her personal lack of academic prowess and this mattered greatly to her. She had pulled out of her education when she was 17 and she feared that the same would now happen to Jason. The psychotherapist initially pursued the line that Nathalie might envy Jason's potential success, suggesting that Nathalie might have a wish to destroy his chances of passing his exams, so that he would not surpass her. The idea was that Nathalie was afraid of her own destructiveness and therefore hid away from the world. This was an unnecessary interpretative side-track, which made Nathalie quite defensive for a bit. It was the kind of intervention that psychotherapists often favour that alienates people from their own experience by mystifying it instead of elucidating it. The intervention was not based on any evidence though. In supervision we considered what the use of such an intervention could be and I encouraged the therapist to listen silently to what Nathalie actually had to say instead of imposing speech and explanations on her client.

What emerged in the next session was that Nathalie felt that if she let Jason keep hiding away from the truth of his own actions, he would remain a passive bystander forever. He would in other words become like herself: afraid to stand up and be counted. This was the real moral dilemma: was she strong enough to stand up and be counted and teach her son to do the same? This was the question she needed to answer in action. The endless debate about whether or not it mattered to let people know about what had really happened to Adam had become irrelevant. It was by then a publicly recognized fact that the bullying had been an important contributing factor to Adam's suicide. Of course it still mattered to tell the truth. It mattered to Adam's family to know the truth and it mattered to Jason and Nathalie to take a truthful stance rather than a cowardly and self-protective stance. Later on, as Nathalie found the courage to say these things to her son she discovered that Jason felt the same. He actually wanted to recover his self-respect by owning up to what he had done and what he knew others had done. He feared the consequences of his silence more than the consequences of speaking out. There was also the issue of doing his duty by his dead friend. It was interesting that both Jason and his mum had at times pretended that Jason could not speak up because it would implicate the other friends. They now found that the idea of protecting friends was not a convincing story, as Adam, a dead friend, needed protecting more than anyone. In the end it was clear that Jason could come clean without attracting particular punishment or even directly implicating anyone else. It also became obvious that such an act would be morally correct and emotionally corrective. When Jason did own up and took his reprimands calmly, this increased his self-esteem and gained him approval from many. He still had to manage his relationship with the old gang, who now banned him, but he found that this was not a major loss and probably an advantage. Nathalie was very proud of him and somewhat reluctantly took some of the credit for helping him to be truthful. She sensed that both she and her son had reclaimed their self-esteem by being truthful. Jason's passing his exams rather more successfully than expected immensely gratified her. Her fate and that of Jason were intrinsically linked. Passing the test of truth together strengthened their relationship. They could now think of themselves and each other as people who were able to do the right thing. This did enough for Nathalie's self-confidence to help her out of the impasse of anxiety and back into the flow of life. Her therapist had helped her to face life rather than facing her pathology. She had steered clear of listening to endless accounts of her anxieties and she had stopped herself from giving psychological explanations. Instead she had helped Nathalie in confronting the moral dilemmas she had to address. Here was a case where philosophical speaking had been the definite way forward out of her predicament, whereas therapeutic silence would have merely condoned her remaining in a place of despair and inaction, where she did not want to stay. It was also a case where a quest for comfort and ease would have backfired whereas doing the hard thing could lead a to some resolution. This is not to say that it led to happiness. There were too many difficulties and conflicts that still needed to be confronted.

Psychotherapy or philosophical consultancy?

All the life stories presented above are examples of people who are quite seriously in difficulties and out of touch with ordinary everyday living. They were in situations where they were overwhelmed by issues of life and death and had to struggle with severe isolation and disconnection from the social world, whilst having to make extraordinary or potentially threatening decisions. Philosophy, in as much as it is willing to contemplate the most pertinent human predicaments, is an invaluable resource at such moments. People who are profoundly distressed and tested by life are generally at a loss for understanding and they welcome philosophical clarity, provided it is experienced as genuine, concrete and directly relevant to their situation. In such dire moments psychological theories or abstract interventions are simply not sufficient and do not scratch the person's itch for real human contact and fresh understanding. Yet when people are upset or in turmoil they may find it difficult to clearly consider the contradictions, objectives and values of their actions: in other words rational philosophizing is not where it is at for them either. When we are alienated and out of touch with ourselves what we need most is to be helped to put our finger directly on the nub of the problem. We need to make sense of life again and think through the issues with someone who can do so calmly and quietly without any religious or scientific axes to grind. We need therapeutic sensitivity and humanity in the person helping us as well as philosophical insight. We need to know the other is at our level, right there with us with empathy and insight. They need to capture our mood precisely and pick up the exact atmosphere with which we are surrounded. We need a pragmatic philosophical intervention that is resonant with our emotional state and needs. We do not need them to make us happy, but rather to tune in to the emotions we do have.

Emotions speak louder than words

Fortunately some philosophers have captured such insights into the role of our emotions and feelings quite carefully. Spinoza (1677/1989) in his book *Ethics*, Sartre in his *Sketch for a Theory of the Emotions* (1939/1962) and Heidegger in *Being and Time* (1927/1962) have all described how the ontic, i.e., the concrete and practical position a person takes in relation to that which they value, determines their emotional state. Heidegger calls this *Befindlichkeit*, literally the way in which you find yourself, though often translated as state of mind. (see van Deurzen and Kenward 2005). Heidegger argued that the way in which we are attuned to the world is the most immediate and accessible bit of information about how we are being human at any one time. It tells us how we are positioned in the world and how we conduct ourselves in relation to what is. Gendlin's experiential method (Gendlin, 1996), called focusing, has elaborated this idea in a lot of detail, providing a pathway for gauging the felt sense a person has at any one time.

The mood we are in is constantly modulated and our moods are like the weather: there is always weather, though we probably only notice it when it gets extreme enough to notice. So it is with the emotions. Heidegger remarks that we are always in a mood and that one mood can only be overcome by being replaced by another. Emotions or states of mind are therefore a good place to start to understand a person's worldview. We are not merely speaking of 'feelings' here but complete attitudes, states of mind that colour our overall mood. To understand our mood in relation to something is to clarify our thoughts about it too. We move from emotional response to thoughtful awareness and not the other way around. To know what makes us tick we need to pay attention to how we are feeling, or sensing, or thinking or intuiting about things. Sometimes it is our actions that speak louder than words and that express our state of mind or attitude. Working with our emotions is never about making ourselves happier but rather about getting to know the whole range of our emotional responses and their significance in terms of the values we hold. Any emotional position in relation to our world tells its own story, but each emotional stance can have a positive or a negative meaning, as I pointed out in *Existential Counselling and Psychotherapy in Practice* (van Deurzen, 2002). So for instance jealousy, the position of suspiciousness, can be experienced as careful vigilance or as absorbing resentment, depending on our inner attitude. Rather than dividing emotions into good and bad ones and aiming for the good ones, particularly of course that elusive and much desired emotion of happiness, we need to learn to get the hang of each position on our emotional compass so that we can guide ourselves through the complexity of life. There is absolutely no magic in aiming for the emotional north on our compass at all times.

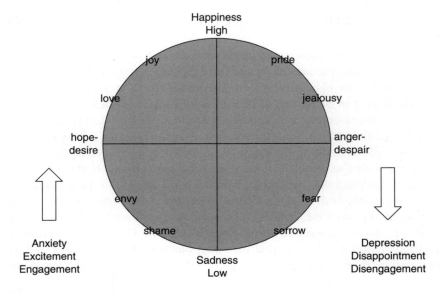

Figure 6.1   The emotional compass

We can learn to understand our emotions by tuning in and working out what they are about and which direction they are taking us in. For this, and basing myself largely on Spinoza's and Sartre's descriptions, I devised the handy instrument of the emotional compass, which can help us get our bearings and elucidate our orientation.

There is no doubt though that when we reach the emotional objective of happiness we exult in our oneness with that which we consider to be the best thing in the world. This feels like the high point of our experience and gives us a sense of fulfilment. The low point is when we feel at rock bottom, depleted and empty, and call this depression. For many therefore the magnetic north of happiness is at the top of our emotional compass. When we point northwards we point towards that which we think will satisfy us and which we feel is most worthwhile. The magnetic north becomes our ultimate value and our northern star by which we navigate. However pointing ourselves north and heading towards something we want is invariably anxiety provoking and demanding of much energy.

All upwards emotions on the left side in the lower quadrant of the compass, from south to west, are such aspiring emotions and they are highly charged with anxiety. First when we are still in the grip of the feeling of our incapacity to attain what we want, we are bathed in the emotional flavour (Tantam, 2002) of shame over what we seem incapable of getting right. From here we move to envy, which is the feeling of wanting what another has. As we become a little bolder in our longings and reach out to our northern star our desire strengthens and allows us to feel hopeful, holding on to the belief that we can actually get what we want and that all may turn out well in the end. Hope is crucial in this regard as we discussed in the first chapter, but it also has the habit of being elusive and we often plunge back downwards at this point: keeping up hope requires dedication and strength and some conviction in ourselves and the rightness of our striving. Such emotions require much energy and can be exhausting. It is often easier to let yourself simply flop back to the well known south of the low regions of depression, where at least we can recognize where we are: at the restful bottom of nowhere. This can be a strangely comforting thought, since we cannot fall lower. If we do persist and commit ourselves to the object of our longing and dedication we arrive in the upper left quadrant of our emotions which take us from west to north. These emotions are effusive, they start with love, a feeling of becoming united with the value we are pursuing, be that a thing or a person or an abstract idea. Love is a demanding emotion, or rather activity, and cannot be done without dedication and commitment. It is hard to maintain and will constantly test us. The chances are that it will lead us to joyful experiences as we get surer of our success in being united with our object of happiness. As we achieve this for sure, very momentarily, we will reach that plateau of satisfaction which we call happiness. A good place for certain, but not a very steady place. On the whole people accept that their bliss is often quickly extinguished when achieved and anyhow none of us can live in the upper spheres of emotional exuberance all the time even when we get good at toning it down to make it more tenable for longer.

The pride we feel in having ownership over that which we most value is already one degree down from the happiness we wanted. It smacks of complacency and is tinged with danger, and it will lead, sure as anything, to a threat to our contentment and smugness in having what we want. Pride indeed comes before a fall. That fall takes us from north to east, slipping by jealousy, that feeling of threat to our most prized value, which someone or something is now preying on and trying to remove from us. When our vigilance slips or circumstances prove stronger than our own caution, we slip east, towards the midpoint on our slippery slope. This is the place for anger: that a last ditch attempt at the east of our emotional compass, where we try to retrieve, forcefully, what we know is slipping out of our reach once and for all. When we fail in this effort to muster our strength, we slip down a bit further towards the lower right quadrant of the compass, where first it is fear that we experience: that odd sensation of losing it, not being able to be in control any more and the sure sense of being in danger. This unease leads to flight or withdrawal. We are now giving up and feel sadder and sadder until we hit the next post on the way down, where sorrow takes over as we count our losses and realize we are beyond saving. This is when we slip back to the bottom of that depressed position in the south of our emotional compass. And so we move from anticipation to disappointment, around the emotions that indicate what we are after or have lost, all the time, relentlessly and whether we like it or not. Any positions that take us towards what we desire and aim for are anxiety provoking, anything that takes us away from our pleasure and most prized possessions takes us down to the bottom of our emotional compass and is depressing or disappointing.

Ebb and flow

On the whole it is best to follow the flow of life and know when to let oneself drift southwards towards letting go and letting be and when to make the effort to reach out for something more. Emotional states are like an ebb and flow of life. Kierkegaard likened it to a process of breathing in and breathing out: anxiety guiding our breathing in and despair our breathing out. Each emotion has its moment and each is indicative of where we are and what we stand to gain or lose. Going down gives us speed and can help us swing back up again, unless we hang on to the low regions for too long. Going up is more elaborate and painful and takes effort and concentration, but obviously has its own rewards. Each of the directions is necessary, instructive and part of our capacity for being fully human. We all have our own patterns of emotion that seem familiar and comforting. To want to play exclusively in one quadrant of our emotional range is to reduce ourselves to stilted robots.

In therapy enabling another person to get in touch with the meaning of their anxieties and depressions is far more helpful in the long run than to help them get rid of them or aim for happiness. Quite clearly the objective cannot possibly be to simply get good experiences in life. Therapists need to model this ease with the whole range of experience and validate these feelings.

This raises the important question about what clients and patients are actually picking up from their therapists, silently and non explicitly but probably very effectively. What do clients learn from their therapy that remains unsaid? What new tricks and values do they pick up with the interventions their therapists make or abstain from making? The issue of influence and indoctrination has to be seriously considered. As long as psychotherapists deny that they are actually influencing the essential ways in which their clients see and experience the world, it remains difficult to systematically investigate how such influence is exerted, let alone to ask how we might do so in a constructive way. It also raises the question of how we can carefully and fairly research the effect of our work on our clients.

Such research is difficult enough as it is, because we do not have clarity on what kind of influence is beneficial and desirable. Erwin in his book *Philosophy and Psychotherapy* (Erwin, 1997) points out that it is not for instance clear whether we should evaluate psychotherapy by the therapist's or the client's standards. Should we consider psychotherapy a success if an unemployed person ends up establishing him or herself as an independent copy-editor using the ability to work as the criterion of success, when perhaps the tendency towards self-isolation which was the problem in the first place has thus been compounded? In other words is what makes the client happy necessarily the right direction to go in?

Ethical questions

Woven in with the personal and psychological problems that our clients bring are deeper layers of difficulty, which are to do with the perennial questions about the meaning of life and the moral issues about how a good human life should be lived. There are some fundamental philosophical, political and educational issues that are regularly dealt with in psychotherapy. They include basic questions such as what is the correct way to raise children or to run a society? They also include existential questions such as why is there something rather than nothing, why am I me and not someone else, what is the meaning of life, is there such a thing as a self and is there such a thing as altruism? There are ethical questions about how my actions make a difference in the world. More profoundly there are metaphysical issues such as what happens after my death, or whether a foetus is a human being, whether there is such a thing as extra-sensory perception or the presence of ghosts. Perhaps most importantly there is the problem of good and evil. Children are intensely preoccupied with the existence of goodies and baddies from an early age as they try to figure out what kind of person they should be themselves. People wonder whether goodness will always win, is it always the best option, or whether sometimes the strong have to be mean and goodness equals weakness. People really want to know whether they must fight evil, or whether they are evil themselves for thinking and doing certain reprehensible things. They are often perturbed because they have or have not done something specific in their lives. Guilt is a source of much human suffering. Quite often people feel that they do not deserve to set this aside and be at ease. Should we treat these conditions medically or psychologically or should we go beyond psychotherapy and tackle them at the root? Is psychotherapy enough to help people return to their essential grasp of human nature, the human condition and the life they want to try and live, or do we need a much more practical form of philosophical enquiry and praxis? Have we gone beyond psychotherapy back into the field of applied philosophy?

It is quite noteworthy that psychotherapists should increasingly be treated by society as the wise people who can show the direction in which culture ought to move. It is often psychotherapists and counsellors who speak on radio and television about a myriad of issues on which they form opinions based on their clinical experience. It would seem important that they reflect upon such issues from a rather more solid foundation in philosophical thinking and argument. Indeed the issue of whether we should credit our feelings, express them, suppress them, or ignore them sends us back to ancient philosophy.

An ancient enquiry

It was 3,000 years ago when people called philosophers were searching for wisdom. Philosophy was about seeking better ways to live. What we now call psychotherapy was originally called philosophy and we would be very wrong to believe that the history of psychotherapy starts merely a century ago. It is actually useful and important to learn from the early Athenian and Roman philosophers. Authors like Nussbaum (1994, 2001) or Vlastos (1991) should be essential reading for therapists.

It is fascinating to consider the contributions of Aristotle and his followers, Epicurus and the Epicureans, the Sceptics and the Stoics. When we pay attention to our forebears we find that there is much of therapeutic value in each of these philosophies. The wide variety of philosophies is like the wide range of therapeutic approaches. Each rethinks essential and existential principles in their own way. Hellenistic philosophy was quite blunt about its objectives, which were definitely to achieve Eudaemonia, the good or flourishing life. As we have said before this means literally: living with the good forces. The definition of what such a life consists of and how it is achieved varies from one philosophical school to another. Paying attention to these matters predictably means that one has to ask a number of searching political questions. Think for instance about the Aristotelian emphasis on the good life as something that can only be taught to the privileged intellectual, although it should be attainable by the many, in contrast with the Epicurean ideals, which are a much less sophisticated product that can be more easily absorbed by the crowd, but that has the drawback of being dogmatic as a consequence. Equally in many of the Hellenistic philosophies, but particularly in the Aristotelian, the condition of an individual's pursuit of the flourishing life is that it should benefit the community at large rather than the individual only.

Guidelines for the Aristotelian practice of Eudaemonia are remarkably compatible with existential psychotherapy (van Deurzen, 1988/2002, 1997; Macaro, 2006; Richardson Lear, 2004). Note for example the prescription that the philosophy teacher's (psychotherapist's) discourse with the pupil (client) should be a cooperative, critical one that insists on the virtues of orderliness, deliberateness and clarity. Teacher and pupil are both active and independent, though the teacher is able to offer experienced guidance. The ethical inquiry that they engage in together is seen as a 'winnowing and sifting of people's opinions' (Nussbaum, 1994: 76). Pupils are taught to separate true beliefs from false beliefs and to modify and transform their passions accordingly. The idea that emotion can be educated, rather than ignored, or merely expressed or suppressed, is also similar. Aristotle's descriptions of the various emotions and what can be done with them is not unlike that of Spinoza, who also showed them to be like a field of opposing forces (Spinoza, 1677/1989).

Finding moral principles

The philosophies of Socrates and Plato are the best known for giving moral guidance. The ideal world described in these philosophies is promised as being obtainable to anyone who is able to rise above the trouble and strife of everyday life by following reason and acquiring knowledge of the good. While Socrates lived his philosophy to the bitter end of his own death sentence, his example is not easy to follow for lesser mortals. Aristotle's critique of Socrates' teaching that virtue is all and can overcome anything is powerful. It is a much more realistic acknowledgement of the realities of everyday life and the recognition that practical wisdom consists not of being sufficient onto oneself but to be connected to the world and to experience all the emotions it that it evokes. Aristotle's idea of moral education remains however an elitist one.

The Epicureans by contrast seek to treat human suffering by removing corrupting desires and by eliminating pain and disturbance in the process. Epicurean pupils are taught to adjust their values in order to retain only those that are attainable and may bring them pleasure. It is a method very much like rational emotive behavioural therapy, which seems to promise a life free of stress. Following this method one relinquishes the unobtainable and adjusts one's expectations to what is realistic, so that with a sleight of hand we can obtain what we think we want. This involves a detachment from one's own desires. The teaching of detachment is similar to that in some forms of Buddhism; though for the Epicureans detachment happens in relation to externals, rather than in relation to self. The Epicurean idea of the good life is unfortunately rather dogmatic. Dialectical investigation and critical thinking are replaced with formulae and communal living enforces the creed. Some schools of psychotherapy similarly stray into prescriptive territory. However Epicurus also understood something that neither Plato nor Aristotle had fully grasped, i.e., that false beliefs are often settled deep in the soul and that they may not be available for argument. This is something not all therapists are cognisant of, although the psychoanalytic tradition promotes the idea forcefully.

Nussbaum indeed credits Epicurus with the discovery of the unconscious and shows how he learnt to use the technique of narrative to contact suppressed and hidden motivations and beliefs. She makes this clear by drawing on Lucretius's work with dreams and emotions. The aim of Lucretian therapy is 'to make the reader equal to the gods and at the same time, to make him heed nature's voice'. In order to do this we are taught how to deal with love, death and anger, but most other topics also get discussed in the process.

The Epicurean view is that pleasure is the only good and we are taught to adjust our needs so as to guarantee the procurement of pleasure from small natural resources. However according to the Sceptics this in itself creates anxieties and the only way to stop pain and suffering is to simply not believe in anything nor desire anything at all. So whilst Epicureans try to get rid of false beliefs, the Sceptics want to get rid of all belief. It is a strategy that is increasingly popular in Western society, as we have seen, and that many people today adopt in order not to get hurt. Nussbaum herself notes that Scepticism is a knack that anyone can learn and which sets out to protect one against intensity. 'But an intense attachment to the absence of intensity is a funny sort of desire, a desire born of troubles' (ibid 1994: 311), she comments incisively.

Whilst Epicureans and Sceptics, unlike Plato and Aristotle, reject reason as a way out of difficulties, the Stoics accept it, but use it in a rather forceful and controlling manner. Again the parallels with contemporary psychotherapy are fascinating. Though no form of therapy today has yet dreamt up the kind of systematic ordering of the self and soul that the Stoics proposed to bring about, I am sure someone will oblige sooner or later.

One thing that all the ancient therapeutic philosophies have in common is their emphasis on education. For the Stoics the pupil's goal is to become his own teacher and pupil and they teach us that in order to improve a person's life the soul must be exercised everyday, for instance by the use of logic and poetry. The objective is wisdom, which is the ultimate value and virtue and which leads to Eudaemonia in turn. Eudaemonia is not the same as happiness, but rather more like the right way to live, literally the flourishing life. We do not have to agree with the Stoical conclusion that such wisdom is primarily achieved through detachment and self-control. Nor need we agree that it is necessary to extirpate our passions as Stoics would like us to do. But we can certainly learn a lot from their thinking about how passions can best be tamed and benefited from. We need not get rid of passions altogether (as the Sceptics do), or minimize them (as the Epicureans do), or increase control over them (as the Stoics do). Perhaps what therapists in the twenty first century can achieve is to not just learn to tolerate their passions, but actually expand them whilst making them safe by understanding. Perhaps in learning from the old philosophers and combining their insights with those of psychology and counselling we can come to a new way of life. There are rich and fruitful interactions to be had between philosophy and psychotherapy. If we are to develop psychotherapy beyond its narrow scope of cure or an aspiration to mortal happiness, we could do worse than to reconnect with our philosophical roots.

Chapter 7

The Meaning of Being: Beyond the Quest for Happiness

But what is happiness except the simple harmony between a man and the life he leads?

Albert Camus (1989)

Happiness is clearly a complex matter. It would seem that Nietzsche was right that happiness cannot be had without unhappiness. And if that is so, then before anything else we need courage in living our daily lives. Facing the paradox of existence requires resilience. And as we have seen for some such resilience seems out of reach. They never achieve the essential harmony between themselves and their lives that allows them to face up to how things stand in reality. They may continue to hope for happiness all their lives without ever understanding that they are out of tune with life itself.

Those who do achieve a sense of rightness about their lives have certain things in common. They do not aim for happiness, but simply for making the most of what they have got. Making the most of life is more about finding or creating meaning than about achieving a state of bliss. It is about finding contentment with the way things are. And meaning is not a gratuitous experience; it can only be created out of difficulty and challenge. So perhaps we can now conclude that the ultimate objective of life is something other than happiness, something like intensity or contact with reality. In the final analysis it may be that we are simply after life itself and want to know and feel that we are really truly alive more than anything else.

Meaning rather than happiness

Living a good and meaningful life is very different to aiming for happiness. Rubenfeld (2006) at the start of his novel *The Interpretation of Murder*, captures the distinction extremely well:

> *The ways of happiness and meaning are not the same. To find happiness, a man need only live in the moment; he need only live for the moment. But if he wants meaning – the meaning of his dreams, his secrets, his life – a man must reinhabit his past, however dark, and live for the future, however uncertain. (Rubenfeld, 2006: 5)*

This capitalizes on the notion of our relationship to time, something Heidegger understood better than anyone. It is one of the cornerstones of existential therapy (Cohn, 1997; van Deurzen, 1988/2002): to help people to live in time, past, present and future in equal measure and to own their capacity for transformation and evolution, if they are to live meaningfully.

We have seen that the same can be said for our emotions: happiness and sadness and the whole range in between are equally important. We can never just choose one. Emotions are only active as long as they keep changing in response to our position in the world, doing their job of letting us know where we stand. Now we can easily see that bad feelings are just as important as good ones. The cycle of our emotions will go around and around and our emotional compass will not set itself to steady happiness ever after. Life is not a fairy tale and feelings are not meant to be unimportant enough to single out only a few of them. Bad feelings are the crystallization of our discontent and we need to take them seriously in order to learn to get things right in our life. Burying them under a cover of joy and fun will not do at all. Upset may be the beginning of a new insight into what is wrong with one's life. Without upsets no human inventions or creativity would exist. Nor are depression and anxiety in themselves symptoms of malfunctioning. We need to learn to celebrate our rebellions against the triviality or unfairness of existence. Instead of treating such feelings as unwelcome symptoms of dysfunction or mental illness we can engage with our sensations, our feelings, our thoughts and intuitions and mine them for all they are worth.

Similarly conflicts, dilemmas and problems are an intrinsic part of the human condition and being alive means learning to deal with them. One of the great advantages of aging is that we have more experience in doing so and do not have to panic at the first sign of difficulty. Indeed we know by the time we are middle aged that being cured of difficulties is the death of possibility and creativity. Continuous and constant problems and troubles are a daily necessity for a well lived life.

Tillich, in his *The Courage to Be* (1952), said:

> *Courage is the universal self-affirmation of one's Being in the presence of the threat of non-Being.*

Quite literally this means that to affirm one's being requires a threat to it. We come to life and to ourselves when under fire and it is in facing challenges that we become strong and show our mettle. To live courageously is what brings depth and vitality and ultimately meaning to our lives. To do so is to transcend ourselves, by loving life, other people and the world and to seek out something more for tomorrow than what we contented ourselves with yesterday. Tillich added:

> *A neurotic person can take on board only a little bit of non-being*
> *The average person can take on a limited amount of non-being*
> *The creative person can accommodate a large amount of non-being*
> *God can tolerate an infinite amount of non-being. (Tillich, 1952)*

This gives us a sense of how to grow stronger: not by avoiding troubles and aiming to be merely happy in the moment, but to face them and integrate them until we learn to thrive on our misery as much as on our elation. Here is a hierarchy of existential strengths, showing us the way towards a better place in our life. But such a climb is a bit like Sisyphus's climb onto his rock: it can never be taken for granted that we will succeed and even if we do we will encounter new contradictions. It is never an easy road up the mountain. On our hero's journey we have to lose illusions all the time and we have to seek truth, in the sense of Heidegger's αληθεια (aletheia), which is the unhidden. We do this by unveiling what at first remains covered up and by remaining open rather than closing off. On the way we lose much and ultimately gain only wisdom and maturity. This is no easy feat and it is no wonder that we often find ourselves anxious and depressed when things are difficult. But those experiences are the *sine qua non* of a successful journey to a worthwhile end.

Existential therapists have shown that anxiety, far from being something to shun and to treat as a symptom to eliminate, is the source of energy that makes us come to life (van Deurzen and Kenward, 2005). Equally our capacity for despair is what makes us deep and capable of feeling empathy, understanding and ultimately creativity. So it is not just a preparedness to live in time that brings meaning, we have to give up on utopia and show a willingness to labour and suffer as well as experience frequent anxieties and despondency. Without suffering our lives would have less meaning. To be human is to be conscious and aware of lack, trouble and strife. Paradoxes, conflicts, dilemmas, contradictions, alternatives, dialectics, and experiments in living are all the very stuff of the human condition and they are ultimately the only stuff that we thrive on. Would we really consider emptying all of this out of our system and making ourselves a vessel of mere abstract detachment? It seems absurd. Why not engage with life instead and learn to live it straight down the line?

So, most people are in some trouble much of the time and none of us are without some preoccupation or problem. That is because things matter to us, for we are alive and we care. Apathy or death is the only remedy for this state of affairs. Similarly the body is rarely in full repose and never more so than when we have expired. Bodies are imperfect and have discomforts, sore spots or actual aches and pains to attend to or live with much of the time. The ego is rarely confident, often bruised, tampered with, tearful or fearful. The self is often lacking in identity or strength. The soul is often confused or distracted and wary. So what? That is what being alive is about. We are not here to rest in peace and suppress all of our experiences and feelings. Nor are we here to express them non stop and bore everyone to tears with our misfortunes. Mostly they have enough of their own and complaining will not get us anywhere. What we can do though is take heed and take notice and learn from our troubles. We can make sense of it all and come to some kind of integration and understanding as we begin to achieve some mastery over our lives.

How to find meaning?

There are authors, like Frankl (1955, 1967), Eagleton (2007) and Baumeister (1991), who have focused on the exploration of the importance of meaning in people's lives. This is an interesting and rather different stance which takes us immediately out of the sphere of individualism and positive emotion to a more socially defined concept which may include positives and negatives in equal measure.

Baumeister (1991) reviewed many theories of meaning and concluded that there are four basic needs for meaning and his findings match those of existential therapists who describe life as taking place in four dimensions. Baumeister speaks of the need for purpose, value, efficacy and self-worth and these can easily be related to the four existential dimensions as follows:

- The need for **purpose** relates to our spiritual needs. We cannot live a meaningful life without having a sense that things are done for a reason and that they amount to something.
- The need for **value** refers to our social sphere, where everything we do is defined as more or less meaningful in relation to the values we attribute to things. No meaning, in the long run, can be constructed outside of this societal framework.
- The need for **efficacy** refers to our physical existence and reminds us of the importance of feeling capable of having an impact on the world. To do so makes life instantly more worthwhile and not to do so is highly problematic.
- The need for **self-worth** is the individual road to meaning on the personal dimension of existence. It is hugely important to feel that you are a good person and that the things you do in some way confirm this goodness.

Baumeister shows quite convincingly that it is the process of going in the general direction of these four objectives that makes for a meaningful life. He adds astutely that happiness is when reality lives up to your desires and you feel you are generally going in the right direction in this fourfold manner.

Baumeister also, more than other authors, understands the key fact that we must not actually achieve Utopia and that fulfilment of our every desire can never be more than an idea. He says: 'It is an idealized notion of a perfect state that one may achieve in the future' (Baumeister, 1991: 34). The point is that when we reach our goals we no longer have them and we need new ones to replace them if we are not to go under through boredom. Long-term goals offer a sense of direction, but it is necessary to have short-term goals in order to derive daily meaning as well. In fact it is the short-term achievable goals that allow us to feel efficient and purposeful and that give us most of a sense of self-worth and the value of life.

Values for Baumeister are a form of motivation. If we live in accordance with our values we are guaranteed a way of life that is going to lead to satisfaction and self-worth. Morality also allows people to live together in harmony and feel in control of their environment.

> *Killing, injuring, stealing, lying, betraying, and various forms of sexual misconduct are all disruptive to group harmony, and so societies regulate and prohibit these acts. On the positive side, sharing, helping others, defending the group, and furthering the group's goals will all improve the group's ability to survive and prosper, and so the collective values encourage and reward these actions. (ibid.: 38)*

Eagleton (2007) and Habermas (1973) also argued that modern society needs values in order for the individual to find meaning or make decisions. We need to know for the sake of what we are doing. A sake is the ultimate value base for which you feel effort is justified (for the sake of God, humanity, my parents, my children, etc.) The destruction of the traditional value base has left people without the justifications they need to find meaning (Baumeister, 1991: 41). As we have seen the simple 'sake' of happiness is not enough. But Baumeister argues that even to live a meaningful life and to have goals and values is not enough: you must also feel you are capable of achieving these things.

> *It is necessary to find moderately difficult tasks to maintain that middle ground between boredom (too easy) and anxiety (too hard). (ibid.: 41)*

It is here that some of the positive psychology exercises come into their own, when they remind us of doing enough meaningful activities each day to keep ourselves motivated. To get away from learnt helplessness (Seligman, Peterson, and Maier, 1995) is undoubtedly a good thing. To plunge ourselves into self- deceptive optimism and positive thinking about ourselves is quite another. It may very well be that some optimistic illusions are necessary for mental health but that does not mean that we need to give in to our desire for self-aggrandizement.

All this does bring home the fact that our happiness is a result of interpretation (Baumeister, 1991: 229). Baumeister shows that we are more likely to consider ourselves happy if we maintain low expectations and rise slowly on the ladder of achievements enjoying each step on the way, making our gains in life a cause for celebration.

> *Thus the final recipe for happiness is as follows: you form and maintain some positive social bonds or human relationships; you satisfy your basic needs for meaning; you maintain goals and aspirations that are low enough to be within reach; you manage to do reasonably well in objective terms; and you cultivate self-flattering, optimistic illusions. (ibidem)*

While, once again, this gives us a handle on some of the practical things that may give us the impression of a good and meaningful life, this does not guarantee them. Threats and unexpected problems can upset the apple cart just as much as before. When life goes wrong, things don't just lose meaning. They take on a dark meaning. In the first instance life may seem drab or boring then insignificant or futile, devoid of our previous motivating project. But eventually I will provoke the world into releasing some further life events and I will set off a crisis regardless of the consequences either to myself or to others. If this goes wrong again and I find myself another rung lower on the ladder, life may actually start to seem dangerous, dark, horrible and unreliable. We have landed in dystopia, depression or despair. This is when our resolve and valour are tested and a much wider range of abilities and insights is needed to come into play.

We discover that we cannot just affirm a positive way of life but have to invent and reinvent ourselves and the world as we go along. As Iris Murdoch said:

> *Freedom is not strictly the exercise of the will, but rather the experience of accurate vision which, when this becomes appropriate, occasions action. (Murdoch, 1970: 67)*

I much prefer to think of the objective of life as finding this radical kind of freedom that allows me to keep going no matter what, always finding new interest in the world and learning more. Sartre in his later work (1960a/1968 and 1960b/1976) defined the human being in exactly that way:

> *Man is characterised above all by his going beyond a situation and by what he succeeds in making of what he has been made. This is what we call the project. (Sartre, 1960a/1968: 91)*

To live like this is to be engaged with life no matter what comes our way. We are active and engaged with what Sartre calls our praxis: the concrete actions and thoughts of our deliberate lives. In this process we constantly need to recreate ourselves, reflect and transcend. We move on with dialectical progression:

learning from our mistakes and past commitments, and summarizing, totalizing everything until it makes sense. An existential approach to human misery is to help people to do just that and get increasingly more lucid in the process, living actively rather than reactively, deliberately rather than by default.

Of course in that process we discover a wealth of other aspects to life, both positive and negative, aspects of human comedy and human tragedy, which we experience with grandiosity and humility, with sadness or humour. We may often feel disorientated or overwhelmed on this great adventure of life, but we will continue to redeem ourselves until we have lived it to the hilt. Almost certainly we will discover that there are greater values in life than happiness: there is love, truth, beauty, loyalty, honour, courage and freedom, and many other things besides.

How to live if not for happiness?

So, in conclusion there are no short cuts in life. We have to live it the long way and our own way lest we lose ourselves and live not at all. But there are some markers on the road that we follow and some things that we learn along the way. On the whole it is probably best:

1 To earn our own keep with our own labour and take pride in this.
2 To not dismiss others as a waste of space but try to understand them and collaborate with them.
3 To not assume that we know ourselves but to question and ponder our own motivations.
4 To reflect on life in order to keep learning and evolve better ways to be.
5 To be in harmony with our own values but transcend them whenever possible and remain ready for this.
6 To be on the lookout for the purpose and truth of human existence and align ourselves with it as much as we can.
7 To aim to contribute something more to the world than we take from it, whenever possible improving it.
8 To have humility and not believe ourselves either invulnerable or superior to nature, respecting it and the universe that holds us.
9 To take awareness of our life as a temporary adventure which we can either fear or turn down or that we can relish so as to make it matter.
10 The more we engage with life, things, others, our selves and the wisdom we can gather the more we learn to love and this is important.
11 In all this we have to be prepared for change and transformation, for that is how existence works: it is dynamic rather than static.
12 Tuning into the laws of life we recognize when to be resolute and when to let go and put our faith in being.

13 So while we learn about rules we will continue to replace them with broader and more encompassing rules when these become available.

There is also much we can do to bring all this about in our lives. Rather than remain passive or despondent we will thrive on some of the following:

1   To look after our body the best way possible, allowing it to be sometimes energetic and sometimes tired, sometimes healthy and sometimes less so. We need to be respectful of our own vitality.
2   To enjoy what is free in the world, for these are the most precious things available, like drinking water from a spring, diving into the waves, breathing clean air in a mountain or a forest and being close to nature which endlessly renews itself.
3   To be loving with others and to pay attention to their needs and concerns and to learn to care for at least one other person deeply.
4   To find a way to respect and esteem yourself, getting to know your strengths and weaknesses and making sure others do too.
5   To find both daily and longer term goals worth putting your whole energy into and which will help you feeling alive and ultimately worthy.
6   To learn to question things and not take anything for granted, unafraid to doubt and explore and discover new things as you go along.
7   To find life interesting enough to relish every minute and savour the progress of time rather than fear it.
8   To be prepared to let things go and lose much of what you value, practising in small ways for what we all have to do sooner or later: being ready to die and let go entirely.
9   To strive for wisdom and excellence in the process of your daily routines and to wonder and ponder until you figure out what you are doing wrong.
10 To savour the moment, the memories of the past you are still struggling with and the future yet to come.
11 To allow yourself to achieve something, whatever, and leave the world a better place than you found it.
12 My conclusion is similar to that of Camus: happiness is simply to live in harmony with your own life and to love it in all its manifestations. This is also similar to Nietzsche's Amor Fati.
13 Challenges, difficulties, crises and conflicts are not the enemy, nor to be avoided but rather to be welcomed as our touchstone. For here we are tested to show our mettle. And here we learn to transcend ourselves.

Not everyone will agree with these points, and I am sure that I will disagree with them myself some time in the future. But I don't think there is an excuse for not trying to formulate the principles one lives by. The point is not to prescribe stagnant and inflexible ways of being but rather to keep light on our feet and seek to improve ourselves continuously in the process.

People can have shallow meanings, deeper meanings, positive or negative meanings. We are not taught early on to create meanings in our lives. We are taught to obey and mostly we just inherit meanings from our environment, culture, era, parents, education, reference group and the media. When people first come to therapy they rarely have a sense of what they truly believe or what they most appreciate and fear about life. They are probably not even aware of the things they attribute the most meaning to and how they might become vulnerable to losing their bearings. They probably do very little to enhance the meaningfulness of their world in an active, deliberate manner. Pathology is one end of the spectrum, positivism is the other. Neither provides a coherent picture of human living and we need to go beyond these old opposing forces to arrive at mobile meanings and dialectical human progress.

This brings us to consider how much of what we do is not opted into actively. We participate in the world, or rather take part in what appears to be presented to us as unquestionable truth or right behaviour and thinking, and we accept what seem like inevitable situations. It takes a lot to become aware of what it is we are part of and opt into and take for granted and much more still to see it in perspective, let alone discover alternatives. After this we also have to find the energy and initiative to disengage from the previous framework of reference and replace it with a new one. Such new ideas take time to successfully develop and constructively engage with. All of this is complicated and cannot be done in a formulaic strategy of a few sessions of CBT. It is a life-long project.

Initially we are always absorbed by our environment, preoccupied with our survival mostly, committed to the narrow challenges of our daily existence. It takes quite a lot to start seeing this clearly. Nearly all the time we coast, or else we are thrown into crisis, unexpectedly (though probably predictably given a more critical awareness of our situation and a better understanding of our own role in the world). We rise to the occasions of our existence, but often sluggishly or against our will. A lot of life feels forced and dutiful or uninteresting and boring or tiresome and exhausting. We continue in this way, occupied and preoccupied until we come to our senses, usually because of a contretemps or a catastrophe, sometimes because our personal reflection has led us to force a way out of the impasse of our daily life. It takes a lot of paying attention and reflection before we become capable of taking heed of what is really the case in our lives. It takes far more to become self-reflective about the role we play in all this. Much of our lives we are merely taken over by circumstances, by the dictates of others' expectations, imagined, perceived or real as these may be, by our own character and inclinations and by the morals and ethics that we feel we have to abide by.

When we say a person is selfish, we usually mean they are merely doing that which suits their own purpose, that purpose usually being about gain of some sort, habitually material in nature. When we say a person is egocentric, we usually mean that they have got into the habit of expecting other people to take second place to them and they expect the world to turn round them. This makes it easy for them also to be selfish. But it is equally common for a person to be apparently self-effacing or even apparently altruistic, but nevertheless to have no clear understanding of what the other really truly needs. Altruistic people, like Sartre's serious people, are just as deceived as egoistic people. They still mostly go about their tasks blindly and without true consideration of either their own motives or the best way to achieve their goals. True self-reflection requires us to become first of all aware human beings. That's the trouble. For this is hard to do. Rushing after self-interest or other interest, or after some duty, or some hedonistic goal can all be done without the slightest hint of self-reflection, or with a mere token awareness that does not question or consider anything in depth, least of all ourselves.

Freud's preoccupation with the unconscious as an entity is interesting in this respect, for in focusing on something termed 'the unconscious' he rather turned reality on its head (van Deurzen, 1997). For what is the most elusive and least practised of human abilities is that of consciousness. Most of our actions and experiences are automatic and fairly unaware, they are certainly not very cognisant of themselves. We do not need to dig very deep at all to notice unconsciousness, forgetting, non remembering or misunderstanding, for human experience is limited and our self-reflection and understanding, remain superficial and ephemeral. No wonder psychotherapy when practised in a committed and in depth manner can become endless and addictive. The process once started becomes compelling for there is always more to find out about our own engagement with the world and the possibilities of misinterpretation are multifold, whilst the discoveries of new insight are miraculous, multifold and untold.

In the process of coming to terms with the manifold meanings of life an ability to live with ambiguity and paradox is essential. The wise person is a person who can creatively process apparent contradictions and conflicted information into a narrative that makes sense, a coherent story that cannot only satisfy our aesthetic instincts but also those of others. It provides a map for future living that is more accurate than the map we had hitherto.

Bad faith is usually the denial of ambiguity: it is the opting for one simple explanation, which allows us to pretend that certain things are not so or do not have to be taken into account. It is the world reduced to the logic of wishful thinking. If we become more adept at being open to the complexity of reality we shall tolerate ambiguity and use irony or sensitivity to the paradoxical and multi-faceted aspects of life to construe our worldview, which will tend to be complex, though coherent and capable of holding the tensions of life.

Such authenticity in living is to 'own' life as it really is, to own up to our responsibilities as human beings, but more than that it is about not refusing life and its vagaries: daring to be 'engaged' with life, a life where we are willing to connect and open our eyes to reality without folding, special pleading or evasion. Authorship on the one hand and courage on the other hand are aspects of such a valiant attitude towards our existence. They are both important and yet different. We will still allow ourselves some comforting illusions, or narratives that soothe, for along the way we need some salvation and safety. But if we become alienated in these illusions, estranged from ourselves and life, time has come to be called back to reality.

Overcoming alienation

Thus therapists will be on the look out for the four ways in which people can be estranged: from their body and the things in the world, from others, from themselves and from life itself. Therapy is not about how to be a better person, or changing one's character and basic ways of being in an essential way, but rather about learning more about life itself and improving our way of living by improving our understanding of the human condition. Often this process does involve a shameful recognition of how wrong we have been getting it. We learn to see ourselves as others see us:

> shame is by nature recognition: I recognize that I am as the Other sees me. (Sartre, 1943/1956: 222)

To be brave enough to see ourselves in all our limitations is often a huge liberation from the tension of behaving ourselves. Giving up on the illusion of perfection is a relief whether it applies to our own character or to the illusion that life will ultimately be happy one day. Utopia is a kind of faith, therefore it is necessarily a bad faith, for it denies the complexity of choices we can make for the future and gives us one outcome for the world: a world disinvested from conflict and obstacles that we will have to concentrate on overcoming. The representation of our options and future is reduced to a manageable reality, which may be useful in the short term as Ricoeur (1986) suggested, but which may also become extremely destructive if we do not remain alert to the forces against it.

Claiming our freedom is an essential component of our capacity for altering the world: therefore the more we let ourselves pipedream about the happiness we long for, the less we are prepared for the harshness of existence. That lack of toughness is precisely what prevents us from claiming our freedom. Simply put: to be free is to liberate ourselves from easy and ideal solutions and to embrace the necessities of the world instead. This is what I call radical freedom: the retrieval of the basic state of availability to our own lives that we all have, but alienate in so many ways. We can only be truly free to the extent we are ready to enjoin the world of necessity and take the difficult with the simple and the good with the bad. To claim freedom is never to set out on an easy or straightforward course of action, it is likely that we need to know a bit about the road ahead and the winds we will be facing if we are to be braced enough to make our journey a success. Without a clear picture and a real vision of the implications of the task and of our own strengths and weaknesses we are quite likely to be thrown off course before we are even half way there.

Life rarely provides us with a Road to Damascus, where sudden insights enlighten us and everything becomes clear at once and we realize we have a mission. Usually our freedom and true action are arrived at by long and hard labour. Work is essential to humanity. At the physical level we need to be prepared to engage with the concrete work of survival. On a social dimension we need to be capable of doing a decent job and exercising our craft or profession to the benefit of ourselves and others. At the personal level we need a commitment to our career and at the spiritual dimension we need to be open to the vocation that will show us the why and wherefore of our work and its wider purpose.

If our life is to be a creative and constructive one, not just a long waiting game, where we try to escape from hardship and hide from reality, then work and labour are an essential part of it in all these guises. Often people who use drugs, alcohol, or other forms of self-evasion and reality forgetting are in search of a utopian space, where they can believe in happiness at least for a while. They are clearly prepared to pay a huge price for even momentary bliss. People who attempt suicide are prepared to pay with their lives for the hope of oblivion and peace. No matter how good we are at facing life and toughing it out we still need calm and reassuring places of safety. We all need good places to let go of our tensions and restore ourselves. Whether those are places of happiness or simply places of recreation and contemplation is a different matter. Certainly therapy itself is a mixed blessing in this way: it is a place of work and a place of rest, a place of safety and a place of challenge. In therapy people discover their strength to hold out against the wars of life but also their ability to make it easier on themselves as they get better at living. They also discover the mildness of good human interaction and the reassurance of sanctuary. The paradox of life is also the paradox of therapy. Perhaps indeed it is because we are prepared for hardship and contretemps that we can truly make our lives work and find our way towards goodness. In order to bring this about therapists need the personal strength of character to stand like a rock in the surf to demonstrate the calm and peace required to face tragedies and troubles.

So we do not flinch, though we do feel the pain. We show how it is possible to either increase our capacity for feeling or decrease it. And we discuss the consequences. If we increase our sensitivity we will be more alive and more open to others, but we will also suffer more. Conversely the price for less suffering is to care less and be less sensitive and less available for depth in relating. So the question always remains ours to answer: do we want to live for real and to the full, or do we want to hide in fear, or pretend to be happy and contented? The choice is that of each human being who is ready to notice that this is their life, to make of it what they want. The choice is mine, the choice is yours. Your life belongs to you. Though we always go back to suffering and effort, we are always strong enough to face our own destiny. We can triumph over our misery and persist in our efforts. Our lives are valid not because we are happy but because we are conscious and continue to make the effort till the end.

Strength

So how to move to a position of strength when we find ourselves in the dumps, down on our luck, or simply desperate? It may be a cliché, but it doesn't make it less true that it is often from those who suffer hardest that we learn our lessons in life when we are despondent. The people coming to couple therapy in constant battle with one another who rediscover mutual respect and the joys of loving each other remind me of having to count my own blessings or try a little harder. The kids I meet unexpectedly in a shanty town in South America, who beg for money but also lose themselves in a game of passionate football, to which they devote themselves with true enthusiasm, exhibiting their indomitable love of life: with the exhibition of their skills they show me the need to be exuberant still, no matter how hard or dark my path.

Like everyone I have my secret doors through which to find my way back home when I have lost my joy and confidence in life: climbing a steep slope, riding a quiet horse in the countryside, skating on a frozen pond, listening to the sea at night, walking towards a wide horizon across a stile, shared intimacy and genuine tenderness, a wood-fire, the smell and taste of home made bread, a starry sky, a special oak tree, a long loving dialogue, the wisdom of others stowed away in books, shared yearnings and projects, a dance full of feeling, a newly composed song, a moving orchestral movement, the comfort of family and friends, a warm and cosy bed. There is no end to it: there is always something old or new to please me, give me heart when I feel I am losing my soul. And I haven't even started on the new discoveries that remain possible, the things I do not even know about yet: new species of animals, other lands, other people, other customs, ideas beyond the ones already within my ken. What wealth the world has to offer to me. It never ceases to astonish me that people exist and can help each other, make each other happy or grateful, or just merely content to be alive and with each other. To discover what makes it work is a privilege: modesty and generosity and understanding and so many other principles that make the task of living a little easier. How amazing it is what my brain and body do for me, how extraordinary that I can breathe, sleep, think, walk. How bizarre that I live and that one day I shall die. The wonder of it all! While I have a chance I aim to make the most of it and not waste my time in regretting what I have or have not got.

Remembering all that is to rise above the one dimensional representations of life. Neither the focus on pathology nor the focus on happiness is where it is at. We can highlight the dark side or we can strive for the light. But in the final analysis it is the contrast between things, the tensions and the polarities, the dynamic of life and death, the variety of things and the interaction between dark and light that defines and determines our lives.

To catch such moments of truth we have to be open to what is. It requires reflection and meditation, deep thinking, as Heidegger called it. Not the calculative thought that only seeks advantage, measurement, pleasure or comfort, but the thought that seeks to know what is real and that anchors itself in the root of one's soul. The thought that allows things to be as they are and learns to know them, gets to see them, gets to be them even. Heidegger said thinking is thanking and there is definitely a deep connection to gratitude in all this. Not forgiveness. No, forgiveness is something much less great which is reserved for dealing with special injustices in life. This is about receptivity to and gratitude for what is and will be, regardless of you and me, regardless of the system, regardless of what we produce and make of the world. True openness to the universe and the cosmos in all their complexity and grandeur, in all their simplicity and splendour is peace. This is gratitude pure and simple for the principle of living, welcoming what is and knowing that it is good. This is not an idealized utopian picture of living, with grazing sheep and fruits in trees against a perfect blue sky with fluffy clouds and endless sweet wine in one's cup which overflows. The living that is true and real is much harsher and paradoxical than that. It is a place where people experience equal measures of despair and hope, aspiration and disappointment. It is a place where life is on a continuous flow, where seasons follow each other and generations of living elements take their turns, animals using and absorbing each other as summer and winter and ebb and flow exchange places in a non stop process of movement and transformation. Pleasures and pains are equally fleeting and short and grandeur and horror stand next to each other, completing the whole scene.

Meaning

There is meaning in this world that it is not for me to invent or ordain. I can find it and recognize it but not create what was there long before me and what will carry on quite regardless of my actions and reactions to it. It takes no notice of me or my presence. Meaning is in evidence precisely because of the play of dark and light. When I look at anything I see the Clair/Obscure of life. The shadings are as much part of the whole picture as the glints of light. It is the entire composition of life that is most satisfactory. And it does not demand excesses or expressly created wonders. The products of the life/death cycle are everywhere, ripe for the picking. The swing in the garden, softly floating on the spring wind, conjures up a whole world of images, memories of days when it was used or made and it equally brings into mind the possibilities still to come. But would it be any less full of meaning on a winter's day in a storm? Certainly not. There is as much deep meaning in any event at any time, but we only open ourselves to it on a good day, when it seems good and easy and safe to let it in. To be wise is to be able to let things in more often than only on a good day and to see beyond the disturbances and excitements of life towards a deeper perspective where the whole of life and its inexorable endings and new beginnings come into view.

How often do we make this our priority? All too regularly we get confused by the welter of facts we try to muddle through every day of our lives. We maintain ourselves amongst the crowd and hurry to keep up with a rushed world that urges us to catch up with progress. In the midst of this flurry we only just manage to remain cogent and coherent and when we don't the jumble of life that seems to attack us on all fronts easily gets the better of us. We find ourselves buried in the sand-dunes of our busy lives before we know it, wary and weary and increasingly snowed under. How are we meant to make sense of things that we cannot even oversee or keep up with? Even when we have time off we tend to fill it with stuff that keeps us from thinking; partying and drinking or holidaying and frantic travelling may become like more chores if we do not allow ourselves to keep some perspective.

Taking stock

And this is what therapy is all about: taking time to take stock of our lives, not in order to accomplish and achieve even more, but in order to relearn to see things and reflect on who we have become and how we want to be. It is about getting out of our hiding places and daring to lift the veil that keeps out the light. Of course this means wondering about which direction we need to take next. It is about daring to decide about the destination of our destiny. If life is a great landscape, therapy provides the charts and the compass and the preparation for travel. It enables people to find their way safely, with an awareness of all the dangers, whilst encouraging themselves to be brave and adventurous again. It makes them think about their dislocation or homelessness and it helps them overcome disorientation. It helps them think for themselves about where they belong. It returns governance to a person and enhances their authority to know what they are capable of so that they dare experiment once more and savour the variety and spice of life without too much fear and too much random desire. It is about learning to lead one's own expedition or captain one's own ship once more.

The whole range

Therapy then is not primarily about providing people with goodness, fun or even well being and authentic happiness. It does not single out positive experiences, but rather encourages resilience and flexibility in the whole range of human experiences necessary to live a good human life. It is about going beyond the superficial pursuits of life towards an in-depth sense of our multiple connections. This is only possible if we are centred and rooted in universal principles rather than in ephemeral fashions and momentary thrills. This requires us to rediscover the way things really are and acquire slow knowledge that takes time to mature. The quest for truth and meaning will then be our guiding principle instead of the quest for happiness. This does not mean that we can ever state categorically what truth and meaning are, but rather that our existence is a journey for discovery for something a lot bigger than ourselves which we will gradually find out more about, if we are willing to collaborate with each other and reflect, communicate and seek to understand.

When we do this we will find ourselves on a dialectical progression: always going beyond our previous understanding and transcending it. Positives and negatives are an equal part of this process. Our deeply considered experience will range from the extremely delicate and delicious through to the dreariest and dankest dread of deepest darkness. Existential therapy values all these and mines them for their particular potency and value.

As part of a therapeutic conversation there will often be an acknowledgement of what is and of the rightness of what is. But there will also be a constant exploration of how we interact with the world and society and life and the people around us, so as to enhance our understanding of how we can affirm more effectively what is right and combat what is wrong. Therapy becomes a moment when we can ponder on the small but important part each of us plays in the universe and become more aware of the ways in which we ourselves affect the course and the flow of life, not just our own but also of others. It is not about becoming either fanatically positive or fatalistically negative but about firmly engaging in our own life project. It is about opting into the role we decide to play: a central part as far as we are concerned, for we are always at the centre of our universe, each of us in our own special right.

The role of unhappiness

So what about unhappiness: should it be borne with forbearance when it is upon us, or should we tolerate it and aim to overcome it, or should we avoid it like the plague or combat it like a warrior? The answer is simple as there is no real question about it: we cannot avoid unhappiness in the same way in which we cannot avoid its opposite. Another evening will always arrive, no matter how pleasant the day has been. The sun always sets and the warmth goes away. As night follows day, so day follows night, whether we like it or not: we learn to live with both and not to hanker after continuous sunshine or avoid the dark. What we can do however is have a receptive attitude towards the negatives and learn to appreciate the advantages of each phase of life. This is not just about populating our evenings with lamplight and warm blankets and safe havens, though it is about that as well, but it is also about facing the fading of the light with equanimity and learning to appreciate the stars. To not have to be in terror is surely one of the main objectives of learning to live a good life.

This could be phrased as I have put it before as cultivating a movement of love in one's way of being in the world: as long as love is defined as engaged and considered commitment. One could have worse objectives than to dedicate oneself to finding the beauty and truth in all our experiences, whether of night or of day, of light or of dark. And in this we need a dose of realism and humility. There is no point in looking for the sun when the stars are shining. There is no point in wanting the stars or the sun or the moon when the clouds veil the skies. There is no point in bemoaning the blue skies that are lost when the rain is upon us. Rain is good and vital and necessary. It re-hydrates and fertilizes the rivers of life. Night is a time for safety and hiding, a time of replenishment and rest. Not only are the seasons necessary, the cycles of night and day and variations of climate and weather are as well. We have to learn to appreciate these things and make the most of each. We have to learn to find our way by the moon sometimes and we also have to learn to protect ourselves from too much sun. And when we have worked and rushed around enough each day we let ourselves sleep and do not demand constant stimulation lest we become fretful. And when we have had our food we do not demand continuous snacks and sweets and goodness, lest we overfeed ourselves and become indolent and useless. Life's journey leads us over varied and often arduous roads and we need to discover the best ways of enjoying their vistas and panoramas, for there is much more to behold than we allow ourselves to see ordinarily. It is often at the moments of greatest suffering and pressure that such unknown beauty is revealed to us.

The true quest of therapy

Quite often psychotherapy is just about that: representing the world to another in a new and more engaging manner. Making it clear again how current difficulties are part of the overall pattern of a life that is going somewhere and that makes sense and where suffering is the background to finding meaning as long as we find a way to use it for the good. It is about returning the person to a sense that they can have a kind of personal worldly wisdom and self-possession that give them a new lease on life. The world is revealed as a place they can live in with confidence and an enjoyment of whatever may come. To help people retrieve a sense of life as a source of much joy and happiness alongside much toil and trouble is what I see as the objective of almost all therapeutic endeavours. It is about helping people to see clearly again and to feel strong in the knowledge of their own ability to make the most of it all. Of course in order to achieve this many defective aspects of a person's existence may need to be addressed first if these have hidden their capacity to see clearly.

Teaching people that they were born to live a valid life but that there can be no promise of it being easy is what it is all about in the first instance. Helping them to get through the narrow places in their lives where their fears and incapacities have paralysed them momentarily is the next thing. All through this process the therapist needs to be able to keep things in perspective as well as having a true understanding of what has gone wrong and right in a person's life. Therapists thus help people to stratify their lives so that they have an overview and an effect on their own problems again. Of course as therapists we need to believe in the possibility of hope and resilience: the human capacity to deal with expected and unexpected problems has to be valued and honoured. Human beings are problem-solving machines; we are creative entities capable of making things better all the time and sifting life in order to make something good out of what has started out with imperfections. That is what we do, for some reason or other, processing difficulties and getting better and better at it. We process misery and turn it into learning. We transcend and overcome and evolve, not by the survival of the fittest, but by the generosity of the wisest.

Perhaps one day we will know what the overall objective of this is and its purpose, but for now it is enough to know that when we do this well we feel a sense of intrinsic value and meaning about ourselves, the world and our personal existence. When we do this with others for the benefit of all we get a sense of belonging and collaboration that adds another dimension of pleasure on top of it all. To be out of touch with our human capacity for making things work is a pity, though many are. Therapists are supposed to know better and be able to help people see their way to a better life. It would, as we have shown, be extremely naïve to believe that people will be helped towards happiness: instead their capacity for better living is increased and they are taught to handle themselves, the world, each other and life itself better than they used to. And that should be enough to keep us busy for a lifetime, for none of us are ever perfect at this business of living. And it is only when the end is in sight that we will know whether we have got it right or have wasted our time.

When clients rediscover the range of experience that has been frozen for so long, they will not flinch from living their own human drama and will be ready to absorb and process tragedy when it strikes them. Equally they will be able to go with the moments of exquisite bliss and delight that are available to us all. Moments of happiness have to be plucked from the ether where they can be found. We have to be on the look out for them and we have to be willing to cultivate them briefly and savour them for all they are worth. Once clients re-establish their ability to delight in the ecstatic moments of life and are also able to be in misery temporarily without going under, we know their elasticity and flexibility have been restored. They are full human beings who can function with natural and aerobic ease again. When a client describes the way in which they are able to arrange good moments for themselves, exploiting their own capacity for relishing life and tasting its good things as well as valuing their strength in standing up to adversity, therapy can usually come to an end. We do not look for happy endings, for they are a clear indication that the whole story has not been told. It is the vigour of a person who takes pleasure in their own vitality and zest for life that is the hallmark of a successful therapy, not the temporary lack of symptoms or the compliant pretence to a complete cure. We all have symptoms of unease: for these are the signs we navigate by. There is always something wrong in our lives, in our hearts and in our bodies, between ourselves and others and between ourselves and our best sense of who we are capable of being. Life means challenge, troubles and difficulties. Sorrows and problems abound everywhere: to become real in therapy means to be prepared to meet these head on and to have an attitude of willingness and eagerness to be in tune with life and to find good in the bad, moving forward courageously and confidently, no matter what may come.

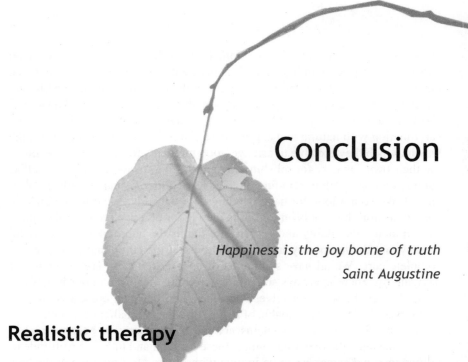

Conclusion

Happiness is the joy borne of truth

Saint Augustine

Realistic therapy

This book has argued for a more realistic psychotherapy profession, one that is not narrowly confined to focus either on psychopathology or on happiness. It is time for psychotherapy to confidently address the whole of existence rather than only one part of it. Many therapists of various orientations are moving in this integrative direction, but they do not always have a clear philosophical framework to guide them on their way. Therapists have nothing to lose and much to gain from acknowledging their implied moral and ethical mission. Psychotherapy is not just a supplementary or complementary health profession. Although it certainly deals with mental health and emotional well being, it goes beyond that to help people redefine their reasons to live. Therapists are at their best when they enable us to be more at ease in the world by helping us to examine our values and beliefs and our deepest experiences and concerns. It is in dialogue and discussion that current predicaments can be changed into new understanding, meaning and purpose: this is an existential rather than a medical task. Ultimately the therapist's role is to lead people to reflect on their existence and improve their mastery of the human condition and of life itself.

The objective of therapy if not happiness

Psychotherapy certainly doesn't cure illness, but if conducted carefully it can make all the difference between a miserable life and a well-lived life. Psychotherapists have at their disposal all the tools and insights of psychology but also those of philosophy in helping people come to grips with their misapprehensions and errors, their misfortunes and their shortcomings. They can enable people to become more realistic about the possibilities and limitations that govern their lives and can help them to bravely and effectively face the trials and tribulations they are exposed to on occasion. It can be an eye-opener to explore everyday experiences in a systematic way and consider the roots and antecedents of events and our reactions to them. It can be equally important to consider what precisely our current outlook is and what the options and actions are that will lead to a worthwhile future. Therapy is about taking stock and finding our own authority to take charge of life and learn to live better. Therapy can help people rethink, reclaim and reorder their existence in such a way that they can make major re-adjustments without being told what to do or made to obey. People have a natural curiosity for the way their lives are going. They like to understand themselves and the world around them better.

Characteristics of good therapists

We have seen that therapists need considerable strength of character and insight into life as well as the courage to face new problems with every new client (and indeed every day in their own lives). Addressing the wider issues cannot be learnt by rote. It requires a certain amount of maturity and self-reflection and a questioning of the status quo. Therapists have to be discerning enough to know when to enhance a person's self-esteem and when to query it. They need fine and subtle judgment and an ability to be equally sensitive to the need for hope in some and the necessity for acceptance of the inevitable in others. This requires considerate and perceptive understanding. Therapists who take up this challenge have to be prepared to soar with anxiety and be deepened by despondency, without coming to grief and without floundering. They have to be nimble, flexible, persistent and patient. They have to understand the whole palette of human emotions and be at ease with each of them. They have to be clear-headed and capable of elucidation. They have to see the links between the feelings and the values and beliefs of those who experience them. They have to be able to succinctly summarize and express these observations. They have to be able to pinpoint precisely what inspires people's lives and what leads them to despair. They have to know about different life philosophies so as not to get fazed when exposed to contradictory and paradoxical information. They make sense of the obscure and the nonsensical. They inspire deep reflection and a desire for ethical decision making. Therapy when practised well is a fine but delicately balanced intervention in another person's life. It requires a devotion to truth and a merciless pursuit of right living. For most therapists their profession is a life long vocation, for which they continue to be in training unremittingly, because life never stops bringing new challenges and exposing new secrets. Expertise in bringing people out of the darkness of a disappointed or bitter life into the light of a new vitality is hard earned. It is a privilege and a pleasure when it works well. But that level of engagement with clients is also extremely demanding and it can never be achieved by trotting out stereotyped tricks from approved textbooks.

Dangers that need to be faced

The art of therapy is in danger of being lost underneath the evidence-based, manualized science of therapy. When we break down the human encounter into a four or twelve step intervention that anyone can make we are in danger of losing sight of the things that really matter in a person's life. We also risk losing the magic of human relations. Accomplished therapists can almost be like magicians when they help to turn a person's life around. But since they are able to do these amazing things, they are also capable of doing much harm in the process. They can hold great personal power and they can be very persuasive. They can abuse the power they yield, or worse, misunderstand it and mislead those who follow them blindly. Clients can have wild interpretations imposed on them and slide backwards into a bewildered state of awestruck paralysis, mowed down by their therapist's supposedly superior knowledge, which was no more after all than a bit of posing or charisma.

So how to wield this power wisely? Is it a case of teaching careful and measured moves, as in a chess game? Or is it a case of tuning into our clients' own desires and wisdom to help them develop a better way of life first with, then without, our assistance? We need to remember that though life is hard for most people it is also essentially liveable. Though it brings catastrophes, hardships and heartaches it also brings delights, joys and unexpected fortunes. It does not require genius or intellectual super strength and all of us are doing it. It does require good will and a willingness to make the most of it often in difficult circumstances. Even if therapists fail them, people left to their own devices may eventually pull themselves together. They may encounter a new friend or have a surprise experience that suddenly jolts them out of their misery and back into the fold. Even without that people have their own way of getting through a crisis and letting themselves slouch back into mediocrity in order to achieve an acceptable state of survival. The trick of good therapeutic intervention is to go beyond the client's default position and enable them to transcend their usual deficient way of coping, taking them to a new level of experience from where they can become self-sufficient again. Some therapies add insult to injury by locking clients into problems instead of releasing them from these. Therapists need a light touch so as not to harm their clients and not make them dependent on therapy. They should also never promise more than they can deliver.

Therapy does not lead to utopia

No therapy can truthfully promise happiness or utopia. Though we may succeed in making a person laugh again, or give them a constructive outlook on life, or provide relief of excessive tension or an escape from boredom, there are no guarantees that this will be sustained in the long term. Nor indeed can we guarantee that this will render the person happier. Happiness is a subjective state which is relative and non permanent. Ultimately it depends on the person, the circumstances of their life and how they choose to live these. Life will never be simple or easy and no one who consults a therapist will end up in the Garden of Eden. Nirvana is not a therapeutic destination. But that should not stop us helping our clients ponder on the improvements they want to effect in their own lives and giving them a clearer and more true sense of what is possible. As long as people are encouraged to actively tackle and repossess their own lives, in harmony with the other people around them, we cannot go far wrong.

We have seen that in this process overcoming passivity is as important as establishing resilience in relation to the life events that are inevitable. Therapy does need to enable clients to think more clearly about their lives and the reasonable or unreasonable expectations they have of them. We can certainly help them gain a real comprehension of what would make their lives better or more interesting and what risks may be taken in the process to achieve such improvements. Clearly we should not assume we already know what is good for our clients and neither should we take the easy option of teaching them to simply go through the motions of the predictable steps of a set routine of self-development or to jump through other hoops. Each person's path is particular to them and they need to progress from where they find themselves. That is why therapy is such a personal matter. No two clients need precisely the same intervention. There are certain things however that all of us have in common and therapy needs to take notice of these. We do need to pay attention to future dangers and past losses. Life's losses and profits need to be balanced against each other. In life it is never a matter of simply getting the good things without the bad ones. All choices require us to give up something. There are no positives without negatives. There is no light without shadow.

Finding the source of light

Accepting that light throws shadows and that we also need night does not mean becoming passive. There is no point in waiting for God, a god or gods to bail us out and give us the good stuff we pray for. No matter what our creed or beliefs, we are never exempt from having to make the most of the modest gifts we have got, be it as a therapist, a client, or as a person. If the new morality dictates that we want the force to be with us, perhaps we should go that extra mile and make sure that we are with the force instead of expecting it to be with us. For that to be possible we have to let ourselves know the powers that run our lives. We must also make distinctions between the forces of life that are at our command and those that are beyond us and that command us: the power of nature, the laws of society, the inclinations and pathways of our own mind and the rules of life and the universe or multiverse. We will fare much better if we learn to live in harmony with these rather than trying to fight or bend them.

This life exploration is one we cannot undertake at random or haphazardly or all by ourselves. We need to base it on facts and on a true understanding of what life brings and how the world works. If we do seek to engage with such an in-depth exploration in therapy, we can certainly expect our therapists to be experts on these matters and lead the way. We don't want them to dictate their truth to us, but rather to help us find our own truth. Better still we would like them to help us critically examine all truths and learn to think for ourselves. We don't want them to direct us but we do need them to show us how to find our own direction and work our compass with a good and accurate map. We don't want them to tell us how to live our life or toe the line, nor do we want to be persuaded to follow any dogmas or holy books. We definitely want them to know something about the different layers and modes of living and the different paths people can take. We don't want them to promise us never-ending happiness or a place in the hereafter. We do want them to live decent lives and be able to model an attitude that is fundamentally sound and attractive. Yes, these are things that therapists should be able to show us and if they do not we should ask ourselves whether they are worth their salt.

Demanding more of therapy

Is it ever good enough when a therapist tells you off or makes you feel worse about yourself? Is it really right when a therapist is competitive with you? Or when she clearly withholds her approval or support without explaining to you why this is or making it possible for you to learn something in the process? Is it ever acceptable for a therapist to cold-shoulder you or constantly outsmart you? Should therapists be trusted if they act as if they are fully analysed and above and beyond the human condition or your criticism? Should you accept their refusal to disclose their own lives to you? If to improve the way we live our lives is the objective of us seeing a therapist, then their ability to manage their own lives becomes a test of their readiness to be our mentor. Perhaps this should be the greater proof of their capacity for being a therapist than anything else. In the same way in which it would be hard to trust a doctor who drinks and smokes at the detriment of his own health, or a surgeon who is clumsy, or a personal trainer who is markedly overweight or whose muscles are under developed and feeble, it would be hard to credit a therapist who is confused or careless in their own conduct. Yes, the therapist has to demonstrate good mental, emotional, relational and existential capability and this has to be obvious from their approach to you too. If they prey on you go elsewhere, if they are needy of you leave them. If they can let you be free and encourage you to find your own dignity they may be able to help. Ask them whether they have current difficulties and if they say they don't or they won't reply, be cautious. If they seem relaxed and confident about the problems they do have and they seem engaged with their own lives and the people in them in an active and searching and engaged manner, the chances are they will be able to help you with your search for problem solving as well.

If you want to learn about living, see a therapist who is willing to teach, but also willing to learn. If you want to get good at living your life look for therapy that can make you stronger and wiser, that doesn't promise utopia, or happiness, but that is prepared to help you sustain your search for something better. Quality of living is not just about contentment and enlightenment, though these experiences will surely be part of the objective. It is most of all about learning to journey, learning to be both resolute in our attitude to adversity and difficulty and surrendered to the laws of life, easy with the limitations and misfortunes we encounter and enthusiastic and passionate about the good things we look out for along the way. It is all about living life as an adventure and understanding about the right and wrong moves to make according to how we want to act. Ethical living is living with morability in a virtual age, conducting ourselves with wisdom and alacrity and an eye for what is true and good and beautiful. But also with a capacity to withstand and transcend what is wrong, ugly or bad. Why should we content ourselves with ordinary human misery? Human evolution can lead us further ahead than that. The therapeutic profession was established to take us beyond the medical or the magic. Let us make sure it progresses. Human freedom and ingenuity can enable people to live well and to the full. It is our task to bring this about whenever possible.

Happiness as emotion

So what of the feeling of happiness in the end? It is only half of the picture. If we want strong emotions, including happiness, we have to be willing to experience the entire emotional spectrum. We can make a decision about how open we want to be to our feelings and state of mind. We can be more or less fluid or frozen. We can be more or less sensitive and more or less reactive. But our attitude cannot always be positive, lest we become sawdust filled puppets or zombies, who fall into submission and cannot disagree or fight. Of course what we love and what feels good makes us happy. But happiness or love alone does not make a world. And not all we love is good for us and not all happiness sets us on the right track. This does not mean we should not aim for love and happiness, merely that we should be more discriminating in what kind of happiness and love we aim for. And of course we need to be prepared to deal with hate and misery as well.

What we have discovered in unravelling the mystery of life is that happiness and love are only truly meaningful if we take them as indicators of our own attitude. They are active experiences and modes of being rather than reactive responses. To love someone or something is to have a committed and dedicated attitude towards the object of our love. To be truly happy is not to relish the simple sensation of happiness, comforting and pleasant though it may be. Happiness is a state of mind, which requires me to be open to the world, to others, to myself and to the ideas that inspire me. The attitude of happiness is one of appreciation rather than condemnation or complaint. Doing happiness rather than being happy is to commune with the world as it is, with life as it comes. In this mode of being my amateur painter's eye beholds the world around me and sees growth and decay in equal measures and finds beauty in each. My amateur singer invents tunes that emerge as by miracle from the trees and the birds and the noise of the factories and the traffic alike. Happiness as an active engagement with the world makes more sense than happiness as a required reward for me to feel contented. When I am actively engaged with life, even if it is challenging rather than purely happy, my skin glows, my blood flows smoothly, my thoughts can cope even with tragedy.

Happiness as truth

I became acutely aware of this when finishing the first draft of this book, as my father's imminent death weighed heavily upon me. In this state of mourning the sunshine illuminating the trees in the garden took on a special meaning and a quality of profound seriousness. I was supersensitive to the ephemeral beauty of nature and became infused with an awareness of the temporary quality of my own existence as something to be grateful for and to let myself come into harmony with. I do not ask or demand for anything to be different to the way it is, and yet I know I have to play my part in making things as best I can. I learn to work in line with what is right and I try to let the world shine for all it is worth in order to be part of its light while I am alive. I know that becoming what I am will sometimes be glorious and sometimes odious and I have peace with it all, no matter what. Losing my father makes me more aware of being a child of life rather than a child of my parents. He is slightly ahead of me in the inexorable coming and going of life, but I now recognize the path and can see its end lit up in the distance. The paradox is always there: in life we are in death. It is not for us to meddle with. I cannot demand a rearrangement. And as I let myself face death, I rediscover life.

Ultimately there is a tremendous sense of peace in that knowledge: a kind of radical happiness that comes from being forlorn and yet founded in a universe that we know must make sense though we do not know how. We hope it is not malignant or malevolent towards us and it is a relief to realign ourselves with it and feel safely held within it. My leap of faith is to trust that life will give me the exact experiences that are most apt for learning to live. And sometimes such experiences will be difficult. At times they may even seem catastrophic. But in transcending them and learning from them we make them into moments of truth.

References

Achenbach, B.G. (1984) *Philosophische Praxis*. Koln: Jurgen Dinter.

Aurelius, M. (2006) *Meditations*, transl. M. Hammond. London: Penguin Classics.

Baumeister, R.F. (1991) *Meanings of Life*. London: The Guilford Press.

Beauvoir, S. de (1972) *The Second Sex*, transl. H.M. Parshley. London: Penguin Modern Classics.

Beauvoir, S. de (2000) *Ethics of Ambiguity*, transl. B. Frechtman. Oxford: Citadel Press.

Bernard, B. (1985) *Vincent by Himself.* New York: Little, Brown and Co.

Binswanger, L. (1946/1958) 'The existential analysis school of thought', in R. May, E. Angel and H.F. Ellenberger (eds), *Existence*. New York: Basic Books.

Binswanger, L. (1963) *Being-in-the-World*, transl. J. Needleman. New York: Basic Books.

Blackburn, S. (2001) *Being Good: A Short Introduction to Ethics*. Oxford: Oxford University Press.

Boss, M. (1957) *Psychoanalysis and Daseinsanalysis*, transl. J.B. Lefebre. New York: Basic Books.

Boss, M. (1979) *Existential Foundations of Medicine and Psychology*. New York: Jason Aronson.

Bracken, P. (2002) *Trauma: Culture, Meaning and Philosophy*. London: Whurr.

Bretherton, R. and Ørner, R.J. (2004) 'Positive psychology and psychotherapy: an existential approach, in P.A. Linley and S. Joseph, *Positive Psychology in Practice*. Hoboken: John Wiley and Son.

Brulde, B. (2007) 'The science of happiness', *Journal of Happiness Studies*, 8 (1) (March): 1–14.

Buber, M. (1923/1970) *I and Thou*, transl. W. Kaufman. Edinburgh: T&T Clark.

Buber, M. (1929/1947) *Between Man and Man*, transl. R.G. Smith. London: Kegan Paul.

Camus, A. (1942/2006) *The Myth of Sisyphus*, transl. J. O'Brien. Harmondsworth: Penguin Modern Classics.

Camus, A. (1954) *The Rebel: An Essay on Man in Revolt,* transl. A. Bower. New York: Vintage.

Camus, A. (1989) *The Stranger*, transl. M. Ward. New York: Vintage Books.

Carr, A. (2004) *Positive Psychology: The Science of Happiness and Human Strengths*. New York: Psychology Press.

Cohn, H.W. (1997) *Existential Thought and Therapeutic Practice: An Introduction to Existential Psychotherapy*. London: Sage.

Cooper, D. (1967) *Psychiatry and Anti Psychiatry*. London: Tavistock Publications.

Csikszentmihalyi, M. (1990) *Flow: The Concept of Optimal Psychology*. New York: Harper Collins Publishers.

Csikszentmihalyi, M. (2007) http://en.wikipedia.org/wiki/Mihaly_Csikszentmihalyi

Curnow, T. (2001) *Thinking Through Dialogue: Essay on Philosophy in Practice*. Oxted: Practical Philosophy Press.

Cutler, H. (2007) http://theartofhappiness.com/

Dalai Lama and Cutler, H. (1998) *The Art of Happiness*. New York: Riverhead Books, Penguin.

Davies, P. (2007) *The Goldilocks Enigma*. London: Penguin Books.

Dawkins, R. (2006) *The God Delusion*. London: Bantam Press.

Dennett, D. (2003) *Freedom Evolves*. London: Allen Lane, the Penguin Press.

Derrida, J. (1967/1978) *Writing and Difference*. Chicago, IL: University of Chicago Press.

Deurzen, E. van (1988/2002) *Existential Counselling and Psychotherapy in Practice*. London: Sage Publications.

Deurzen-Smith, E. van (1997) *Everyday Mysteries: Existential Dimensions of Psychotherapy*. London: Routledge.

Deurzen, E. van (1998a) *Paradox and Passion in Psychotherapy*. Chichester: Wiley.

Deurzen, E. van (1998b) 'Beyond psychotherapy', in Psychotherapy Section of the *British Psychological Society Newsletter*, 23 (June): 4–18.

Deurzen, E. van (2000) '*The Good Life: New Values for an age of Virtuality*', key note speech for the International Conference on Existential Psychotherapy in Arhus, Denmark, published on the internet: www.existentialtherapy.net

Deurzen,. E. van and Arnold-Baker, C. (2005) *Existential Perspectives on Human Issues: A Handbook for Practice*. London: Palgrave.

Dickinson, E. (1994) *The Works of Emily Dickinson*. London: The Wordsworth Poetry Library.

Diener, E. (2000) 'Subjective well-being: the science of happiness, and a proposal for a national index', *American Psychologist*, 55: 34–43.

Diener, E. (2007) Satisfaction with Life scale. http://www.psych.uiuc.edu/~ediener/hottopic/hottopic.html

Diener, E. and Suh, E.M. (eds) (2000) *Culture and Subjective Well-being*. Cambridge, MA: MIT Press.

Dreyfus, H. (1964) in M. Merleau Ponty, *Sense and Non Sense*. Evanston, IL: Northwestern University Press.

Eagleton, T. (2007) *The Meaning of Life*. Oxford: Oxford University Press.

Eliot, T.S. (1954) *Selected Poems*. London: Faber and Faber.

Erwin, E. (1997) *Philosophy and Psychotherapy*. London: Sage Publications.

Foucault, M. (1965) *Madness and Civilization: A History of Insanity in the Age of Reason*. transl. R. Howard. New York: Random House.

Frankl, V.E (1967) *Psychotherapy and Existentialism: Selected Papers on Logotherapy*. Harmondsworth: Penguin.

Frankl, V.E. (1946/1964) *Man's Search for Meaning*. London: Hodder and Stoughton.

Frankl, V.E. (1955) *The Doctor and the Soul*. New York: Knopf.

Garland, A. (1997) *The Beach*. London: Penguin Books.

Gendlin, E.T. (1996) *Focusing-Oriented Psychotherapy: A Manual of the Experiential Method*. London: Guilford Publications.

Graves, R. (1992) *Greek Myths*. London: Penguin Books.

Habermas, J. (1973) 'Dogmatism, reason, and decision: on theory and praxis in our scientific civilization', in *Theory and Practice*, transl. J. Viertel. Boston: Beacon Press.

Heidegger, M. (1927/1962) *Being and Time*, transl. J. Macquarrie and E.S. Robinson London: Harper and Row.

Herrestad, H., Holt, A. and Svare, H. (2002) *Philosophy in Society*. Oslo: Unipub Vorlag.

Hoggard, L. (2005) *How to be Happy? Lessons from Making Slough Happy*. London: BBC Books.

Holmes, T.H. and Rahe, R.H. (1967) 'Holmes-Rahe life changes scale', *Journal of Psychosomatic Research,* 11: 213–218.

Hoogendijk, A. (1991) *Spreekuur bij een Filosoof*. Utrecht: Veen.

Hubbard, S. (2004) Eurydice, in *Ghost Station, Salt.* First commissioned by the Arts Council and the BFI for Waterloo underpass 1999.

Huxley, A. (1932/2003) *Brave New World*. London: Vintage, Random House.

James, H. (1986) *The Ambassadors*. London: Penguin Books Ltd.

James, O. (2007) *Affluenza: How to be Successful and Stay Sane*. London: Vermillion.

Jaspers, K. (1951) *The Way to Wisdom*, transl. R. Manheim. New Haven: Yale University Press.

Jaspers, K. (1963) *General Psychopathology*. Chicago: University of Chicago Press.

Jaspers, K. (1964) *The Nature of Psychotherapy*. Chicago: University of Chicago Press.

Kierkegaard, S. (1843/1974) *Fear and Trembling,* transl. Walter Lowrie. Princeton: Princeton University Press.

Kierkegaard, S. (1844/1980) *The Concept of Anxiety,* transl. R. Thomte. Princeton: Princeton University Press.

Kierkegaard, S. (1846/1941) *Concluding Unscientific Postscript,* transl. D.F. Swenson and W. Lowrie. Princeton: Princeton University Press.

Kierkegaard, S. (1855/1941) *The Sickness unto Death,* transl. W. Lowrie. Princeton: Princeton University Press.

Kierkegaard, S. (1999) *Papers and Journals: a Selection* trans Hannay A. London: Penguin Classics.

Lahav, R. and Venza Tillmanns, M. da (1995) *Essays on Philosophical Counselling*. Lanham: University Press of Maryland.

Laing, R.D. (1960) *The Divided Self.* London: Tavistock Publications.

Laing, R.D. (1961) *Self and Others*. London: Penguin Books.

Laing, R.D. (1967) *The Politics of Experience*. London: Tavistock Publications.

Laing, R.D. and Esterson, A. (1964) *Sanity, Madness and the Family*. London: Penguin Books.

Layard, R. (2005) *Happiness: Lessons from a New Science*. London: Penguin Books.

LeBon, T. (2000) *Wise Therapy*. London: Continuum Press.

LeBon, T. (2007) http://www.timlebon.com/BeyondAuthenticHappiness.html

Levin, I. (1972) *The Stepford Wives*. New York: Random House.

Levinas, E. (1989) *Ethics as First Philosophy*. Duquesne: Duquesne University Press.

Lewin, K. (1999) *The Complete Social Scientist: A Kurt Lewin Reader*. New York: American Psychological Association.

Linley, P.A. and Joseph, S. (eds) (2004) *Positive Psychology in Practice*. Hoboken, NJ: Wiley.

Luther King, M. (1963) *Strength to Love*. Glasgow: William Collins and Sons.

Macaro, A. (2006) *Virtue Ethics and Psychotherapy*. Chichester: Palgrave.

McGrath, A. and McGrath, J.C. (2007) *The Dawkins Delusion*. London: SPCK.

Mankell, H. (1994) *The Man who Smiled*, transl. L. Thompson. London: Harvill Press.

Mann, T. (1924/1996) *The Magic Mountain*, transl. John E. Woods, Everyman's Library. London: Random House.

Martin, J. (2006) *The Meaning of the 21st Century: A Vital Blueprint for Ensuring our Future*. London: Transworld Eden project books.

May, R. (1969a) *Love and Will*. New York: Norton.

May, R. (1969b) *Existential Psychology*. New York: Random House.

May, R. (1983) *The Discovery of Being*. New York: Norton and Co.

May, R., Angel, E. and Ellenberger, H.F. (1958) *Existence*. New York: Basic Books.

Merleau Ponty, M. (1945/1962) *Phenomenology of Perception*. transl. C. Smith. London: Routledge.

Merleau Ponty, M. (1964) *Sense and Non-Sense*, transl. H. Dreyfus. and P. Dreyfus. Evanston, IL: Northwestern University, Press.

Merleau Ponty, M. (1968) *The Visible and the Invisible,* transl. A. Lingis. Evanston, IL: Northwestern University. Press.

Midgley, M. (2004) *The Myths We Live By*. London: Routledge.

Morioka, M. (2003) *Painless Civilization: A Philosophical Critique of Desire*. Mutsu Bunmei Ron, Tokyo, Transview, English translation, http:/www.lifestudies.org/painless00.html: 21

Murdoch, I. (1970) *The Sovereignty of Good*. London: Routledge.

Nagel, T. (1986) *The View from Nowhere*. New York: Oxford University Press.

Nietzsche, F. (1881/1987) *Daybreak: Thoughts on the Prejudices of Morality*. transl. R.J. Hollingdale. Cambridge: Cambridge University Press.

Nietzsche, F. (1882/1974) *The Gay Science*, transl. W. Kaufman. New York: Vintage Books.

Nietzsche, F. (1883/1933) *Thus Spoke Zarathustra*, transl. A. Tille. New York: Dutton.

Nozick, R. (1974) *Anarchy, State and Utopia*. New York: Basic Books.

Nussbaum, M.C. (1994) *The Therapy of Desire: Theory and Practice in Hellenistic Ethics*. Princeton: Princeton University Press.

Nussbaum, M.C. (2001) *Upheavals of Thought: The Intelligence of Emotions*. New York: Cambridge University Press.

Orwell, G. (1949) *1984*. London: Penguin Books.

Oxford Dictionary (2005). Oxford: Oxford University Press.

Plato (405 BC/1998) *Gorgias*, transl. James H. Nichols Jr. Ithaca: Cornell University Press.

Redelmeier, D. and Singh, S. (2001) 'Survival in Academy Award winning actors and actresses', *Annals of Internal Medicine*, 124: 955–962.

Richardson Lear, G. (2004) *Happy Lives and the Highest Good: An Essay on Aristotle's Nicomachean Ethics*. Princeton: Princeton University Press.

Ricoeur, P. (1986) *Lectures on Ideology and Utopia*. New York: Columbia University Press.

Rubenfeld, J. (2006) *The Interpretation of Murder*. London: Headline Publishing Group.

Sartre, J.P. (1939/1962) *Sketch for a Theory of the Emotions*, transl. M. Warwick. London: Methuen & Co.

Sartre, J.P. (1943/1956) *Being and Nothingness: An Essay on Phenomenological Ontology*, transl. H. Barnes. New York: Philosophical Library.

Sartre, J.P. (1960a/1968) *Search for a Method*, transl. H. Barnes. New York: Random House Vintage Books.

Sartre, J.P. (1960b/1976) *Critique of Dialectical Reason*, transl. A. Sheridan-Smith. London: Methuen and Co.

Sartre, J.P. (1965) *What is Literature?*, transl. B. Frechtman. New York: Philosophical Library.

Sartre, J.P. (1983/1992) *Notebooks for an Ethics,* transl. D. Pellauer. Chicago: University of Chicago Press.

Sartre, J.P. (1992) *Truth and Existence,* transl. A. van den Hoven. Chicago: University of Chicago Press.

Seligman, M.E.P., Peterson, C. and Maier, S. (1996) *Learned Helplessness: A Theory for the Age of Personal Control.* New York: Oxford University Press.

Seligman, M.E.P. (2002) *Authentic Happiness.* New York: The Free Press.

Selye, H. (1974/1991) *Stress Without Distress.* New York: Signet.

Selye, H. (1978) *Stress of Life.* New York: MacGraw Hill.

Snow, J. (2005) *New Ten Commandments.* London: Channel Four.

Solnick, S. and Hemenway, D. (1998) 'Is more always better? A survey on positional concerns', *Journal of Economic Behaviour and Organization*, 37: 373–383.

Spinoza, B. de (1677/1989) *Ethics*, transl. R.H.M. Elwes. New York: Dover Publications.

Spurrell, M.T. and MacFarlane, A.C. (1992) 'On stress', *Journal of Nervous and Mental Disease,* 180: 439–445 [Medline].

Szasz, T.S. (1961) *The Myth of Mental Illness.* New York: Hoeber-Harper.

Tantam, D. (2002) *Psychotherapy and Counselling in Practice: A Narrative Approach.* Cambridge: Cambridge University Press.

Tantam, D. and Deurzen, E. van (2001) *Cycle of Crisis.* SEPTIMUS course, www.septimus.info

Tillich, P. (1952) *The Courage to Be.* Newhaven: Yale University Press.

Tillich, P. (1966) *On the Boundary.* New York: Charles Scribner and Sons.

Tolstoy, L. (1886) *The Death of Ivan Ilyich.* London: Penguin. Red Classics.

Tolstoy, L. (1983) *Confessions*, transl. D. Patterson. New York: Norton and Company.

Veenhoven, R. (1984) *Conditions of Happiness.* Dordrecht/Boston: Kluwer Academic Publishing.

Vlastos, G. (1991) *Socrates: Ironist and Moral Philosopher.* Cambridge: Cambridge University Press.

Wikipedia (2006) *Dictionary on the Internet*, www.Wikipedia.com

Worden, W. (2002) *Grief Counseling and Grief Therapy: A Handbook for the Mental Health Professional.* Frankfurt: Springer Publishing Company.

World Health Organization (1946) *Constitution of the World Health Organization.* WHO records, 2: 100, New York.

Yalom, I. (1980) *Existential Psychotherapy.* New York: Basic Books.

Zeigarnik, B.W. (1967) 'On finished and unfinished tasks', in W.D. Ellis (ed.), *A Sourcebook of Gestalt Psychology.* New York: Humanities Press.

Index